The Importance of Being Poirot

Other Books of Interest from St. Augustine's Press

Joseph Bottum, *The Decline of the Novel*

David Ramsay Steele, *The Mystery of Fascism*

James V. Schall, *On the Principles of Taxing Beer:
And Other Brief Philosophical Essays*

Promise Hsu, *China's Quest for Liberty: A Personal History of Freedom*

Rémi Brague, *The Anchors in the Heavens*

Rémi Brague, *Moderately Modern*

Marvin R. O'Connell, *Telling Stories that Matter: Memoirs and Essays*

Josef Pieper, *Traditional Truth, Poetry, Sacrament:
For My Mother, on her 70th Birthday*

Peter Kreeft, *Socrates' Children: The 100 Greatest Philosophers*

Peter Kreeft, *Ethics for Beginners: Big Ideas from 32 Great Minds*

John von Heyking, *Comprehensive Judgment and Absolute Selflessness:
Winston Churchill on Politics as Friendship*

Alexandre Kojève, *The Concept, Time, and Discourse*

David Lowenthal, *Slave State: Rereading Orwell's 1984*

Gene Fendt, *Camus' Plague: Myth for Our World*

Nathan Lefler, *Tale of a Criminal Mind Gone Good*

Nalin Ranasinghe, *The Confessions of Odysseus*

Will Morrisey, *Herman Melville's Ship of State*

John Poch, *God's Poems: The Beauty of Poetry and Christian Imagination*

Roger Scruton, *The Politics of Culture and Other Essays*

Roger Scruton, *The Meaning of Conservatism: Revised 3rd Edition*

Roger Scruton, *An Intelligent Person's Guide to Modern Culture*

Gabriel Marcel, *The Invisible Threshold: Two Plays by Gabriel Marcel*

Stanley Rosen, *The Language of Love: An Interpretation of Plato's Phaedrus*

Winston Churchill, *The River War*

The Importance of Being Poirot

JEREMY BLACK

THE WEIGHT OF WORDS SERIES

ST. AUGUSTINE'S PRESS

South Bend, Indiana

Library of Congress Control Number: 2021939683

St. Augustine's Press
www.staugustine.net

For
Crawford Gribben
A Sleuth after Truth

Table of Contents

Preface ix

Acknowledgements xiii

Note on Sources xiv

1.   Introduction: The Writer as Moralist 1

2.   Post-War Turmoil 24

3.   The Middle-Class Milieu 42

4.   Xenophobia 68

5.   Class and Nation 84

6.   War 109

7.   Recessional, 1945–51 123

8.   The New Elizabethan Age, 1952–63 137

9.   The 'Sixties', 1964–9 161

10.   To the End, 1970–6 172

11.   Retrospectives, 1971–2021 184

Index 191

PREFACE

For Bond the (American) publishers insisted that I add James. Apparently there would be doubt otherwise, although (another) James Bond, as you all know, is the protagonist in Christie's witty short-story 'The Rajah's Emerald' (1934). But surely not for Poirot. Hercule is the name, but Poirot is all that is required to conjure up a world of order and morality, the clarity of reason in the search for safety from a renewed stability.

The music immediately triggers a response. The graphics follow. And then there is David Suchet. For thirteen seasons in Britain, from 1989 to 2013, there was a comfort blanket for very many, and one that presented them with Agatha Christie. Such style, such a world of ease and order.

Well no, of course. Read the books of the best-selling novelist of all time. There was little such ease in the novels which were, at once, more complex and insightful than some lazy modern critics might suggest, but also far more interesting than the television made them.

We deal here not only with Hercule, but with the entire Christie detective genre, including the Jane Marple novels and the others without a famous detective. Christie's world is one that is the usual fictional mélange of fact and invention. Whereas science fiction rewards the latter and the detachment from the factual groundings of the present, detective fiction is very different. It grounds its imagination in the understanding, by writer and reader alike, of the facts and conventions of the world. Indeed, the crimes in question, their motives and consequences, both reflect these conventions and are a breach of them, the combination producing both understanding and shock.

And so, despite Edith de Haviland's comment in *Crooked House* (1949), about Philip Leonides who '"Writes books. Can't think why. Nobody wants to read them. All about obscure historical details"', that situation offers a role for the historian. He or she can explain this world, and thus the context for the Great Detective, and also for the author seeking to work within a sense of the conventions of their times. An historian can also take the stories to throw light on the world. And for Poirot, this is particularly necessary because so much of our understanding of him comes from the subsequent presentation on screen. As with Bond and Sherlock Holmes, that situation poses a number of problems, and not least that Christie was writing for the audience of her today, not posterity; and we are posterity. So, again, another task for the historian.

And lastly, this historian. Each to their task. I am not a writer of detective novels, and for that it is better to turn to Martin Edwards who, from that perspective, has written very ably on his predecessors. But I have written extensively on twentieth-century British history, and have a long fascination with detective fiction, lecturing on it at a number of places including Cambridge and, on both Doyle and Christie, for the Great Lives Series at Mary Washington University.

The locked room, no entry by anyone, even to that floor, bar by the victim. No windows, no chimney, a door that is flush to the surround, and has a fixed handle and a covered keyhole. How did I kill Sir Gerald, my uncle? The 'tec of course works it out, a dissolvable poison dart in the dumb waiter. Instead of drawing myself up to my full height (which you should rarely do – most men hate looking up) and saying "'I have never heard anything so ridiculous. If you repeat that you will be hearing from my attorney/solicitor'", I, of course, self-incriminate, by pulling a shooter/pistol, trying a runner, or blubbing that I had to as he was cutting me out of his will as a result of his intended marriage. Consider the degree to which the traditional novel relies on self-incrimination, and that most Poirot solutions or indeed those by others, including for example Rex Stout's Nero Wolfe, would not stand up a moment in court, not least due to their reliance on hearsay and on uncorroborated evidence.

My idea is to make the protagonist-narrator a dumb copper, for him to solve the case, and make the arrest, and for the novel to end as the case proceeds towards trial. Crucially, that solution is to work for about 60 percent of the readership, but about 25 percent realise that I have made a mistake but do not know who did it, and about15 percent can work out who did it, but will not know if the villain will get away with it. For this lover of detective novels, who put reading them in a hot bath as one of his hobbies in his *Who's Who* entry, there is the great pleasure of the serried ranks of past works as well as the ever unfolding present.

Having written this book, I am left feeling rather like Poirot at the start of *Third Girl* (1966): 'He had enjoyed this literary achievement and enjoyed the vast amount of reading he had had to do'. So, set your spats to the fore, and let us follow Poirot into his world.

ACKNOWLEDGEMENTS

I am most grateful to the late P.D. James for advice, to Donald Sturrock for letting me share his account of meeting Agatha Christie, to Graham Stewart for arranging a most stimulating podcast interview on Christie, to 'Reels of Justice' for inviting me to do a podcast judging *Murder on the Orient Express*, and to Bill Crawley for asking me to speak on Christie at Fredericksburg. I also benefited from speaking on the subject at Torquay Museum. For biographical guidance to Christie, I recommend Janet Morgan's *Agatha Christie: A Biography* (1984; revised edition 2017). In the care of the National Trust, her lovely holiday house at Greenway is well-worth visiting, not least with its fine grounds down to the Dart. Above all, though, read.

Sharing drafts of this book with friends has been good fun. I would like to thank Eileen Cox, Bill Gibson, Crawford Gribben, Lothar Höbelt, Philip Kiszely, Nigel Saul, Peter Spear, Richard Wendorf and Neil York for their observations. None are responsible for any errors that remain.

NOTE ON SOURCES

There is no definitive edition of Christie works. References are to the British titles, and then, if necessary, to the chapter, and not the page number.

1. INTRODUCTION: THE WRITER AS MORALIST

The standard approach to detective fiction is one that begins with nineteenth-century writers, usually Edgar Allan Poe. Horror, however, is more commonly his puzzle, as in 'The Cask of Amontillado' (1846), for which it is worth reading the haunting sequel by John Jakes, 'The Opener of the Crypt' (1952). For Britain, Wilkie Collins is in the vanguard of detective fiction with the brilliant, multi-narrator *Moonstone* (1868). We then move on to the commanding presence of Sherlock Holmes, who first appeared in *A Study in Scarlet* (1887), before approaching the Golden Age, a period generally dated between the two world wars, and one in which Agatha Christie stars.

Writing in *The Saturday Review* on 7 January 1939, John Strachey, a Communist journalist, originated the phrase: 'This is, perhaps, the Golden Age of the English detective story writers. Here suddenly we come to a field of literature – if you can call it that – which is genuinely flourishing'. He referred to the 'old masters': Sayers, Christie, and Freeman Wills Croft, and described Christie as 'the most prolific and efficient professional of them all, turning out innumerable highly competent, if sometimes irritating books, with an occasional classic'.

From an upper middle-class family background at Torquay, Christie (1890–1976), the youngest of three children, was born Agatha Mary Clarissa Miller. The best-selling fiction writer of all time and the most-translated individual writer, Christie is the most significant author of detective novels. Her mother, Clara, married an American, Fred Miller, in 1878, and had three children. They bought the leasehold of a Torquay villa in 1890 and Agatha was born and grew up there. She was taught at home, becoming an industrious reader. After her father died in 1901, Agatha went to school in Torquay and later Paris. She visited Egypt with her ill mother in 1907–8 and thereafter began writing. Marriage in 1914 was followed by hospital work as a nurse and then a dispenser, and in 1916 she wrote her first detective novel, although it was not published until 1920.

Christie and those who wrote on similar topics dominated the genre in the inter-war years, but World War II then brought a more significant change in mood and content to the genre than its predecessor. Post-1945 novels, such as those of Julian Symons or Ruth Rendell, are usually seen in terms of greater realism, both social and psychological, and also, partly due to this, as more unsettling. In contrast, their predecessors are sometimes held up for obloquy, or at least presented as dated.

However, in practice, the Golden Age writers were far from having the limitations and conceits that harsh critics so readily discern in what they do not like.[1]

That critical view has also affected the response to the depiction on screen of Golden Age stories, a depiction in which the Poirot[2] and Marple stories have consistently been foremost in Britain. There is a claim that audiences are eager abettors in a false world that tells us little about the past and deliberately ignores the present. The depiction of Poirot is certainly frequently highly stylised, as well as crowded with an elegant period detail that seems to be the prime focus of attention. Indeed, this critical view has led to attempts to rework Christie's plots of late, or, rather, to transform the ambience and tone to an extent that has little or nothing to do with the original novels. Some may see this as bringing past texts to new life; but others see it as an aspect of the 'culture wars'. At any rate, the process certainly does not help in understanding the world in which the stories are set.

It is to that which we will turn, but, first, it is necessary to suggest a somewhat different history for detection. The detective novel, as classically conceived, dates from the nineteenth century, but novels in which detection plays a role have a longer genesis, as even more do stories about crime and detection. Indeed, Simon Brett's humorous spoof 'The Literary Antecedents of Agatha Christie's Hercule Poirot' begins with the Anglo-Saxon classic *Beowulf*.[3] This was set in the sixth century, although dates from between then and the tenth.

---

1 M. Edwards, *The Golden Age of Murder: The Mystery of the Writers Who Invented the Modern Detective Story* (London, 2015).
2 On Poirot, see also M. Aldridge, *Agatha Christie's Poirot: The Greatest Detective in the World* (2020).
3 S. Brett, *Crime Writers and Other Animals* (London, 1998), pp. 72–82.

Moreover, the notion of crime had a moral component from the outset, and notably so in terms of the struggle between Good and Evil, and in the detection of the latter. Indeed, it is this detection that is the basis of the most powerful strand of detection story, because Evil disguises its purposes. It has to do so in a world and humanity made fundamentally benign and moral by God. Thus, as with the Serpent in Eden, a classic instance of malign disguise, Evil seeks to exploit weakness and, to do so, has to lie, or to challenge Good by violence.

These sinister purposes and malign acts are disclosed, at the time or subsequently, and, accordingly, in all religions and religious cultures, tales developed, as did the conventions that affected their contents, framing, and reception. So also did processes to find the truth, some, such as physical trials, extraordinarily rigorous, others, such as the understanding of oracular testament, a challenge of frequently obscure clues that offers much for those interested in Golden Age detective novels in particular. Priesthoods had special functions in discerning, confronting and overcoming Evil, and guidance accordingly, as in confessional handbooks. Campaigns against the menace and deceit of witchcraft saw such anxieties rise to murderous peaks, as in seventeenth-century Europe. This echo of the priesthood as the detector of Evil was seen in G.K. Chesterton's homely, but clearly moral, clerical detective, Father Brown, who first appeared in print in 1910.

Drawing on the same mental world, a different form of story of detection related to the journey to Salvation, as in John Bunyan's epic *The Pilgrim's Progress* (1678), as individuals had to detect snares en route. In part as a result, there was a clear overlap between writing about this world and the next, the struggle with Evil being foremost. John Buchan used the Bunyan epic in his *Mr Standfast* (1919), a World War I story in which a German agent in Britain is a major threat and needs uncovering and vanquishing.

The development of the novel in England in the eighteenth century saw the notion of secrecy pushed to the fore, with an opening up of such secrets being a key theme in the plot of many novels, secrets related to behaviour, as in the exposure of hypocrisy, or to origins. This could be in a comic context and to comic effect, as in Henry Fielding's *Tom Jones* (1749), with the unveiling of his parentage; but there were also novels that were darker and more troubling. This style came to the fore with the Gothic novels of the late eighteenth century, notably those by (Mrs) Ann Radcliffe, especially *The Mysteries of Udolpho* (1794) and *The Italian* (1797), and also Matthew Lewis's *The Monk* (1796). These novels had elements of both the thriller and the detective novel. The fears to which they could give rise could be a source of fun, as clearly with Jane Austen's *Northanger Abbey* (1817), but the popularity of Gothic fiction is instructive.

In many respects, the Gothic novels were the precursors of the more classic detection fiction that was to be so important to the Victorians, with deep secrets for example crucial in such Dickens masterpieces as *Nicholas Nickleby* (1838), *Bleak House* (1852), and *Little Dorrit* (1855). There was also a continuation of Gothic fiction in 'penny dreadful' serials such as the work of George Reynolds (1814–79), notably the highly popular *The Mysteries of London* (1844–8), in whose pages the Resurrection Man, a serial killer, stalks. This was followed by *The Mysteries of the Court of London* (1848–52). The relating of crime to foreigners was a significant theme in Gothic fiction and from the eighteenth century onwards. Reynolds wrote about vampires, and Bram Stoker's *Dracula* (1897) drew on these ideas. Invasive contagions linked to sexuality were in part an aspect of this equation.

Crime was also a central subject in the press which, after an unsettled seventeenth-century beginning, grew rapidly and consistently into the twentieth century. This was a press that Christie was apt to disparage, as, at length, with the foolish and pompous, but commercially highly successful, press proprietor, Lord Whitfield, in *Murder Is Easy* (1939).

Accounts of the actions of criminals not only served to excite newspaper readers, but also provided warnings that were regarded as valuable, as when the *Taunton Courier* of 12 March 1828 warned against swindlers. Nevertheless, it was interest in a good story that primarily helped encourage inserting details of crime. The lives of villains were frequently discussed, often in moralistic and voyeuristic terms, while there were regular reports on assizes and executions, each of which provided easy copy for the newspaper. Four-and-a-half columns of the *Birmingham Chronicle* of 6 November 1823 was devoted to the 'Gill's Hill murder' near distant Elstree on 24 October. In addition, the editorial, which noted that the reporting had driven out news items from abroad, commented on the wealth and respectability of the principal accused, adding a note of drama:

Another trait in the evidence brings the affair into a resemblance with those banditti establishments, hitherto peculiar to the Continent, and which have been known to us only as the plots of our melo-drames. Incredible as it may appear … a fraternity existed for the express purpose of robbery and murder.

The following issue (13 November) devoted two entire pages, including four sketches and a map, to the murder, as well as an editorial.

The massive attention given to crime by the daily and provincial press showed that it was not only the Sunday newspapers that covered it extensively. Prurience and sensationalism attracted many. *Drewry's Staffordshire Gazette* of 2 August 1827 devoted one of its twenty columns to the calendar of prisoners for trial at the Staffordshire summer assizes, and also provided details of a trial at the Oxford assizes, two attempted break-ins, and a London poisoning; for poisoning was a staple of murderers well before its popularity in the pages of Golden Age detective writers, notably Christie. The *Gloucester Journal* of 9 April 1836 noted: 'our columns are so extensively occupied by assize intelligence that we have been compelled to omit many advertisements and articles of a local nature'. Interest in crime was national as well as local and encouraged the printing of items from other newspapers. The *Taunton Courier* of 6 February 1828 carried an account from the *Bath Journal* under the heading 'The Murder in Marlborough Buildings, Bath – Confession of the Murderer'. The *Courier*, a London daily evening paper, in its issue of 18 September 1832, printed a story headlined 'Shocking Murder', with the *Bolton Chronicle* as the source. The extent to which crime rates reflected social and economic trends, including post-war demobilisation and economic depressions,[4] understandably did not attract comparable attention.

The Sunday newspapers proved particularly keen to report crime. Papers such as *Lloyd's Weekly Newspaper* (1842), the first English paper with a circulation of over 100,000, which, by 1896, was selling over a million copies, and the *News of the World* (1843), extensively reported crimes and readily added moral strictures. Periodic moral panics, many provided by,

4   J.M. Beattie, *The First English Detectives: The Bow Street Runners and the Policing of London, 1750–1840* (Oxford, 2012).

or linked to crimes, were frequent. Thus, in 1895, when 14-year-old Robert Combes was convicted of the murder of his mother in London, the murder was blamed by part of the press on his reading of 'penny dreadfuls' or 'cut-throat newspapers'. Press reporting of crime meanwhile employed novelistic styles, as in 1888 with the 'Jack the Ripper' murders. Fear of the poor, of the East End of London, of outcasts, and of criminality all played a role in creating a sensational narrative, while in the aftermath of these murders there was an even more sensationalist, crime-oriented journalism.[5]

And so into the 1920s. Crime proved a prime topic in the popular press, one that spoke in particular to the social, ethnic and gender anxieties of the period,[6] as well as providing human interest, and with a frisson and, often, excitement. Alongside national newspapers spreading stories, local newspapers covered crimes across the country. Thus, the *Devon and Exeter Gazette* in January 1930 reported on a murder at Bradford.[7]

Novelists responded to the press coverage. In his short story 'The White Murder' (1925), Chesterton has the wise Adrian Hyde: 'pishing and poohing over the newspapers. "Lord, what rubbish!" he cried. "My God, what headlines! Look at this about White Pillars 'Whose Was the Hand?' They've murdered even murder with clichés like clubs of wood"'. Chesterton had experience of the press as a columnist for the *Daily News* and *The Illustrated London News*, and in his newspaper, *G.K's Weekly* (1924–36).

Criticism of the press as a whole had become more striking in the latter stages of World War I. In February 1918, Austen Chamberlain, a leading Conservative politician, attacked the government of David Lloyd George for being so closely linked to major newspaper proprietors. The assertiveness

5   J. Stokes, *In the Nineties* (Chicago, 1989); L. P. Curtis, *Jack the Ripper and the London Press* (New Haven, 2001).
6   C. Emsley, 'Violent Crime in England in 1919: Post-war Anxieties and Press Narratives', *Continuity and Change*, 23 (2008), pp. 173–95.
7   J. Rowbotham, K. Stevenson and S. Pegg, *Crime News in Modern Britain: Press Reporting and Responsibility, 1820–2010* (Basingstoke, 2013); J.C. Wood, '"The Third Degree": Press Reporting, Crime Fiction and Police Powers in 1920s Britain', *Twentieth Century British History*, 21 (2010), pp. 464–85; H. Shore, 'Rogues of the Racecourse: Racing men and the press in interwar Britain', *Media History*, 20 (2014), pp. 352–67; 8 Published in 1960 but an expanded version of *The Mystery of the Baghdad Chest* (1932).

of Alfred, 1st Viscount Northcliffe, who owned the *Daily Mail* and the *Times*, proved a particularly major issue. Subsequently, Stanley Baldwin, the Conservative leader, was to attack two leading press proprietors, Harold Harmsworth, 1st Viscount Rothermere, and Maxwell Aitken, 1st Lord Beaverbrook, in 1931, not least for "'direct falsehood, misrepresentation, half-truths'".

In an instructive theme that related to the commonplace coverage of crime, and thereby provided a counterpoint to the skill, tone, and methods of Poirot, Christie repeatedly held up the treatment of crime in the press for ridicule. This was notably so in *The Man in the Brown Suit* (1924) with Lord Naseby and his assertive *Daily Budget*. Again, with *The ABC Murders* (1936):

> The newspapers were full of nothing else. All sorts of 'clues' were reported to have been discovered. Arrests were announced to be imminent. There were photographs of every person or place remotely connected with the murder. There were interviews with anyone who would give interviews.... The population of Great Britain turned itself into an army of amateur sleuths. The *Daily Flicker* had the grand inspiration of using the caption: HE MAY BE IN *YOUR* TOWN.

Christie may be assumed to reflect through Poirot on this situation:

> The spoken word and the written – there is an astonishing gulf between them. There is a way of turning sentences that completely reverses the original meaning.... If our madman reads what I am supposed to have said to the *Daily Blague* today, he will lose all respect for me as an opponent.

In the same novel, with Mrs Marbury, Cust's sympathetic landlady in London, there is a reference back to a former serial killer on whom the press had focused: "'Nothing but this murdering business in the papers nowadays.... It's like Jack the Ripper all over again'". In *Sad Cypress* (1933), Poirot ignores the newspaper reports owing to their ever-inaccuracy. In the Detection Club's parodic novel of that year, *Ask a Policeman*, a press lord was the victim. Christie's short story 'The Augean Stables' (1940) has Percy Perry, the editor of *The X-Ray News*, as a dangerously disruptive force.

In Christie's *Death in the Clouds*, the *Weekly Howl* is the paper in question, offering to buy or make up the story of Jane Grey and then fabricating an interview. We are in the satirically critical world of Evelyn Waugh's brilliant novel *Scoop* (1938), with its *Daily Beast* and its proprietor Lord Copper. In Christie's *The Body in the Library* (1942), George Bartlett responds to the murder by remarking: "'Sort of thing one reads about in the Sunday papers – but one doesn't feel it really happens'". Lady Angkatell in *The Hollow* (1946) notes that the wealthy landed Angkatells pretend they get the *News of the World* for the servants, but that the very understanding butler, Gudgeon, never takes it out for the latter until after the owners have read it with their tea. She remarks about the incredible number of suicides mentioned in the paper: women putting their heads in ovens. Near the close of the novel, old Mrs Crabtree is lent the papers so that she can read about the murder in which she takes ghoulish pleasure.

In *A Murder is Announced* (1950), the press offered headlines such as 'Bloodhounds seek blonde typist's killer', while, in *A Pocket Full of Rye* (1953), the 'very superior' intellectual Gerald Wright complains about "'how incredibly bloodthirsty our public press … our newspapers delight in reporting brutal murders'". In 'The Mystery of the Spanish Chest',[8] Poirot distinguishes between the press printing news and truth. More generally, this is a distinction in Christie's work: it is a distinction not only about crime but also relating to character and emotions.

In Christie's *Three Act Tragedy* (1934), the elderly Mr Satterthwaite notes 'we can't expect young ladies to sit at home and sew and shudder at the idea of crimes of violence in these enlightened days'. In practice, readership for detective novels was high among both men and women. Children also feature in the world of Christie. Thus, nine-year-old Peter Carmody, an attractive character, in *The Body in the Library*, tells Superintendent Harper that he likes detective stories: "'I read them all, and I've got autographs from Dorothy Sayers and Agatha Christie and Dickson Carr and H.C. Bailey'". Sir Henry Clithering, the former Commissioner of the

8   Published in 1960 but an expanded version of *The Mystery of the Baghdad Chest* (1932).

Metropolitan Police, who had a frequent appearance in the Marple stories, in which he plays a positive role, later says to Peter, "'The head of Scotland Yard is usually a complete dud in books, isn't he?'", earning the rejoinder "'Oh no, not nowadays. Making fun of the police is very old-fashioned'". The previous year, in *Evil Under the Sun* (1941), with a placement in past coverage, Horace Blatt uses Holmes as a lodestar, as when he observes that Poirot is: "'in on this. Oh well, I suppose you would be. Sherlock Holmes *v* the local police, is that it? Ha, Ha! Lestrade – all that stuff'", Inspector Lestrade being a character in the Holmes stories.

The large number of detective novels and short stories ensured that it was not necessary to read popular newspapers in order to follow an interest in crime. There was a different parallel with books about 'true crimes'. At any rate, with detective fiction drawing on its resonances, there was a constant series in the 'real world' of news stories about crime, stories which provided links to new forms of crime, to alarms about the competence, and even integrity, of the police, and often references to ideas in the popular fiction of the period. Christie's world therefore was unreal, but recognisable.

There could be a pronounced xenophobic dimension in the press reporting of crime, with particular attention devoted to crimes by, or allegedly by, foreigners, a theme matched in much popular fiction. There was a widespread assumption, frequently reiterated in popular fiction, as with the murderous villain Rigaud in Dickens' *Little Dorrit* (1855–7), that foreigners were particularly associated with crime in London. Detective novels often contrasted rugged British heroes with foreign residents of London, the latter generally presented in terms of supposedly undesirable physical characteristics such as shifty looks and yellowish skin. The manly heroes relied on their fists, and their devious opponents on knives. Christie's espionage thrillers were in that tradition.

Drugs were also associated with foreigners. In the early 1920s, the *cause célèbre* of note was the case of 'Brilliant' Chang (b. circa 1886), a well-educated Chinese restaurant owner and drug dealer in London, who focused on young women and was held responsible for the death through a cocaine overdose of Freda Kempton, a dance hostess. 'White slavery' was a major theme in the press coverage. Chang was convicted in 1924 for drug-dealing, the judge denounced him for 'corrupting the womanhood of this country', and after prison he was deported in 1925.[9] Christie addresses this milieu in 'The Lost Mine' (1923), with an opium-den in London's Limehouse, its trapdoor, and Limehouse's evil-smelling streets all part of the setting. Limehouse, in London's Dockland, drew on fears of the East End and of Chinese immigrants, and on the popular Fu-Manchu stories. Doyle had made use of the sinister reputation of Chinese-run opium-dens in London. Christie, however, does not fall for the easy theme of Chinese villainy. The victim, Wu Ling, was indeed killed by Chinese gangsters in Limehouse, but the plot was that of Pearson, a British director of Burma Mines Ltd. with substantial gambling debts.

In practice, London's key gangsters included the Sabinis, led by an Anglo-Italian, Charles 'Darby' Sabini (1888–1950), who focused on race-course and, later, West End protection rackets. The Cortesi Brothers of Stamford Hill were rivals. As in the United States, there were Jewish gangs, notably one led by Alfie Solomon. Alongside upper-class criminals,[10] other gangs included Freddie Gilbert's Finsbury Boys, the Camden Town gang of George Sage, the White Family gang, the Bethnal Green Boys under Dodger Mullins, and the Elephant and Castle Mob under the McDonald Brothers. The gambling and cash linked to racing made the latter a focus for crime, including protection rackets.[11] In *The Body in the Library*, the shop girl working herself into the good graces of Mr Badger the chemist '"was carrying on with a *very* undesirable young man connected with the racecourses"'. Drugs are a topic covered by Christie, one example being a killer in *Why Didn't They Ask Evans?* (1934). In *Endless Night* (1967), there are references still to 'race-course gangs' as well as to 'dope gangs'.[12]

Prostitution in London was largely seen as a problem with foreign origins. The Maltese Messina brothers dominated prostitution from 1934, opening a large number of brothels and creating a system that lasted for

9   M. Kohn, *Dope Girls: The Birth of The British Drug Underground* (London, 2001), pp. 123–9.

10   A. McLaren, *Playboys and Mayfair Men: Crime, Class, Masculinity, and Fascism in 1930s London* (Baltimore, 2017).

11   H. Shore, 'Rogues of the Racecourse: Racing Men and the Press in Interwar Britain', *Media History*, 20 (2014).

12   B. McDonald, *Gangs of London* (London, 2010).

several decades.[13] This affected the perception of Soho. In Christie's 'The Kidnapped Prime Minister' (1923), set during World War I, Lord Estair, Leader of the House of Commons,[14] tells Poirot that the Prime Minister's car was '"discovered standing outside a certain unsavoury little restaurant in Soho, which is well known as a meeting-place of German agents"'. Soho was described by Alec Waugh, a London-based novelist, in 1926 in terms of 'a swarthy duskiness, and oriental flavour; a cringing savagery that waits its hour'. In *Dead Man's Folly* (1956), Poirot suggests that the Italian murderess has taken refuge in Soho where underworld affiliations can provide her with the necessary papers.

Crime, meanwhile, responded to technological change, for example with new methods of fraud. More dramatically, the spread in the 1930s of large numbers of affordable cars with reliable self-starter motors, so that it was not necessary to crank up the motor by hand, led to a wave of 'smash and grab' raids, as criminals took advantage of the new technology and its speed. In response, the Metropolitan Police experimented with mounting ships' radios in cars, and was able to develop a fleet of Wolseley cars thus equipped to launch an effective response.

Gangsters used guns, knives, razors, and coshes. Guns were seen as particularly American, although there were many in Britain not least due to those retained from military service in World War I. Gangsters did not use the poison seen in a small number of murders and also in detective novels, whereas Christie's war work in a pharmacy had left her with knowledge about medicines and poisons, knowledge she was both to employ ably in her plots. Poison was a sign of preparation and a conspiracy against truth that was different from the demonstrative violence of gangsters. The notion of conspiracy against truth defined detective novels and thrillers alike, and indicated how Christie spanned the two genres.

Crime overlapped with other aspects of public morality, notably sexual

---

13 J. Laite, *Common Prostitutes and Ordinary Citizens: Commercial Sex in London, 1885–1960* (London, 2011); S. Slater, 'Pimps, Police and Filles de Joie: Foreign Prostitution in Interwar London', *London Journal*, 32 (2007), pp. 53–74.

14 A Lord could fulfil this role if the title was a courtesy one as heir to a member of the House of Lords.

conduct and drug-taking. Drug-taking and female independence are linked in Christie's *Lord Edgware Dies* (1933) when Donald Ross, a young actor, remarks 'Idiotic the way all these girls dope'. A very different tone, misogynist, philistine, and sneering, was taken by Rupert Croft-Cooke, writing as Leo Bruce, in *Case of Three Detectives* (1936): 'I do not mean that it was all rather self-conscious and arty, like those awful parties in London at which women with unpleasant breath advocate free love and nudism'.

The press sought to be the definer and policer of public morality.[15] Particular concern with the sexuality of young women was a key element, with social reform joining human interest. The press found ready copy in the matters of every day, not least thanks to problem pages, which brought together the older practice of reader correspondence with a particular interest in sexuality. The *Daily Mirror* had such a column from 1935, and the *Daily Mail* from 1936. They were variously informative and repressive; although attitudes toward them depended in part on personal preference.

The moral framework of any society is one we need to consider when assessing literature as a whole, and fiction in particular, because in fiction it is possible to alter the story to drive home a moral lesson, a method that is not so simple when dealing with fact. Thus, we need to consider the changes in religious belief and sensibility in this period. Despite *Murder in the Vicarage* (1930), *At Bertram's Hotel* (1965), and several other appearances, clerics do not play a major role in Christie's novels.

Nevertheless, in *Three Act Tragedy* (1934), there is a positive account of Christianity from the dynamic young Egg Lytton Gore referring to a recently dead clergyman.

'... He prepared me for confirmation and all that, and though of course a lot of that business is all bunkum, he really was rather sweet about it.... I really believe in Christianity – not like Mother does, with little books and early service, and things – but intelligently and as a matter of history. The Church is all clotted up with the Pauline tradition – in fact the Church is a

---

15   A. Bingham, *Family Newspapers? Sex, Private Life and the British Popular Press, 1918–1978* (Oxford, 2009).

mess – but Christianity itself is all right … the Babbingtons really *were* Christians; they didn't poke and pry and condemn, and they were never unkind about people or things'.

Canon Prescott, in *A Caribbean Mystery* (1964), is positive. In a gentler age, it was possible to say that Prescott is extremely fond of children, especially small girls, without that being seen as sinister.

Moreover, even though clerics are not thick on the ground, that does not mean that religion is absent, either in terms of the lay religiosity of the characters or with reference to the role of the author. Far from it. A similar discrimination to that of Egg Lytton Gore, in favour of a true Christianity as the basis for judgment, is offered in Christie's *Appointment With Death* (1938), when Sarah King observes in the symbolic setting of Jerusalem:

'I feel that if I could sweep all this away – all the buildings and the sects and the fierce squabbling churches – that I might see Christ's quiet figure riding into Jerusalem on a donkey – and believe in him'.

This leads Dr Gerard to reply gravely: '"I believe at least in one of the chief tenets of the Christian faith – *contentment with a lowly place*"'. He goes on to claim that ambition is responsible for most ills of the human soul, whether realised or not. Asylums are filled, he argues, with those who cannot cope with their insignificance.

In a way, Christie presents murder in the same way, and the implication throughout is that it defies the true message of Christianity, not least the acceptance of suffering and the significance of the soul. Some ghost stories, for example those of M.R. [Montague Rhodes] James (1862–1936), explored similar themes. At the close of *In Search of England* (1927), H.V. Morton meets a vicar who tells him:

'We are, in this little hamlet, untouched by ideas, in spite of the wireless and the charabanc. We use words long since abandoned. My parishioners believe firmly in a physical resurrection…. We are far from the pain of cities, the complexities…. We are rooted in something firmer than fashion'.

In *Three Act Tragedy* (1934), the disabled Mrs Milray refers to '"The Lord's will"'. At the denouement, there is also a social dimension, one that Christie brings up when Sir Charles Cartwright responds to Poirot: 'He radiated nobility and disgust. He was the aristocrat looking down at the ignoble canaille.... Hercule Poirot, the little bourgeois, looked up at the aristocrat. He spoke quietly but firmly'. Speaking truth to power, or rather to social eminence and fame, Poirot is observed as taking a moral line, both in stopping murder and also in thwarting a would-be bigamist. The dubious morals of much of the 'smart set' have recently been highlighted in the 2021 first volume of a projected complete edition of the diaries of 'Chips' Channon.[16] Poirot is more generally against crime, in *The ABC Murders* comparing murder to gambling. In 'The Chocolate Box' (1924), Poirot's sole professional failure, he refers to himself as being '"*bon catholique*"'.

Religion is present again in *Triangle at Rhodes* (1937). Poirot goes to the Mount of the Prophet where he meditates on God permitting 'himself to fashion certain human beings' and advises Marjorie Gold to 'leave the island *before it is too late*', a moment recalled in the closing lines when he refers to being 'on the Mount of the Prophet. It was the only chance of averting the crime ... she chose – to remain....' Thus, Poirot as prophet, and Gold as the sinner with free-will, who has rejected, through pride, the possibility of safety, are clearly revealed, with the message underlined in case the reader has missed it. Furthermore, as another aspect of morality, Poirot is convinced that, if the wicked escape, as in the case of 'The Mystery of Hunter's Lodge' (1923), it is at a price. In that story, and the capitalisation is in the original, the murderers gain the huge fortune of the victim, Harrington Pace, but Nemesis overtakes them. They crash in an aircraft and Justice is satisfied. In the penultimate scene in *Death on the Nile* (1937), Mrs Allerton and Poirot join in thanking God that there is happiness in the world. Earlier in that novel, Poirot has referred to a parable in the Bible when chiding Linnet Ridgeway.

Reference to God is part of everyday conversation; as in *Murder Is Easy* (1939) when Mrs Pierce reflects on the death of her young Emma Jane: '"a sweet little mite she was. 'You'll never rear her'. That's what they said. 'She's

16 S. Heffer (ed.), *Henry 'Chips' Channon: The Diaries I: 1918–38* (London, 2021).

too good to live'. And it was true, sir. The Lord knows His Own'". However, in the same novel there is bitter criticism of the pompous press magnate, Lord Whitfield, who has a great faith and trust in Providence, with enemies of the righteous (the latter a group with whom he identifies) struck down by swift divine wrath. Luke Fitzwilliam finds excessive Whitfield's retribution on the drunken chauffeur, and Whitfield's comparison of himself with the Prophet Elisha is obviously inappropriate. Christie is clearly with Fitzwilliam, although, in a typical case of misdirection, the proud and pompous Whitfield is not in fact the villain.

The references to religion continue. *N or M?* (1941) takes its title from a catechism in the *Book of Common Prayer*, while in *Evil Under the Sun* (1941), Stephen Lane, a cleric, complains that "'no one believes in evil'", whereas he firmly sees it as a powerful reality that "'walks the earth'". Poirot agrees with this longstanding view. In *Destination Unknown* (1954), the villainous impresario of evil evades justice on earth, but Jessop comments "'I should say he'll be coming up before the Supreme Justice before very long'". The link between crime and evil is thus reiterated. Very differently, the continuity of ordinary Christian society is presented as significant in *A Caribbean Mystery* (1964), in which Inspector Weston of the St Honoré CID notes that there are few marriages on the island, but that the children are christened.

A practising Anglican, Christie was far from alone as a detective novelist with a strong religious sensibility. Others of this type included Freeman Wills Croft, as in *Antidote to Venom* (1938). The detective fiction of the period presupposed a providentially governed universe that could provide meaning. This was a key aspect of the religious necessities of such fiction and of the contemporary reporting on crime. At the same time, standards were more general. Thus, the world of Sherlock Holmes required a very striking stability so that clothes, routines, and other factors had a fixed and knowable meaning. These ideas of order, epitomised in character and behaviour, were an aspect not only of particular detective novelists, such as Dorothy L. Sayers, but also of the genre as a whole and, indeed, of social norms and practices.

Christie did not restrict her morality to crime. 'Magnolia Blossom', a magazine story of 1925, was not a crime piece but a three-way drama of a marriage under strain and of how people react. The role of the author in terms of judgment is not of course synonymous with the life of the author. It is well-established that some of the great detective writers had somewhat rackety personal lives.[17] Yet, that rarely stops moral grandstanding or indeed simple conformity. And so with detective fiction, much of which relates to morality, directly or by reflection, and with both the author and the reader offering moral frameworks. Indeed, in one respect, fiction is an attempt to offer guidance in a post-Providential world. In an urgently-religious age, Providence brings an instant fate to the wicked, but, by the 1920s, the religious environment was somewhat different. Judgment in life came to be seen more as a matter of human agency and agencies, and the detective was to the fore. Yet, there could be a religious aspect to the moral dimension, a perspective vividly demonstrated in J.B. Priestley's play *An Inspector Calls* (1945), a haunting drama of discovery.

Christian morality is applied by Christie in part in terms of the newly-fashionable psychological insights and in terms of the belief in heredity Poirot mentions in 'The King of Clubs' (1923), and in which he follows other detectives including Holmes. These insights provide both a subject for discussion and explanation and a particular *modus operandi* for Christie and her detectives. This is true not only of the 'foreign' Poirot, but also, albeit using a different language, the very English Jane Marple, who is first introduced in 'The Tuesday Night Club', a thoughtful short story of December 1927. In *The ABC Murders*, Poirot insists that it is crucial to treat the murderer as '"a psychological study"' and '"to get to know the murderer"'. Subsequently he adds, '"A madman is as logical and reasoned in his actions as a sane man – *given his peculiar biased point of view*"'. *Cards on the Table* (1936) also sees an emphasis on the psychology of the suspects, which is a theme underlined in Christie's Foreword. A total misunderstanding, one that is all-too-typical of responses by critics, was offered by Camilla Long in a television review in the *Sunday Times* on 16 February 2020 in which she claimed: 'Christie didn't do personalities; she felt any hint of psychology could distract from the plot lines'.

So also for others. In *Three Act Tragedy*, Lady Mary Gore, who, in a Christie-like autobiographical touch, had fallen for 'a certain type of man', foolishly thinking 'new love will reform him', explains to Satterthwaite that:

17 Edwards, *The Golden Age of Murder.*

'Some books that I've read these last few years have brought a lot of comfort to me. Books on psychology. It seems to show that in many ways people can't help themselves. A kind of kink.... It wasn't what I was brought up to believe. I was taught that everyone knew the difference between right and wrong. But somehow – I don't always think that is so'.

Satterthwaite adds that: '"Without acute mania it may nevertheless occur that certain natures lack what I should describe as braking power ... in some people the idea, or obsession, holds"'. In 'The Red Signal' (1933), Sir Alington West, 'the supreme authority on mental disease', explains: '"suppression of one's particular delusion has a disastrous effect very often. All suppressions are dangerous, as psychoanalysis has taught us"'.

The methodical and intelligent Superintendent Battle, who first appeared in *The Secret of Chimneys* (1925), acknowledges a debt to Poirot's psychological methods in *Towards Zero* (1944). The language varies, but the theme is constant. In *Death in the Clouds* (1937), the young Jane Grey challenges the '"very old-fashioned idea of detectives"' as involving disguise (as Holmes had done), as nowadays they simply think out a case psychologically.

Christie was far from alone in her interest in psychology. Thus, in *The Mystery of a Butcher's Shop* (1929), Gladys Mitchell, who was up on Freud, introduced as her detective Mrs Beatrice Bradley, the author of *A Small Handbook of Psycho-Analysis*. Yet, Christie had a much more Christian feel for psychology. At the brilliant end of *Crooked House* (1949), where there is one of the more outstanding reveals, there is a psychoanalytic explanation in terms of 'retarded moral sense' and heredity, including of 'ruthless egoism'. More bluntly, this becomes "There is often one of the litter who is 'not quite right"', and Christian judgment and justification are offered: '"I do not want the child to suffer as I believe she would suffer if called to earthly account for what she has done.... If I am wrong, God forgive me... God bless you both"'. In *Hallowe'en Party* (1969), Mrs Goodbody, the very pleasant local witch, or, at least, fortune-teller, is clear on the real presence of evil:

'wherever you go, the devil's always got some of his own. Born and bred to it ... those that the devil has touched with his hand.

They're born that way. The sons of Lucifer. They're born so that killing don't mean nothing to them…. When they want a thing, they want it…. Beautiful as angels, they can look like'.

Mrs Goodbody contrasts this with black magic: "'That's nonsense, that is. That's for people who like to dress up and do a lot of tomfoolery. Sex and all that'". At the same time, Honoria Waynflete, in *Murder is Easy*, is compared to a goat which is presented as an apt symbol of evil, as also in Miles Burton's *The Secret of High Eldersham* (1931). In Honoria's case, her behaviour is discussed as an instance of the touch of insanity allegedly present in old families, and she is definitely seen as unhinged. Being a '"wrong 'un"' is the problem for Roger Bassington-Ffrench in *Why Didn't They Ask Evans?* (1934).

Although there was no equivalent to Doyle's strong interest in Spiritualism, the occult plays a role with Christie, one that is understated in television treatments. 'The Harlequin Tea Set' (1971) very much offers the idea of the mixing of this world with a spirit world, as the dead Lily joins Harley Quin from the other world to help Mr Satterthwaite protect the living in a combination that Christie described in her autobiography as her favourite characters. So also with the protection of many ghost stories both of this period and of earlier ones, such as those of Sheridan Le Fanu (1814–73). An altogether more menacing moral framework is on offer in Christie's *The Hound of Death* (1933). The occult is to the fore in this mysterious and disturbing tale of an alternative 'Brotherhood', but a moral retribution is delivered on the vulpine Dr Rose. The hound is very different from that of the Holmes story about the Baskervilles, while in the title-story of the collection there is a religious dimension not present in the latter.

Not black magic, but a good equivalent, can be deployed, as with the kindly nurse in *Towards Zero* (1940) who comes from the West Coast of Scotland where some of her family had 'the sight' or 'Second Sight'. Possibly because the nurse, like Christie, can see what will occur in the novel, she tells the suicidal Angus MacWhirter that God may need him, and is proven correct.

In many respects, Christie adapts psychological views to match Christian morality. That itself may appear to be one answer, but it is not so, for on matters such as free will Christianity offers a range of explanations. As a consequence, Christie's work can in part be seen as an aspect of debate within inter-war Christianity, including English Christianity. In *A Pocket Full of Rye* (1953), the Calvinistic, very elderly Miss Ramsbottom, who is committed to missionary work as the "'Christian spirit'", refers to Marple as "'frivolous, like all Church of England people'". Christie was Church of England. Alongside Poirot's concern for psychoanalysis, there is Marple's blunter focus on, and denunciation of, wickedness, one that is more to the fore than with most of the clerical detective novelists of the period such as Ronald Knox and Victor Whitechurch: they generally left their cassocks at home. In *A Pocket Full of Rye*, Marple remarks "'This is a wicked murderer, Inspector Neele, and the wicked should not go unpunished'", and Neele replies "'That is an unfashionable belief nowadays. Not that I don't agree with you'". Christie is speaking through both of them.

Aside from wickedness, the frequency with which murderers are castigated for 'conceit and self-confidence', as in *The ABC Murders*, is instructive. In that novel, Poirot seeks to psychoanalyse and profile the murderer after his first murder:

> 'In one sense we know nothing about him – in another sense we know already a good deal…. A great need to express his personality. I see him as a child possibly ignored and passed over – I see him growing up with an inward sense of inferiority – warring with a sense of injustice – I see that inner urge – to assert himself – to focus attention on himself ever becoming stronger….'

This approach is very deliberately contrasted with what is presented as a Holmesian one; although Sherlock also relied heavily on pre-Freudian psychology. This is to a degree that not all television and film versions of Poirot stories have fully represented. The point is very much driven home in 'The Plymouth Express' (1923), with the emphasis for Poirot on psychology, and not 'scene of the crime' footmarks and cigarette-ash. Inspector Japp, in contrast, focuses in this story on finding clues along the route. Based on Lestrade, Japp was introduced in the *Mysterious Affair at Styles* and appeared in seven Christie novels, always alongside Poirot, finally appearing in *One, Two, Buckle My Shoe* (1940); although being mentioned thereafter. In *The ABC Murders*, Poirot jests with Hastings:

'The crime was committed by a man of medium height with red hair and a cast in the left eye. He limps slightly on the right foot and has a mole just below the shoulder-blade'…. For the moment I was completely taken in.

'You fix upon me a look of dog-like devotion and demand of me a pronouncement à la Sherlock Holmes … it is always the clue that attracts you. Alas that he did not smoke the cigarette and leave the ash, and then step in it with a shoe that has nails of a curious pattern'.

In 'The Kidnapped Prime Minister', Poirot, to the anger of all, refuses to leave Boulogne to search for clues to the kidnapping such as tyre marks, cigarette-ends, and fallen matches because he must focus on a logical solution, which he does successfully. Similarly, in *Death on the Nile*, the murderer, as Poirot notes, is not so obliging as to drop a cuff link, a cigarette end, cigar ash, a handkerchief, lipstick, or a hair slide. Instead, in a comparison that would have come naturally to Christie, Poirot compares himself to an archaeologist clearing away the extraneous matter. This involves, as he notes in *Mrs McGinty's Dead* (1952), using a hunting image, starting, as it were, several birds in a covert, as if seeking to create a form of creative disruption that will lead to the revelation of the truth. The misdirections provided through, and by, possible culprits are a form of this creative disruption as well as a response to it.

In practice, Christie offers a degree of caricature, as the Holmes stories include psychological insights, but she is correct to draw attention to a contrast. And not always simply with the detective. In 'The Market Basing Mystery' (1923), Dr Giles tells Japp that he cannot give the time of death to an hour as '"those wonderful doctors in detective stories do"'.

And so also with other novelists. In J. Jefferson Farjeon's *Seven Dead* (1939), Inspector Kendall, a figure of brusque intelligence and determined drive, remarks, '"When you don't play the violin, or haven't got a wooden leg, smartness is all you've got to fall back on"', and says of Inspector Black: '"a good man. He doesn't play the violin, either, or quote Shakespeare"'.

In a conversation in *The Clocks* (1963), not one of Christie's better novels, Poirot gives Colin Lamb a long account of what he likes in '"criminal

fiction"'. Anna Katharine Green's *The Leavenworth Case* (1878) is praised
for "'period atmosphere … studied and deliberate melodrama"' and "'an
excellent psychological study"' of the murderer. Poirot then moves on to
Maurice Leblanc's *The Adventures of Arsene Lupin* (1905–7), which he finds
preposterous and unreal, but also as having vigour and humour, which is
indeed the case. Gaston Leroux's *The Mystery of the Yellow Room* (1907–8)
is approved of from start to finish, not least for its logical approach. Charges
that the novel is unfair are dismissed as there is truth concealed by a cun-
ning use of words, which is very much Christie's technique. Poirot notes
that that masterpiece is now almost forgotten. The selection Christie offers
in the account is scarcely insular, nor the approach xenophobic.

In *The Clocks*, Poirot then skips twenty years or so to consider a range
of fictional choices by imaginary detectives, which gives Christie free rein,
beginning with Ariadne Oliver. Christie rejects what she sees as improbable
happenings and an over-use of coincidence, but she is for originality of
mind and for learning more in recent years, notably on police procedure,
firearms, and the law. The last is in an instance of self-reflection by Christie.
The pipe-smoking Mr Cyril Quain, a reference to Freeman Wills Crofts, is
referred to as dull but a master of the intricate alibi, although Poirot then
draws attention to the formulaic character of the latter. In contrast, Garry
Gregson offers thrillers with excessive bloodshed and lurid implausibility.
The American Florence Elks is praised for order, method, and wit; the
"'tough school"' rejected as "'violence for violence" sake', but American
crime fiction is approved of for being more ingenious and imaginative than
English writing while being less atmospheric and over-laden with atmosphere than most French writers. Louisa O'Malley is commended for "'deep
unsuspected seams of crime"' in New York society, before Poirot pulls up
The Adventures of Sherlock Holmes and utters reverently the word "'Maître"'.
Lamb asks if he refers to Holmes, but Poirot says no:

> 'It is the author, Sir Arthur Conan Doyle, that I salute. These
> tales of Sherlock Holmes are in reality far-fetched, full of falla-
> cies and most artificially contrived. But the art of the writing –
> ah, that is entirely different. The pleasure of the language, the
> creation above all of that magnificent character, Dr Watson. Ah,
> that was indeed a triumph'.

Christie, like Doyle, spanned to include in her writing what is too readily seen as an alternative or at least less significant strand of the fiction of detection, that directed in defence of the state against organised foes. This thriller literature was a significant adjunct of the pre-war sense of international menace, whether the war panic with France in 1898 or the naval race with Germany of 1906–12. Novels of detection and adventure, such as Erskine Childers' *The Riddle of the Sands* (1903), sat securely in this context. Puzzles about extra-terrestrial threats played a related role as they also focused on the invasion of England, and notably so with H.G. Wells' *War of the Worlds* (1897–8). So also did those novels of detection directed against conspiracies that lacked a clear state background, notably the Fu-Manchu stories which drew on the idea of a criminal mastermind, acting as a precursor to the SPECTRE of Ernst Stavro Blofeld in Ian Fleming's James Bond novels of 1961–4.

The creation of Arthur Sarsfield, a crime reporter who wrote under the pseudonym of Sax Rohmer, Fu Manchu, 'the greatest genius which the powers of evil have put on earth for centuries', and the foe of the British empire and of British civilisation, combined great cruelty with advanced scientific research, as in *The Mystery of Dr Fu-Manchu* (1913) and *The Devil Doctor* (1916). Wide-ranging conspiracy played a role in many novels, but in some cases, for example the mysterious Spider in Anthony Gilbert's *Death in Fancy Dress* (1933), the result was very weak.

Anarchist conspiracies were also involved in detective novels. These had many forms, including Edgar Wallace's *The Four Just Men* (1906), in which, despite extensive precautions for his safety, the Foreign Secretary is assassinated. During World War I, these anxieties and the related detection very much focused on Germany, as with John Buchan's Richard Hannay stories, notably *Greenmantle* (1916) and the post-war *Mr Standfast* (1919). Hannay takes on features of the detective, although Buchan's plots were held together more by coincidences than by logic and deduction.

International malice and domestic conspiracy is an important context for some of Christie's early work, and to this we will turn shortly. There is no but here, for categories overlapped, strands interacted, and there was no tightly defined set of parameters. Yet it is also important to see Christie in terms of the strength of a middle-brow reading public who wanted good stories and found detective fiction an established means to that end. This public was the key to the genre. At the same time, what this interest would mean in the post-war world was unclear, and authors developed their characters, plots, and styles, in the context of probing a readership that was re-setting after that cataclysmic conflict.

And that probing was necessary in order to earn money, as Christie recorded making only an advance of £25 from *The Mysterious Affair at Styles*, and that from a half share of the series rights which were sold to *The Weekly Times*. Her novel, however, had introduced two stars, herself and Hercule.

2. POST-WAR TURMOIL

> 'Don't pay attention to wild stories of disorders, rioting, out-
> rages and the like. Evil tongues are deliberately inventing these
> to scare you'.
> *Daily Mail*, 6 May 1926, during the General Strike.

'The triumph of law and order over the forces of Revolution', with 'the swift efficient proclamation of martial law' and the collapse of the 'untrained rabble' is the background to the largely unknown 'The Wife of the Kenite', which Christie published in Australia's *Home Magazine* in September 1922. The story was set against a true event, the backdrop of the Rand Rebellion, an uprising of white gold mine workers, backed by the newly-formed Communist Party of South Africa, that began in December 1921. This rebellion was suppressed by troops supported by aircraft, tanks and artillery, under Jan Smuts, the Prime Minister, and a key figure in World War I.

The story repays reading. It joins several of Christie's lodestars of value. The radical agitators, who are unsympathetically described as 'the Reds', are linked to a German veteran who had shown cruelty in the war, brutal-ising and then murdering a child. Retribution is powered by a reading of the Bible, with a woman delivering the harsh, but fair, killing of the villain. This is Old Testament in its forcefulness, and it is abundantly clear where Christie's sympathies lie. Moral judgment, and the working out of an ap-propriate vengeance, are necessary and possible. The Rand Rebellion clearly had an impact on Christie, as it recurs in *The Man in the Brown Suit* (1924), and, far more briefly, in *Death on the Nile* (1937). Christie had visited South Africa in 1922 as a spouse accompanying her husband who was on official duties.

Written and set during the Great War (World War I), although not published until afterwards, *The Mysterious Affair at Styles* (1920) offers the Dr John Watson-like perspective of a man of integrity, Captain Arthur

Hastings, who indeed appeared in eight Christie novels, making him less of a presence than Watson had been for Holmes or than Hastings was subsequently to be in the David Suchet television series. A pre-war Lloyd's broker, Hastings somewhat surprisingly says, in *The ABC Murders* (1936), "'I've never been able to afford to hunt'": in practice friends would lend horses. Hastings, moreover, as is revealed in a novel in which he does not appear, *Death on the Nile*, wears "'an O.E. Tie'", in other words is an Old Etonian. The Poirot stories show Christie focused on attire. At any rate, Hastings became an army captain, and then "'our wounded hero … invalided home from the Front'", the Western Front. In 'The Kidnapped Prime Minister', Hastings records that after being invalided out of the army, he had been given a recruiting job.

His wartime record is more realistic than that of Intelligence work behind German lines given by Dorothy L. Sayers to Lord Peter Wimsey, whose would-be brother-in-law in *Clouds of Witness* is another veteran, Captain Denis Cathcart. Other detectives were from the same stable, including Colonel Anthony Ruthven Gethryn, the protagonist of Philip MacDonald's *The Rasp* (1924), who, after being wounded in action, did Intelligence work in wartime Germany. In Miles Burton's *The Secret of High Eldersham* (1931), a key role is played by Desmond Merrion, who had also been wounded in the war, before, in his case, moving to Naval Intelligence. A number of detective novelists indeed fought in the war, including Anthony Berkeley (in reality Anthony Berkeley Cox), who was wounded, and Cecil Street, who wrote under the names of Miles Burton and John Rhode. Christie's first husband, Archibald, served in the war, becoming a colonel and was mentioned in despatches five times.

Hastings was from the group that took the highest casualties in the war. References to that conflict are frequent in Christie's work. Indeed, as with the description of character in the Bond novels for Ian Fleming, in that case with reference to World War II, it serves as a placing of value. Introduced into English society by Hastings, he adds a wartime note in his description of Poirot: 'I believe a speck of dust would have caused him more pain than a bullet wound'.

In *The Murder on the Links*, Hastings' 'many memories' of the war are reawakened as his train from Paris to the English Channel passes through Amiens, a key British base for the Western Front. The sympathetic response of 'Cinderella', his unexpected companion, emerges clearly. She elicits from the private man his history: "'I was wounded once, and after the Somme they invalided me out altogether'". They eventually marry and have a happy marriage, before she dies leaving him a widower.

In *The Secret Adversary*, Tommy and Tuppence are located by their war work, Tuppence leading the comfort of home life to work in an officers' hospital where Tommy, a Lieutenant, was convalescing. 'Mr Carter' was, like Tommy, in 'the Intelligence' in France. The Communist plot in that novel has a German backstory. The Prologue to the book begins describing a prominent German wartime atrocity, with the U-boat sinking of the liner *Lusitania* in 1915, and, in response, the nobility of allowing women and children to go first into the lifeboats. There is a resulting need in this story for a woman to play a key role in delivering a secret message.

Very differently, the war plays a role in *The Hound of Death* (1933), the title short-story of that collection. In this, the 'uhlans', rampaging 'impious' German cavalry, who ignore Sister Marie Angelique's attempt to stop them entering a convent in 1914, are destroyed by the lightning she calls down: "'I stood on the altar steps and I bade them to come no farther. I told them to depart in peace. They would not listen…. And so I loosed the Hound of Death on them'". In 'The Red Signal' in the same collection, Jack Trent is validated as 'the man who had saved his life in Flanders and been recommended for the VC for doing so'. More minor characters also make reference to the war, as with Mrs James at Mill House in *The Man in the Brown Suit*, who makes reference to her nephew who was affected by a war wound.

In contrast, in a sure highlighting of a lack of values, the feline doctor, James Sheppard, and his gossipy sister, Caroline, in *The Murder of Roger Ackroyd*, are condescending about Colonel Carter who is reminded by the very cold evening of 'the Afghan passes'. This is presumably, as with Holmes' Watson, a reference to the difficult Second Anglo-Afghan War of 1878–80, and one of the numerous references to the Holmes corpus in Christie's early works. Doctor Sheppard records:

> 'It is the private opinion of both Caroline and myself that Colonel Carter has never been in the Shanghai Club in his life. More, that he has never been farther east than India, where he juggled with tins of bully beef and plum and apple jam during

the Great War. But the colonel is determinedly military, and in King's Abbot we permit people to indulge their little idiosyncrasies freely'.

World War I goes on to have echoes in the Christie novels, as would indeed have been the case, and to provide a ready frame of reference. In *Sad Cypress* (1933), Sir Lewis Rycroft was killed in 1917, while Major Somervell becomes the new Conservative MP. In *The ABC Murders*, the commissionaire of the Regal at Doncaster, 'very stiff and military', is asked by Colonel Anderson, the Chief Constable, to provide an account of a murder there, whereupon he salutes. In the same novel, the unfortunate and incommunicative Alexander Bonaparte Cust lightens up when asked by Poirot about the war: '"I enjoyed the war.... I felt, for the first time, a man like anybody else. We were all in the same box. I was as good as anyone else"'. In 'The Second Gong' (1932), a successful puzzle of a short story, Captain John Marshall, the Lytcham Roche's agent, lost an arm in the war. In *Death in the Clouds*, George Leman, Giselle's husband, was killed in its early days, while in 'Dead Man's Mirror' (1937): 'The brother, Anthony Chevenix-Gore, was killed in the war'. In *Murder in Mesopotamia* (1936), the Swedish-American archaeologist Eric Leidner turns out really to be Frederick Bosner, a German spy in the US State Department, who had been arrested during World War I, sentenced to death, escaped and allegedly died in a train crash; whereas, in practice, he had swapped identities with Leidner who had been killed in that crash. In 'In a Glass Darkly' (1959), Neil Carslake is killed in 1916 and Charles Crawley in 1918; but the narrator survives, although one bullet nearly got him below the right ear and the other was deflected by a cigarette case in his pocket. That is an instance of the wartime chance that greatly affected Christie's generation, and she captures it well. It would also have been natural for readers to wish to know what had allegedly happened to characters during the war.

The *Mysterious Affair at Styles* is a good first novel, albeit not as good as Christie was to offer when she came into her stride. The plot followed the standard Victorian pattern of dealing with people who are not what they seem. This captured a lasting issue in detection, provided an effective plot device of mystery, and also reflected the extent to which the greater mobility of the nineteenth-century world brought people into new settings where they could present themselves in a very different way. Alfred Inglethorp "'is an absolute outsider, anyone can see that. He's got a great black beard, and wears patent leather boots in all weathers!'" Financial pressure is not to the fore in the novel, but it is present. Hastings suggests that his married friend John Cavendish "'would have preferred his mother to increase his allowance, which would have enabled him to have a home of his own. John's mother, however, a widow who married Inglethorp, was a lady who liked to make her own plans, and expected other people to fall in with them, and in this case she certainly had the whip hand, namely the purse strings'". Styles was the name given to the house Christie and her family purchased in 1926 in fashionable Sunningdale.

In practise, the immediate post-war years were to see a major crisis hit landed society, one that led to many estates changing hands. This was when Bridget Conway had to leave Ashe Manor in *Murder Is Easy* (1939). Instead, Gordon (Lord) Whitfield, a self-made press lord is able to buy and remodel the Waynfletes' family house. Indeed, many of those living in rural splendour during the Golden Age would have been not the scions of long-established families but, rather, new men (and their wives) who had bought into landed status, either pre-war or immediately after it. Moreover, the process is shown by Christie to be continuing. Thus, with her very large inherited American funds, Linnet Ridgeway spent £60,000 to buy Wode Hall, launching *Death on the Nile* (1937). The previous owner, Sir George Wode, lost on the horses. Linnet puts in a swimming pool (to which end she is rehousing tenants), Italian gardens and a ballroom, all with a projected bill of another £60,000. In *Sad Cypress* (1933), Edmund Seddon advises the acceptance of £12,500 for Hunterbury as large properties are extremely difficult to sell; and Hunterbury itself has been modernised with gas, electricity, and good servants' quarters. In 'The Case of the Perfect Maid' (1941), Old Hall, a big Victorian house surrounded by woods and parkland, proves both unlettable and unsaleable. Instead, a speculator divides it into four flats with a central hot-water system, and with the use of the grounds to be held in common by the tenants. Other detective novelists also noted the change in estate ownership. In Anthony Rolls' *Scarweather* (1934), the 'great estate of Aberleven Manor' had been acquired by Arthur Macwardle, a businessman who 'aimed at the bonhomie, the tempered rusticity of the landed gentleman', only to be revealed as a vulgarian.

Alongside demolitions (such as Haldon House in Devon, between Torquay and Exeter, in 1925) and sales, many stately homes not only remained in private hands but also those of pre-war owners. These included Abney Hall, the home of Christie's elder sister Margaret Frary Miller and her husband James Watts. Built in 1842–7, and greatly extended in the 1890s, this was frequently visited by Christie. It was the basis for Chimneys, which appeared in her *The Secret of Chimneys* (1925) and *The Seven Dials Mystery* (1929), and, also, to a lesser extent, for both Styles and Stonygates, the latter the Victorian stately home of Carrie Louise in *They Do It with Mirrors* (1952).

The changing ownership of estates was part of the disruption of traditional society that·had always existed, but that had become more apparent with the agricultural depression that gathered pace from the 1870s. In the 1910s, the impact of war, combined with taxation, including death duties, and (following the return to peace) with international competition in foodstuffs, all hit hard. That was not an element that is captured in some of our impressions of the period, but it was one that was highly significant. There had never been a golden age, but, certainly, the simulacrum had ceased in 1914, and it was never really restored. Thus, in *The Secret of High Eldersham* (1931) by Miles Burton, Hugh Dunsford, a rural publican, remarks that the times before the war, when ordinary workers could afford a couple of pints of beer, were gone. In Christie's *The Body in the Library* (1942), Raymond Starr, the hotel dancer, was allegedly one of the Alsmonston Starrs from Devon. Their estate was sold:

> 'after it had been in the family for three hundred years ... our kind have to go I suppose. We've outlived our usefulness ... it's hard to get a job nowadays when you've nothing to say for yourself except that you've had a public-school education! Sometimes, if you're lucky, you get taken on as a reception clerk at a hotel'.

Echoes of a more ordered past are presented by Christie as anachronistic, as with a Kent village in *Three Act Tragedy* (1935): 'Gilling was a village which the world had left behind. It had an old church, a vicarage, two or three shops, a row of cottages, three or four new council houses and a very attractive village green'. This was as if we were with H.V. Morton at the close of his *In Search of England* (1927), with his depiction of a true, but precarious and religious, old heart of England located in the Midlands, or, earlier, with Charles Dickens taking Little Nell at the close to rural Shropshire in *The Old Curiosity Shop* (1840–1). At the level of towns, there were similar left-behind settings in Christie, as with other writers. In *Dumb Witness* (1937), there is:

> the little town of Market Basing. Originally on the main road, a modern by-pass now left it some three miles to the north of the main stream of traffic, and in consequence it had kept an air of old-fashioned dignity and quietude about it. Its one wide street and ample market square seemed to say, 'I was a place of importance once, and to any person of sense and breeding I am still the same. Let this modern speeding world dash along their new-fangled road; I was built to endure in a day when solidarity and beauty went hand in hand'.

In *The Moving Finger* (1943):

> somewhere in seventeen hundred and something, the tide of progress swept Lymstock into a backwater. The castle crumbled. Neither railways nor main roads came near Lymstock. It turned into a little provincial market town, unimportant and forgotten, with a sweep of moorland rising behind it, and placid farms and fields ringing it round.

A static, ordered society, dependent largely on established means, including rentier income, was a background to the tensions repeatedly portrayed by Christie and, also, by others who wrote about this particular milieu. Indeed, financial problems made inheritance a more urgent one for those who otherwise were condemned to genteel dependence, as with John Cavendish in *The Mysterious Affair at Styles*, or, even, genteel poverty, with all the loss of status this entailed including the opportunity to find partners. Opportunities for cadet (younger) and collateral (related) family branches were always an issue in all landed societies, but financial crises had brought these to the fore, while also encouraging members to seek a livelihood abroad. Inheritance was the single most important motivation in Christie novels, which was a reflection of writing about a particular social tranche as well as a ready way to structure relationships within a small group of people readily defined as potential heirs. Inheritance could bring together people of different ages and experiences, and, as a prospect and lure, was not restricted to family groups.

Setting the context for Christie's readers, the political situation was tumultuous, both at home and abroad. A theme of the uncertainty of the early 1920s might appear surprising, given the subsequent emphasis on the period as one of prosperity before the Depression of the 1930s. However, there was a profound sense of political and economic crisis in the aftermath of World War I. The sense of victorious triumph at the end of the conflict was muted by the heavy casualties and by new crises in international relations. Ireland, labour relations, and public finances contributed to an overall sense of foreboding that Christie represented very well.

Britain was one of the victor nations in 1918, and its political system had survived the war without excessive strain. Instead, a successful coalition had been created in 1915, with David Lloyd George becoming the Prime Minister in December 1916, a post he held until October 1922. The coalition brought together the pre-war Liberal government with the Conservatives and Labour. Politics, however, had not been thereby banished for the war. In particular, there were Liberal divisions, many refusing to accept Lloyd George's leadership, while Labour was concerned about consequences of the conflict, including food shortages and rising prices, as well as a rise in workers' grievances. These were directed both against aspects of the war, such as wage controls, labour direction, and profiteering, and against facets of social difference that appeared less acceptable in a period of total war.

Christie wrote in the thriller tradition in 'The Kidnapped Prime Minister', published in *The Sketch* magazine on 25 April 1923. The Prime Minister in question, David MacAdam, was clearly based on Lloyd George, an opponent of those calling for a negotiated peace with Germany. They included, in 1917, both Henry, 5th Marquess of Lansdowne, a former Conservative Foreign Secretary, and Arthur Henderson, the Labour leader and the Labour member of the War Cabinet, whose attitude was a response to the possibility that Russia would leave the war, as it indeed did in 1918.

Henderson was unsuccessful and resigned from the War Cabinet, although Labour remained in the government. MacAdam is described as England, which is a classic instance of Christie's tendency to present Britain as England. Readers are told that there are "'German agents in our midst'", and Poirot has for a while been in pursuit of Frau Bertha Ebenthal, who turns out to be in league with MacAdam's secretary, Captain Daniels. The linguistic skill of the latter is not a good sign.

Held in the aftermath and the relief of victory, the general election of 14 December 1918 saw the Coalition strongly re-elected, with those Liberals in opposition doing badly while, benefiting from an extension of the male franchise, Labour gained 60 seats. This election represented a change from the politics of Christie's youth. Prior to the war, the Liberals were in the ascendant, having been in government from 1905. However, by Christie's maturity, they had been hit both by long-term trends and by short-term pressures, not only divisions but also the essential illiberalism of the war years. State action had become coercive during the war with the introduction of the Defence of the Realm Act in 1914, and conscription in 1916. Individual liberties which Liberals had long thought sacrosanct were trampled underfoot owing to the requirements of total war. Furthermore, much of the traditional Liberal concern with temperance (restrictions on the drink trade), Church schools, and Church disestablishment, no longer seemed of relevance or interest to much of the electorate. Separately, the social welfare platform of pre-war Liberalism had in part been achieved and, anyway, now seemed better, and certainly more popularly, represented by the Labour Party. The Liberals lacked new or attractive policies and leaders.

In turn, the Conservatives had recovered from their pre-war electoral failures in 1906 and (twice) 1910. Having moved then to the Right, they had been offered by the war an unexpected way back into government from where they were able to benefit from widespread concern about developments as well as their own skill in flag-waving. An active tranche in writing, notably that of thrillers, reflected this combination.

The Coalition under Lloyd George continued until 1922. This might appear a stable background for Christie's first forays into publication, but that was not the case. Lloyd George's attempt to give the Coalition coherence by creating a new centre force that would accommodate the Conservatives, who, thanks to the 1918 election, dominated the Coalition in Parliament with the social reform of the Lloyd George Liberals, fell foul of incompatible views, especially the determined liberalism of his supporters.

The Conservatives limited Lloyd George's freedom of action over peace terms with Germany, as well as towards Ireland and labour relations. They were also unenthusiastic about social reform policies that would lead to high taxes. Taxes had already risen greatly during the war, and the number of income-tax payers had been considerably increased. Nevertheless, Lloyd George used the Conservatives' fear that if they broke with him that might pave the way to a Labour government, in order to retain power and have some leeway over policy, which served to give his government an aura of progressiveness. Most of the Conservatives were initially keen to maintain the Coalition in order to strengthen opposition to Socialism. They were disturbed by Labour's success in the recent election, by trade union militancy, and by the spectre of Communism sweeping Europe. Yet, some conservative opinion was very opposed to the Coalition. In 1918, the National Party ran about 26 candidates against the Coalition. They were opposed to Indian and Irish nationalists, trade unions and 'Bolshevism', and became part of the die-hard tendency which affected Conservative support for the Coalition and fed into the paranoia seen in the thriller literature.

The Coalition was put under stress both by the settlement of the Irish question and by the problems of post-war social policy. The Anglo-Irish Treaty of 1921 gave effective independence to what became the Irish Free State. A government dominated by Unionists (Conservatives) thus ended the Union, not a move that won their enthusiasm for the Coalition, and one that particularly harmed Lloyd George's position among the backbench Conservative MPs who were to turn against him in 1922. Forty voted against the Act. Liberals, in turn, were angered by the tough tactics used earlier to fight the Irish Republican Army which had waged an insurrectionary war against the Union with Britain. Christie's only references to this conflict are unsympathetic to the Irish republicans.

Post-war economic problems were serious. A world-wide depression in 1921–2 hit British exports. In 1921, unemployment rose markedly (to 1.8 million insured workers), as did industrial disputes, including an unsuccessful miners' strike. Lloyd George no longer seemed able to control social unrest or ensure industrial peace. His value to the Conservatives was now far less clear. At home, the level of government expenditure could not be sustained. In 1922, a committee under the chairmanship of the business-man Sir Eric Geddes, appointed to recommend government cuts in the face of an anti-waste campaign in the Conservative heartlands, urged de-flation. The armed forces were cut, as was expenditure on social services, education and housing, the last the policy of building council houses and thus providing homes for the demobilised troops. This 'Geddes Axe' did not improve Lloyd George's popularity and the social politics of the gov-ernment seemed clearly different from what Labour offered. Indeed, the Labour Party made important gains in council and by-elections in 1921–2.

Abroad, the government was over-extended, with its interventionism in the Russian Civil War against the Communists, and also new commit-ments in the Middle East, both in Iraq and, more seriously, Turkey. In June 1920, Sir Henry Wilson, the Chief of the Imperial General Staff, wrote to Winston Churchill, the Secretary of State for War from January 1919 to February 1921, 'I cannot too strongly press on the Government the danger, the extreme danger, of His Majesty's Army being spread all over the world, strong nowhere, weak everywhere, and with no reserve to save a dangerous situation or to avert a coming danger'. Churchill agreed.[1] As Secretary of State for the Colonies in 1921–2, he urged colonial governors to be wary of Communist infiltration and stirring up of nationalism, which was very much Christie's theme.

It was possible to withdraw from external commitments, but that was not a remedy at home. Labour unrest led to concern about political and so-cial stability. The police forcefully dispersed unofficial strikers in George Square in central Glasgow on 'Bloody Friday', 31 January 1919, the Scottish Secretary talked of a 'Bolshevist uprising', and 12,000 troops were deployed, as were tanks, although they were not required. There were strikes more gen-erally in 1919, including a national one by bakery workers, as well as a police strike that gained significant support in Liverpool. The latter led to looting there in early August, and troops were sent to restore order alongside the use of those police who had not rioted. Elsewhere, fewer police went on

1   Wilson to Churchill, 9 June, Churchill to Cabinet, 15 June 1920, NA, CAB. 24/107 fols 253, 250.

strike, although a portion, up to 10 percent, of the London police supported the opposition to the government's banning of police from joining a trade union.[2] In 1921, troops were deployed in response to unrest among South Wales coal miners. Concern on the part of government did not only lead to such action. Under the Firearms Act of 1920, gun ownership was made dependant on licences issued by the police and renewed annually.

Christie was to voice the fears seen with other writers, notably John Buchan in *The Three Hostages* (1924), in which he discerned 'wreckers on the grand scale'. In *The Secret Adversary* (1922), Christie's second novel, 'Bolshevist gold is pouring into this country for the specific purpose of procuring a Revolution', 'the Bolshevists are behind the labour unrest', and a Labour government would be dangerous. Although set in South Africa, the theme of deadly revolutionary organisation behind strikers is prominent in *The Man in the Brown Suit* (1924). Anxieties continued. The paranoia of the period focused on Socialism as well as Communism. In 1929, *Partners in Crime*, a collection of very different short stories, finds Tommy Beresford and Tuppence up against Moscow's agents again. There is reference to Bulldog Drummond, while Colonel Kingston-Bruce complains about "'A most pestilential fellow – an arrant socialist … a dangerous sort of fellow'".

The international situation appeared more bleak as a result of the extent to which the domestic position was made more threatening by the example of the Russian Revolution and by the way in which Communism could apparently draw on domestic support. Britain had intervened in the Russian Civil War in 1918–20, but without success. In 1921, there was a shift in policy with an Anglo-Soviet trade agreement. Winston Churchill, a fervent anti-Communist, complained that Lloyd George had grasped the 'hairy hand of the baboon' in welcoming the Soviet representative, Leonid Krassion, to his office at No. 10 Downing Street.[3] The British government in fact hoped that engagement, in the shape of trade, would moderate the Communist regime and also be a way to dissolve Communism in Russia. These hopes proved fruitless, although so did Soviet hopes of world revolution.

2   R. Bean, 'Police Unrest, Unionization and the 1919 Strike in Liverpool', *Contemporary History*, 15 (1980), pp.633–53.
3   Lord Beaverbrook, *The Decline and Fall of Lloyd George* (London, 1963), p. 292.

Buchan offered a sense of domestic menace linked to international threat, as did 'Sapper', Lieutenant-Colonel Herman Cyril McNeile, in *Bulldog Drummond: The Adventures of a Demobilized Officer Who Found Peace Dull* (1920), *The Black Gang* (1922), and *The Third Round* (1924). These are accounts of imperial and cultural crises that are turned into a civilisational one. In the opening chapter of *The Three Hostages* (1924), Buchan refers to '"all the places with names like spells – Bokhara, Samarkand – run by seedy little gangs of Communist Jews"'. The 'Bolshevik Jews' return again in the following chapter. The writing style is to a degree satirised by Christie in 'Jane in Search of a Job' (1924). Very differently, T.S. Eliot, in his Modernist poetic epic *The Waste Land* (1922), presented London as the latest in a series of doomed world cities with 'Falling towers'.

Particular suspicions were directed both against foreigners living in Britain, allegedly rootless, but also at dishonest members of the Establishment; both themes to be seen with Christie and linked to the theme of betrayal seen with thrillers. Cosmopolitanism was presented as un-English at best, but, more commonly, as anti-English. Detective fiction frequently returned to this theme. In Georgette Heyer's 'Linckes' Great Case', published in the magazine *Detective* on 2 March 1923: 'Knowledge of our doings is being sold to Russia and to Germany.... The Soviets got wind of our new submarines'. Indeed, the secret plans of submarines also brought in Conan Doyle in 'The Adventure of the Bruce-Partington Plans' (1908) and Poirot in 'The Submarine Plans' (1925). In the last, the Z-type submarine is able to revolutionise modern naval warfare, and a foreign power's attempt to copy it is thwarted by providing fake plans. The aftermath of World War I secrets about a new submarine play a role in Christie's *Postern of Fate* (1973), which is very much a retrospective thriller. The Soviet Union and Germany indeed allied under the Treaty of Rapallo of 1922. Yet, as an instance of unpredictability and conspiracy, in 1923, the Soviets planned war with Germany in support of a Communist revolution there which, in the event, did not occur.[4]

Another dimension is that of Ireland. At a meeting of agitators in *The*

4   D.R. Stone, 'The Prospect of War? Lev Trotskii, the Soviet Army, and the German Revolution in 1923', *International History Review*, 25 (2003), pp. 799–817.

Secret Adversary, the 'Sinn Feiner' promises, if funded, 'I will guarantee you such a reign of terror in Ireland as shall shake the British Empire to its foundations'. There is also discussion at this meeting of a loan to an English newspaper in order to secure favourable coverage, as well as links with the unions, notably the coalminers and the railwaymen, both of which were very radical. A general strike is sought, and one was to occur in 1926.

Yet Lloyd George was to fall because he lost Conservative support, not because he increasingly alienated radicals. Much of the Conservative leadership, including the leader from March 1921, Austen Chamberlain, did not want to divide the anti-Labour vote. Nevertheless, concern about Lloyd George and his policies led many Conservatives in 1921 to decide that they would not fight a second election in alliance with him. Support ebbed further in 1922 as Lloyd George's sale of honours – peerages and baronetcies – led to a public scandal, and, in September, Chamberlain was informed that 180 Conservatives would not fight the next election as Coalition candidates. He wanted to continue the Coalition; but a meeting of Conservative MPs at the Carlton Club on 19 October 1922 decided otherwise by 185 to 88 votes. The energetic and talented, but inconsistent and dishonest, Lloyd George was no longer trusted, admired, or felt necessary by the majority of the MPs, and they also lacked confidence in party leaders who seemed too close to him, particularly the aloof Chamberlain. The National Union of Conservative and Constitutional Associations was also against the continuation of the Coalition, as were the executives of many constituency associations. They put pressure on MPs and, in part, the fall of the Coalition reflected the pressure of activist politics. The Newport by-election victory for an independent (i.e. Anti-Coalition) Conservative confirmed the anxiety of many Conservative MPs about the Coalition. After the meeting decided that the Conservatives should fight the next election as an independent party, not as part of the Coalition, Lloyd George resigned as Prime Minister and Chamberlain as party leader. The Conservatives took office, their new leader Andrew Bonar Law, earlier their leader in 1911–21, who had spoken against the Coalition at the Carlton Club meeting.

The returned party system had to adjust to a new electorate. The Fourth Reform Act of 1918 had brought universal male suffrage, and given women the vote, albeit at a higher age than men. A more broadly-based Labour had replaced the divided Liberals as the leading party of opposition. Labour was therefore the party that opposition to the Conservatives had to cohere round were it to be successful. Although there were important exceptions, for example in Liberal-dominated Cornwall, Labour benefited from the rise in class politics and from the growing prominence of class issues such as industrial relations. It had become the natural first-choice party of the working class, and, as such, was strong in all major conurbations and industrial areas. The greater prominence that the trade union movement had won during World War I, and shifts within the movement so that it was more clearly aligned with Labour, helped the latter. Arthur Henderson, the effective Labour leader in 1908–10, 1914–17 and 1931–2, had been a trade union leader. Labour also enjoyed a measure of support in rural areas among agricultural workers, although that was to ebb as the agricultural workforce declined, while the rural workforce anyway tended to be less unionised than their urban counterparts. Labour benefited from the weakness of its radical challengers, Communism and the Independent Labour Party (ILP). Yet, to the anxiety of outside commentators, Labour also contained both Communism and Socialism.

The Liberals were also hit by the nature of the electoral system, specifically the absence of proportional representation. Winning from 18 to 30 percent of the vote in the elections of 1922, 1923, and 1924, the Liberals suffered because their electors were evenly spread across the country, far more so than Labour, and thus were perennially coming second to Labour victors in working-class seats and to their Conservative counterparts in middle-class areas. Thus, despite the continued liveliness of liberalism as an intellectual philosophy, seen, for example, in the writings of the economist John Maynard Keynes, the Liberals failed to recover their pre-war position.

The decision to abandon Lloyd George helped the Conservatives to victory in the general election of 15 November 1922, with 344 MPs elected. Bonar Law had fought on the platform of stability and 'tranquillity', and, in office, he sought both, promising, in order to lessen the divisiveness and unpopularity of plans for tariff reform, not to introduce protectionism without seeking a mandate in a second general election. Bonar Law served only for 209 days before resigning in May 1923 as a result of the throat cancer that killed him that October.

Bonar Law was succeeded not by Austen Chamberlain, who was discredited by his support for the Coalition, nor by the Foreign Secretary,

George, Marquess Curzon, a peer who felt that he had the strongest claim to the post, but by the less grand (and less experienced), Chancellor of the Exchequer, Stanley Baldwin. Baldwin remained leader of the Conservative Party until 1937. He was crafty, not sparkling, but his tactical skill helped prevent the Conservative divisions from having the same damaging effect as those of their Liberal counterparts. He also played a major role in making the Conservatives appear to much of the electorate to be conservative, but not reactionary, consensual, not divisive, and the natural party of government. Baldwin was to prevail in the General Strike of 1926, the financial-political crisis of 1931, and the abdication confrontation of 1936 with Edward VIII.

Initially, however, Baldwin was less successful. He swiftly lost office, because his call for tariffs in order to protect industry and reduce unemployment was distrusted, unpopular, and widely perceived in class terms as a measure that would help the few, not the many. Both Liberals and Labour supported free trade. Furthermore, Baldwin campaigned poorly and did not make sufficient effort to lessen public anxieties. In the general election of 6 December 1923, the Conservatives took 38 percent of the votes, but only 258 seats, while Labour took 191 and the Liberals 159. The shift in the share of the vote had been small, but this was sufficient to give the Conservatives a net loss of 88 seats. The Baldwin government was voted out by the new House of Commons in January 1924, and Labour took office as a minority party. A Labour government depended on the Liberals, not, as before World War I, vice versa.

National politics were there in the background, and their rapidly-changed nature helped encourage a sense of tumult and unease. There was much more to do with Christie's success, however, than reflecting the troubled tone of national politics as she did in her thrillers. Her ability to write a classic puzzle novel was more significant, and notably so with the skill of misleading her readers. *The Murder on the Links* (1923), with its multiple confusions about identity, and the highly-ingenious hijacking of a false-murder plot by a real one, thus creating an effective red herring, was a masterpiece of this type. It reflected also a move away from the anxieties of post-war Britain in that, although one of the significant scenes occurs in Coventry, most of the action is set in France, and the policing is French. This cosmopolitanism befits Poirot, a Belgian, and Hastings rises to the occasion. The background is the recent co-operation between all three powers in the world war, and that co-operation is to be repeated in *The Mystery of the Blue Train* (1928), which is a far more exotic trip in and to France, although essentially based on her 1923 short story 'The Plymouth Express'.

The fictional Merlinville-sur-Mer between Calais and Boulogne in *The Murder on the Links* is really the English Home Counties moved to nearby France, and not least with a golf course next door. The police are treated as if British counterparts. Christie's range, however, as with the South African setting of the short-story at the outset of this chapter, was far wider. Her ten-month-long round-the-world-tour in 1922, on which, with her husband from 1914 to 1928, Archibald, she had indeed visited southern Africa, had expanded her experience. In her autobiography, she described it as one of the most exciting things that ever happened to her, and so exciting that she could not believe it was true.[5] This British Empire Exhibition Tour was intended to promote the British Empire Exhibition which was held at Wembley in 1924–5. The tour entailed a voyage to Cape Town, travel by train to Rhodesia and within South Africa, a voyage on to Melbourne, and travel in Australia and, via New Zealand, Fiji and a very expensive Honolulu, before travelling to Canada and New York, from which they sailed back to Britain. Although Christie met American relatives, this was very much an imperial tour and for an imperial purpose. Similarly, a round-the-world voyage by a powerful squadron was very much used by the navy in 1923–4 as an attempt to strengthen imperial consciousness.[6]

The British empire was one of Christie's contexts, the empire including the new British presence in the Middle East. The region fascinated Christie. In her author note in *Miss Marple and the Thirteen Problems* (1953), Christie referred to having a great love of the desert. Max Mallowan (1904–78), her second husband, whom in 1930 she met in Ur and married, was an archaeologist specialising in the Middle East. He subsequently was prominent in excavations in Iraq and Syria, and was knighted in 1968.[7] The Middle East provided the setting for *Murder in Mesopotamia* (1936); *Death on the Nile*

5   A. Christie, *An Autobiography* (London, 1977; 1978 edn), p. 298.
6   J. C. Mitcham, 'The 1924 Empire Cruise and the Imagining of an Imperial Community', *Britain and the World*, 12 (2019), pp. 67–88.
7   A. Christie, *Come, Tell Me How You Live* (London, 1946).

(1937), dedicated to a friend who also loves wandering about the world; and *Appointment with Death* (1938). So also with short stories. 'The Adventure of the Egyptian Tomb' (1924) draws on Howard Carter's discovery in November 1922 of the tomb of Tutankhamun. Poirot refutes '"a fury of superstition"' and finds a killer in the present, while also praising Egyptian belief and thought, in contrast to what is presented as the conceit of modern science.

Christie's interest in the Middle East extended to a return to Egypt in *Death Comes as the End* (1945; US 1944), but the action takes place in about 2000 BCE, being inspired by documents of the period found by American archaeologists. The book is a triumph and shows an authorial range, as the only one of her novels to have an historical setting, and a non-European one as well. This is a startling and continually arresting book, although the number of killings is excessive. There is an overlap here between Christie's interest in ancient Egyptian religion and her concern with the occult, as in the stories in *The Hound of Death*. In these, the occult can appear as fraud, as in 'The Mystery of the Blue Jar', but other aspects are also considered, as in the metamorphosis of humans into animals in 'The Strange Case of Sir Arthur Carmichael', in which divine judgment is delivered.

The Man In the Brown Suit (1924), was very much an adventure of Empire. It begins in Paris but most of the action takes place on a voyage to Cape Town and, thereafter, and in, southern Africa. Christie's experiences were reflected in the description of an Atlantic cruise, including seasickness and recovery, the views of Atlantic islands and Table Mountain, and once in southern Africa, the journey to Victoria Falls and to Cecil Rhodes' grave. While reflecting the political anxieties of the early 1920s, the story of an international gang able to kill and capture at will is part of this larger-than-life setting. So were lion stories, crocodiles, and heroic men, notably Harry Rayburn, a Rider Haggard figure, fighting off numerous assailants from an island on the Zambezi River, and discovering a source of diamonds in the heart of British Guiana's jungles. This is Empire as quest, truth, and valorous struggle. Colonel Race, a key defender of Empire, describes Africa as 'simple, primitive, big'.

It is time, however, to turn to the middle-class England of the 1920s that Christie was also to depict. She did so notably, and most successfully, in *The Murder of Roger Ackroyd* (1926).

3. THE MIDDLE-CLASS MILIEU

'Who's Who in King's Abbot', the second chapter of *The Murder of Roger Ackroyd* (1926), is a scene-setter designed to suggest ordinariness: 'Our village, King's Abbot, is, I imagine, very much like any other village.... We are rich unmarried ladies and retired military officers.... There are only two houses of any importance', this phrase indicated the snobbery of the speaker, but one that also captured a commonplace approach of the time, including an approach taken by other detective novelists. Christie then reveals the extent to which this identikit village sees social change, as Roger Ackroyd, who seems and acts like a country squire, is in fact 'an immensely successful manufacturer of (I think) wagon wheels'.

In practice, society had both lasting conventions as well as change, and the interplay of the two was present both for the middle class and more generally. People in novels were classically described in terms of occupations. These were a matter of income, status, living standards, education, and assumptions. There could, however, be tension between these aspects, not least when there was a precarious character to the status and/or income, and this provided much of the back plot in the Christie novels. Underlining this, to be 'middle' class meant very different things at particular stages of life, and this situation challenged any notion of class coherence, let alone unity.

The Victorians employed an occupational classification, and it was continued in many subsequent surveys, as in the 1911 *Fertility of Marriage Census*. Occupational classifications centred on a difference between 'middle'-class, white-collar (non-manual) workers, and the 'working' class, blue-collar (manual) workers. Occupational classification was weakened by a focus on male, and not female, activities, and there could be a tension accordingly in many detective stories. In part, this was a consequence when women were the holders of the wealth, as in *The Mysterious Affair at Styles*.

Meanwhile, social attitudes did not return to the pre-war mould. It would be inaccurate to suggest any pre-war rigidity, but, allowing for that, society was less deferential in the 1920s than hitherto. Although Christie tended not to focus on the young, there was more of a cult of youth and novelty in society. With relatively low rates of juvenile unemployment, the young were able to choose jobs and did not need to be deferential at work. They also had their own leisure choices, especially the cinema and dance halls.

Yet new practices did not necessarily lead to radicalism which, in part, indeed, they were designed to temper. After achieving equal suffrage with men in 1928, when they reached the age of 21, women, as a result of wartime casualties and differing long-term death rates, comprised a clear majority of the electorate, but they were not a united bloc with a shared interest and sense of identity. Having won the vote, the women's movement lost a measure of unity. Instead, aside from the customary divisions that also affected men, on social, ethnic, religious and ideological lines, there were also specific differences between, for example, housewives and employed women, married and unmarried, older and younger, feminists and non-feminists; and these categories clashed, not coincided. In 'Street Haunting: A London Adventure', a 1927 essay, the writer Virginia Woolf suggested that London threatened the established order by offering liberation and delight to women who had formerly, she argued, been marginalised. In the event, many of the new female voters supported the Conservatives and were closer to Christie than Woolf. Dominick Medina, the villainous politician in Buchan's *Three Hostages* (1924), was very keen on a Conservative revival based on the female vote.

Women continued to suffer discrimination in most fields. This related to the jobs they were expected to do and the tasks allocated to them in these jobs. Thus, women teachers were required to resign when they married, while women police officers were essentially expected to deal with women and children. They do not play a role in Christie novels, which reflects the degree to which they were not integrated across a wide range of policing until the 1960s. Or any Chief Constables until 1995. The strengthened ideology of domesticity that followed World War I affected attitudes towards women workers, and, indeed, women in general. So did male unemployment, as in Ethel Lina White's detective novel *Some Must Watch* (1933). White (1876–1944) was a prolific and successful detective novelist writing very varied works, but who is now largely unknown.

At the same time, the women's movement continued to press for equality. Under the leadership of Eleanor Rathbone, the National Union of Societies for Equal Citizenship sought by parliamentary lobbying, not by the Pankhursts' militant tactics, to gain legislative goals, such as welfare benefits for married women. There were certainly advances. Women were allowed to enter the legal profession and become JPs (magistrates) in 1918, and to serve on juries, and divorce law was liberalised. Conservative female movements such as the Mothers' Union were also important in improving the position of women.[1] The position, experience, and views of women varied. An emphasis on this diversity helps explain why feminism was not focused on one cause, why many women were not feminists, and why activists were not only involved with causes such as trade union activity, abortion law reform, and pacifism. Thus, alongside attacks on birth control (and abortion) for evading motherhood, birth control in particular was presented more sympathetically than in the past.

Service on juries was directly related to women's response to murder trials. The *Times* on 16 January 1921 referred to the trial at Aylesbury Assizes of George Bailey, on the charge of murdering his wife at Little Marlow, with the first mixed jury in a murder trial. The judge emphasised that 'however unsavoury the evidence may be, it must be given in the same way as it has always been given to juries composed of men.... There can be no such thing as delicacy if it interferes with our arriving at the truth'. The defence claimed that the death was a suicide by poisoning, while the prosecution established that Bailey had designs on another woman. In his summing-up, reported on the 18th, the judge, Mr Justice McCardie, addressed the three women on the jury and emphasised their need for giving the proper verdict even if they disliked the consequences: 'A jury with women in it has as fully to vindicate the law and guard the security of human life as when the jury was composed of men alone'. The case reflected the presumed fragility and delicacy of women, something that Marple countered. Such newspaper reports both helped encourage a need for more complex plots and also for the extrapolation of the drama into more interesting social settings. The reports also underlined the role of

1   C. Beaumont, *Housewives and Citizens: Domesticity and the Women's Movement in England, 1928–1964* (Manchester, 2013).

women, not only as likely victims but also, whether as juror, or reader, as the deciding observer.

The justice, Sir Henry McCardie, was a reformer who, in 1931, supported the liberalisation of abortion. He was to commit suicide in 1933, in part due to gambling debts over which he was being blackmailed. Yet, in what enhanced the mystery, depression, illness, occult beliefs, and legal quarrels, all played a role. Like most murder cases, then and now, the Bailey case, however, was not a complex one nor at an 'exalted' social level. Bailey was a dairyman and claimed that he sought to buy poisonous drugs in order to become a vet. The jurors were unimpressed and, after their conviction, Bailey was sentenced to death by McCardie and hanged.

Novelists, including detective novelists, responded to the challenge of depicting interesting and strong women. The wide-ranging and prolific Helen Simpson (1897–1940) provided women of independence in *Acquittal* (1925) and *Enter Sir John* (1928); the latter co-written with Clemence Dane (1888–1965) who also wrote plays and non-detective novels. Introduced in *Strong Poison* (1930), Dorothy Sayers' Harriet Vane was an independent-minded female character who had a lover before she married another man. These women were relatively unusual among a host of female characters who mostly reinforced stable sexual and class identities, such as Marple and the heroines created by Ivy Compton-Burnett (1884–1969) and Daphne Du Maurier (1907–89). Nevertheless, Christie was perceptive on the drives and pressures of emotional and sexual appeal and could offer a complexity that matched the situation of the period.[2] In contrast, some male writers frequently offered a crude contrast between a dull heroine and a villainess who has a sexual frisson with the hero, as in Edgar Wallace's characteristically implausible *The Angel of Terror* (1922).

The notion of a villainess was very much seen in 1935, when the 67-year-old Francis Rattenbury was battered to death in Bournemouth by George Stoner, who was Rattenbury's chauffeur as well as the lover of his considerably younger wife, Alma. Aged 39, she had already been married twice. Alma confessed, before retracting her confession; Stoner was sentenced to death, only to have his sentence commuted to life imprisonment after a

2   C. Langhamer, *The English in Love: The Intimate Story of an Emotional Revolution* (Oxford, 2013).

petition signed by over 300,000 people. Alma was typecast as a manipulative older woman,[3] but was acquitted of murder and of being an accessory after the fact only to commit suicide shortly after. This was not a Christie-type murder story.

The law moved over women's issues, albeit often slowly. The Matrimonial Causes Act of 1937 was the brainchild of the Independent MP A.P. Herbert, who was shocked at the inequality of women in divorce cases. The Act allowed women to divorce men on the grounds of desertion for three years or more, insanity, cruelty, adultery, rape, and sodomy. Doyle complained about the earlier situation in the Holmes stories. The difficulties of divorce on the grounds of insanity were a key issue in Christie's *Three Act Tragedy* (1935), whereas, in *Murder Is Easy* (1939), Luke Fitzwilliam refers to '"these days of easy divorce"'. As a result of her husband's infidelity, Christie had separated in 1927 and divorced in 1928.

Legislation was important for women, although it was possibly less consequential than both the realities of economic opportunity and the norms suggested by popular culture. Novelists reflected these factors, albeit to very varied extents. Aldous Huxley's *Antic Hay* (1923) depicted, in the aftermath of the wartime challenge to social values, a new London society of jazz clubs, drug-taking, and birth control. He also noted the pressures of a harsh economic system, social snobbery, and exploitative gender relations: Porteous is supported by 'the weariness and the pallor of a wife who worked beyond her strength', and had 'ill-dressed and none too well-fed children'. Gumbril Senior lived 'in a decaying quarter' near Paddington:

> The houses, which a few years ago had all been occupied by respectable families, were now split up into squalid little maisonettes, and from the neighbouring slums, which along with most other unpleasant things the old bourgeois families had been able to ignore, invading bands of children came to sport on the once-sacred pavements.

Archibald Joseph Cronin, a Scottish doctor who practised in London from 1928 to 1930 before becoming a novelist, described, in his novel *The*

3   S. O'Connor, *The Fatal Passion of Alma Rattenbury* (London, 2020).

Citadel (1937), a practice in Paddington, 'a baddish locality' with 'all these moth-eaten boarding-houses' full of 'seedy, even doubtful characters, and afflicted by winter fogs. In his autobiography, Cronin contrasted the opulent image of London in springtime with a reality of seediness, noting that he and his wife 'never imagined that there were so many alcoholic or broken-down doctors in London, or so few houses that were not dingy and damp, with cavernous basements and attics like mousetraps'.[4] It is such derelict old houses near Chelsea that are being cleared away to build modern flats in Christie's short story 'Four-and-Twenty Blackbirds' (1940). The London described in Cronin's *Citadel* was much like that presented by Robert Louis Stevenson in *The Strange Case of Dr Jekyll and Mr Hyde* (1886), a spectral detective story.

At the same time as misery, there was significant economic growth in the 1920s, the increase in gross national product per head being about 1.5 percent, compared with 0.4 percent in 1900–13. This reflected the expansion of high-productivity consumer industries, although it also owed much to recovery after wartime disruption. Growth helped ensure recovery from the sense of crisis in the early 1920s, and also funded non-essentials such as the purchase of books.

Meanwhile, the country was changing, not least in transport. In 1920, Hounslow, the first civil aerodrome in England, closed as Croydon was made the London Customs Airport. In 1928, it was officially opened as the new Airport of London, and by the end of the decade about twenty aircraft daily were leaving. Paris was a popular destination. At a very different scale, road traffic increased and casualties rose. An editorial in the *Devon and Exeter Gazette* on 20 May 1930 pressed for more safety on Exeter's roads.

In 'The Coming of Mr Quin' (1924), reprinted as part of *The Mysterious Mr Quin* (1930), Lady Laura Evesham is worried about the 'grave uncertainty' of the political situation. However, in a valuable corrective to the implications of some of the post-war thriller writing, the Labour government of 1924 had demonstrated that Labour could rule without bringing in Socialism. There were no serious upsets and financial policy was particularly

---

4   Cronin, *The Citadel* (London, 1983 edn), pp. 220, 225; Cronin, *Adventures in Two Worlds* (London, 1952; 1977 edn), pp. 161–2.

prudent, with the orthodoxy of Philip Snowden making him an ideal Treasury-minded Chancellor of the Exchequer. Far from introducing a capital levy or wealth tax, Snowden was a supporter of tax cuts. The Labour government kept the TUC at a distance and used emergency powers to defeat a strike by London tramwaymen. In 1924, John Hoode, the Minister of Imperial Finance, was murdered in the library of his country house in Philip MacDonald's detective novel *The Rasp*, only for the killer to be unmasked by Colonel Anthony Gethryn, formally of the Secret Service. MacDonald (1900–80), a World War I veteran, wrote detective novels and screenplays including *Love from a Stranger* (1947), which was based on Christie's short story 'Philomel Cottage' (1923). Gethryn's last appearance in a MacDonald novel was in 1959.

Although dependent on the Liberals in Parliament, and drawing, in part, on the ideas of radical Liberalism, the Labour government of 1924 was no coalition, and that October the Liberals turned on Labour in a crisis that looked to elements of thriller fiction with its implication (to critics) of a traitor within. The government had had a charge of inciting soldiers to disobedience brought against a Communist journalist, John Campbell, dropped, and this led to a political furore. Earlier that year, the formal recognition of the Soviet Union had resulted in controversy, while, in August, the proposal to make a trade treaty with the Soviet Union, and to include a British loan, was unacceptable to both Liberals and Conservatives.

The supposed (in practice *very* limited) sympathy of Labour for the Soviet Union and Communism was an issue in the following general election. In terms that matched many of the thrillers of the age, including those by Christie, it was claimed, that a letter published on 25 October in the *Daily Mail*, supposedly by Grigory Zinoviev, a member of the Politburo, demonstrated that the Soviets sought the overthrow of the established order in Britain, including in the army, and therefore wanted Labour to win. The letter was probably forged by White Russian *émigrés*[5] and, despite Labour claims, does not appear to have influenced the results in the general election held on 29 October. Labour lost 40 seats, leaving them with 151; but the Liberals, who

5   G. Bennett, *'A most Extraordinary and Mysterious Business': The Zinoviev Letter of 1924* (London, 1999).

lacked a viable alternative strategy, suffered far more. The number of their seats fell from 158 in the December 1923 election to 40 in October 1924. They were hit by serious financial problems in the 1924 election (the third in quick succession) and did not contest 207 seats, helping the Conservatives to dominate the anti-Labour vote. Liberal weakness cost Labour seats.

The Conservatives appeared as the party best placed to protect property and defend the Empire, which was very much Christie's position. During their months in opposition, the Conservatives had ended the division that had stemmed from the Carlton Club meeting, abandoned tariff reform, and improved their organisation. In October 1924, they took 48.3 percent of the votes and 412 seats, winning the largest majority (223 seats) for a single party since 1832. Insofar as one party could lay claim to the position, this was the national party and one that provided solid support for themes of continuity. They were overwhelmingly the middle-class party, and benefited from the expansion of this sector of society; but the Conservatives also received a large share of the working-class vote.

Yet, the new, larger electorate was potentially volatile, and winning its support posed a considerable challenge to politicians, both Conservatives and others. Under Baldwin, the media were harnessed to create a political image for a mass electorate, with frequent radio broadcasts helping to cultivate the folksiness which the Conservative leader sought to project, while Conservative Party propaganda, often geared towards the female electorate, emphasised the dangers of Socialism to family life and property in general. Unlike in much of Europe, Britain had a strong and confident Centre-Right party that did not reject democracy. Equally, again unlike most of Europe, the Left was willing to work within the system and ignored the type of conspiracy discussed by Christie.

A fan of detective novels, including in 1928 American writers such as Anna Katharine Green, Baldwin offered in his speeches a vision of England in which Christian and ethical values, an appeal to the value of continuity, pastoral and paternalist themes, and a sense of national exceptionalism, were all fused. This was not intended to exclude the Scots, Welsh, and people of Ulster, each of whom were presented as possessing a distinctive character and tradition, but also qualities that had enriched, and been enriched by, the English. Although the rural themes in Baldwin's speeches and their impact can be over-emphasised, he frequently employed rural imagery as an important way to address the issue of the national character, not least in his stress on the country as representing eternal values and traditions, which could sustain 'peace in our time'. The countryside symbolised the natural fecundity that was important to his romance of a stable prosperity without serious problems. In Christie's favoured Devon, the *Devon and Exeter Daily Gazette* of March 1930 included a photograph of Sir Alfred Godson with the huntsman of the South Devon Hounds, alongside a news item on the relevant meet. Ironically, Neville Chamberlain's knowledge and interest in rural matters was far greater. He loved nature, fishing, birdwatching, and the countryside and was a little put out that Baldwin had the reputation of a countryman.

In an account of society and politics that left only a limited role for the other political parties, notably the Liberals, Baldwin was particularly keen to promote peace between the two sides of industry in the 1920s. Striving to bring masters and men together in one industrial nation, he believed that his own background in industry – he had run the family iron works before entering politics – gave him a unique insight into the world of industrial relations. On 4 December 1924, speaking to a Conservative gathering at the Royal Albert Hall in London, Baldwin declared: "'We stand for the union of those two nations of which [Benjamin] Disraeli[6] spoke two generations ago: union among our own people to make one nation of our own people at home'". Baldwin indeed opposed the Trade Union (Political Fund) Bill in 1925, which proposed to replace 'contracting-out' with 'contracting-in', thereby modifying the political levy on trade union members in a way disadvantageous to the Labour Party, on the grounds that it would provoke an unnecessary confrontation between capital and labour.

The importance which Baldwin attached to continuity did not mean that he and his 1924–9 government were opposed to reform. Indeed, Baldwin, restorer of order in a disordered society, was not an aristocrat like Curzon, but in the eyes of such individuals, a middle-class outsider, although not a foreigner like Poirot. As a non-aristocrat, Baldwin was more attractive to those such as Christie who were uneasy about much of fashionable society and its vices. Two of the prominent members of his government sought important changes. Neville Chamberlain was Minister of Health in

6   Conservative Prime Minister, 1874–80.

1923 and 1924–9, and his Housing Act of 1923 provided a subsidy per house to housebuilders – both local authorities and private – for two years, which was designed to deal with the housing problem and to help the economy and the unemployment figures. Chamberlain also sought to improve the provision of pensions, with the Widows', Orphans' and Old Age Contributory Pensions Act of 1925, which introduced contributory pensions to cover those aged from 65 until they reached the non-contributory scheme at 70. With the Local Government Act of 1929, Chamberlain created a new structure for the provision of social welfare. Local authorities – counties and county boroughs – took over the bulk of the responsibilities of the Poor Law Guardians.

Chamberlain's schemes were helped by the support of the Chancellor of the Exchequer, the ex-Liberal Churchill, as he reorganised the financial relationship between central and local government. However, by returning Britain to the Gold Standard in 1925, and fixing the exchange rate at the pre-war rate of $4.86 to the £, Churchill overvalued sterling, and helped deflate the economy. The return to the Gold Standard has long been regarded as a central reason why the British economy experienced so many problems in the inter-war period.

As the pound was over-valued, exports suffered, which exacerbated difficulties in the coal industry, by pushing up the price of coal exports, and thus played a role in causing the 1926 coal strike and the General Strike. Coal exports had also been hit by the development both of competing sources of power and of coal production in other countries, and, as exports fell, the employers tried to cut wages. The miners rejected the report of a Royal Commission under a Liberal MP, Sir Herbert Samuel, that recommended the rationalization of the numerous pits many of which were uneconomic, and a cut in wages. In support of the miners, the Trades Union Congress (TUC) called a selective 'General' Strike. They feared that otherwise the TUC would be seen as weak and that this might lead to the rise of more radical options, such as Syndicalism.

Beginning on 3 May, the strike had variable support, and most of the South of England, outside London, did not strike. While the dock, rail, and tram workers gave good support to the strike, the Seamen's Union did not, and there was only limited backing in the road haulage industry. There was a firm government response that included moving police, deploying troops and warships, and encouraging about 100,000 volunteers. The last were most numerous in London and the South-East. There was also a vigorous government propaganda campaign, with Churchill editing the *British Gazette*. Not wanting revolution, the TUC called off the strike on 12 May. The miners were left to continue the strike alone, and they eventually had to accept the owners' terms.

All of Christie's Chief Constables, mostly former colonels, and all the senior police officers would, in reality, have been involved in planning during the strike. *The Murder of Roger Ackroyd* came out the following month, but *The Big Four*, published in January 1927, better captured the atmosphere of disquiet and, in the case of the novel, international conspiracy. Poirot presents the conspiracy as his great case. The commercially very successful novel in fact was based on short stories published in *The Sketch* from January to March 1924, but, for the readers, the background was the General Strike. Poirot refers to 'the world-wide unrest, the labour troubles that beset every nation, and the revolutions that break out in some.... There is a force behind the scenes which aims at nothing less than the disintegration of civilization.... Lenin and Trotsky were mere puppets'. This theme, which suggested that the centre of conspiracy and action was closer than the Soviet Union, as indeed is revealed to be the case, is not a tangential one to the plot or the tone, but is developed throughout the book, and helps give it a character toward the end that is similar to that of the Fleming novels. The theme of Li Chang Yen, the malevolent Chinese master-criminal in *The Big Four*, echoes Dr Fu-Manchu and prefigures Fleming's Dr No.

That is not, however, the approach that is taken today toward Christie novels. Indeed, this is one of the many respects in which subsequent presentation, while often successful in its own terms, artistically and/or commercially, does not necessarily take you far toward an appreciation of the original work, or, indeed, offer anything for that. *The Big Four* is the classic instance of this process. It was presented in 2013, in the BBC David Suchet Poirot series, which has acquired a form of definitive, or at least iconic, status for the visual Poirot, not least as providing the largest number of Poirot performances. In that series, the story, set on the eve of World War II and with the Peace Party playing a major role, was presented in part as a delusion. This made the text pointless, and, therefore, was worse than if a new, albeit misleading, story had been invented, as in the Poirot continuation novels, notably by Sophie Hannah.

In large part, this failure reflects not just the difficulty of confronting the problems of producing a screenplay but, more profoundly, a lack of engagement with the challenge of addressing the values of the author and text. So also in content and/or tone with many of the Suchet Poirot series, as in, for example, 'The Dream' (1989), which was the adaptation of a 1938 short story. In Britain at present, this process of representation or, often, misrepresentation, is more persistently seen with authors who can be regarded as conservative in disposition and with this conservatism taking a variety of forms. These writers are either disparaged on that ground, as with Fleming, or their conservatism is underplayed or generally ignored, as with Jane Austen.[7] Shakespeare provides another instance of the latter. A host of methods and arguments are pushed to the fore in arguing for an inherent radicalism, notably the search for hidden or subversive meanings, including by means of intertextuality. However, that approach poses the major problem of a tendency to misrepresentation. The search for changes in authorial views during their writing career can be more fruitful.

Christie's reputation is harshly affected by much of the discussion. In part, there is the disparagement referred to above, notably of the very idea of producing conservative work. There is also a tendency to underplay or ignore the specific traditionalist views she offers. This book seeks to show that this approach is mistaken, misrepresents her work, and decontextualizes both her and the audiences for which she wrote, and to some members of whom she dedicated individual novels. If that misrepresentation is done in terms of the supposed sensitivities of a later audience, and supposed is a point because this may be partly or largely a matter of the views of a group of producers and commentators, then that does not help us to understand the original situation.

Returning to the political narrative that provides the context for Christie and for readers at the time, a striking aspect of the short-lived General Strike of 1926 was the extent to which both sides, government and trade unions, went out of their way to avoid antagonizing each other. This accorded with Christie's view of an underlying national identity and sense. Baldwin resisted Conservative back-bench pressure for retribution against the trade unions

7   J. Black, *England in the Age of Austen* (Bloomington, IN, 2021).

until tempers had cooled, and the Trades Disputes Act of 1927 was a relatively moderate measure. However, it still left a sour taste in trade unionists' mouths, and helped Labour and the trade unions recover cohesion, unity, and morale after the General Strike. Furthermore, thereafter Conservative measures continued to be modest and uninspiring, winning the government little popularity. Baldwin's lack of energy had a detrimental effect insofar as creating any impression of drive was concerned.

Nevertheless, the Conservative leadership was confident of winning the next election due in 1929, which was, in the event, to be its major interwar electoral failure. Prosperity had not been achieved. The return to the gold standard was damaging, industrial relations remained cool, and unemployment above a million led to repeated opposition attacks, and it also pressed hard on government finances. Chamberlain's reforms in the Poor Law and local government brought scant popularity. There was a widespread sense that it was time for a change: The government, and certainly many of its ministers, seemed tired and lacking in direction. Some individual policies, such as the Low Church Home Secretary's attack on 'vice' in nightclubs, failed to rouse widespread support.

Labour, meanwhile, benefited from a desire for new ideas and faces. It seemed moderate, and the defeat of the General Strike helped lessen anxiety about Socialism, which can be related to the eventual reassurance of Christie's *The Seven Dials Mystery*. MacDonald, still the Labour leader, did not arouse fear or anger, as Christie's plots make clear. Indeed, in his *Where is Britain Going?* (1926), the prominent Communist Leon Trotsky attacked MacDonald for being ideologically confused and barren, as well as dull and untalented.

In *The Seven Dials Mystery* (1929), the impressive Superintendent Battle appears for the second time. One of her talented policemen, he is present in five novels from 1925 to 1944. Battle has a list of secret societies in London. They include:

> 'The Blood Brothers of St Sebastian. The Wolf Hounds. The Comrades of Peace. The Comrades Club. The Friends of Oppression. The Children of Moscow. The Red Standard Bearers. The Herrings. The Comrades of the Fallen – and half a dozen more'.

'The sinister Mr Mosgorovsky' is proprietor of the Seven Dials Club, and one of the members is an American with 'an inflection of Irish', another a German, and one 'the lady who may be any nationality – for choice Russian or Polish'. The dangerous international gang, is, Bundle Brent, the young heroine, notes, "'the sort of crowd I always imagined until tonight only existed in books'", which is a type of reference that Christie frequently makes as a locator of action and attitudes. Secret papers are part of the plot.

And then Christie subverts it, Superintendent Battle revealing that secret criminal organisations headed by a "mysterious super-criminal", while "common enough in books", are less so in real life. Moreover, Mosgorovsky in fact is Britain's secret "anti-Bolshevist agent", while the American is pro-British, rather than the IRA sympathiser he appeared.

Labour and the TUC were vindicated on 30 May 1929, when the Conservatives lost power in the election, the first contested on a fully democratic franchise, for in 1928 the age at which women could vote had been brought into line with that of men (21). Fighting on the platform of 'Safety First' (which was suggested by an advertising agency), but with little else to offer by way of policy, the Conservatives won more votes, but Labour won more seats, although, again, not sufficient for an absolute majority. Their number of MPs rose from 29 in 1906 to 288 in 1929, and, the same year, they contested their highest number of constituencies so far: 569, compared to 427 in 1923. Furthermore, for the first time, Labour was the largest party in the Commons. MacDonald formed his second minority Labour government.

1929 was also the Liberals' last serious bid for power. They put up 513 candidates and overwhelmingly failed. Lloyd George, leader after Asquith died in 1928, had managed to unite the Liberals momentarily with a Keynesian-influenced programme designed to conquer unemployment, but the number of Liberal MPs only rose from 40 to 59. Its appeal, even on the pressing issue of the day, was insufficiently strong to challenge the hegemony of the two main parties. The Liberal post-election alliances with Labour in 1924 and 1929 were in part tactical, although there was also a common hostility to protectionism, but these alliances cost the Liberals part of their middle-class support.

The increase in the Liberal vote was insufficient to win many seats, but it sufficiently hit the Conservatives to let Labour win numerous seats.

Conservative working-class support was far from solid. Nevertheless, the Conservatives remained the party with the largest percentage of the popular vote. The conservatism of the period, also revealed in local elections, represented a continuation of the consolidation of the propertied that had begun in the 1880s as growing Liberal radicalism led to middle-class disaffection and a rallying to the Conservatives. This was very much Christie's context.

However, as with other novelists, both detective writers and others, much of her writing, other than her thrillers, had little to do with politics. Instead, the second chapter of *The Murder of Roger Ackroyd* had allowed Christie to play with the idea of detective stories. In this story, she challenged the standard methods of the genre, although fairly so, despite the views of some critics. Ackroyd's housekeeper, Elizabeth Russell, is a reader of them, and Dr Sheppard facetiously comments:

> 'The essence of a detective story is to have a rare poison – if possible something from South America, that nobody has ever heard of – something that one obscure tribe of savages uses to poison their arrows with. Death is instantaneous, and Western science is powerless to detect it'.

The 'arrow poison of the South America Indians' was a conscious and witty echo of Doyle's 1924 use of curare in 'The Adventure of the Sussex Vampire', and is a reminder of the overlaps between Doyle and Christie and Holmes and Poirot. Wielded in a hypodermic, this poison returns as an implausible solution in *Three Act Tragedy* (1934). It is an instance of ingenuity being mocked.

Dr Sheppard in *Roger Ackroyd* continues in this tone later: "'The super-detective always has his rooms littered with rubies and pearls and emeralds from grateful Royal clients'". Indeed, 1926 also saw the publication of Dorothy L. Sayers' *Clouds of Witness* with Lord Peter Wimsey's elder brother, Gerald, Duke of Denver, being tried in the House of Lords for murder and Wimsey flying the Atlantic to his rescue. In *Lord Edgware Dies*, the new peer remarks of his predecessor: "'Lord Edgware dies. Good title that, by the way. Lord Edgware dies. Looks well on a bookstall'", where many books were sold, especially in and near rail stations in W.H. Smith kiosks. Christie has a policeman refer to a secret passage as "'Edgar Wallace stuff"', a term frequently employed to suggest the implausible, but also a testimony to Wallace's tremendous commercial success. In 'The Rajah's Emerald' (1934), James Bond rejects the idea of sending back the emerald he has unwittingly purloined because:

> 'he had read too many detective stories for that sort of thing. He knew how your super-sleuth could get busy with a magnifying glass and every kind of patent device. Any detective worth his salt would get busy on Jane's parcel and would in half an hour or so have discovered the sender's profession, age, habits, and personal appearance'.

In *Hercule Poirot's Christmas* (1938), Colonel Johnson, the Chief Constable of Middleshire, a role classically given to colonels in detective fiction, asks whether "'this is one of those damned cases you get in detective stories where a man is killed in a locked room by some apparently supernatural agency?'" The appearance of jewels has a somewhat predictable quality, but also represents easily-understood wealth that has a social role and can be readily stolen. In *Three Act Tragedy*, in an exchange in which Christie is clearly having fun, Sir Charles Cartwright remarks:

> 'Dash it all, in detective stories there's always some identifying mark on the villain. I thought it was a bit hard that real life should prove so lamentably behindhand'.
> 'It's usually a scar in stories', said Miss Wills.
> 'A birthmark's just as good', said Sir Charles.

Later, after Poirot proposes a sherry party, Egg remarks: "'It's lovely – just like detective stories. All the people will be there, and then he'll tell us *which* of them did it'". In 'Mr Eastwood's Adventure' (1934), the detective novelist Anthony Eastwood, planning *The Mystery of the Second Cucumber*, knows that his editor wants a story about mysteriously dark women, all murdered, unfair suspicions on a young hero, and the fixing of the guilt on the least likely by the means of wholly inadequate clues. The last is the aspect of the scenario where Christie clearly departs, although many of her proofs would not have stood up to cross-examination in court.

With a self-satirical device also to be used successfully by Michael Innes, including in *A Night of Errors* (1947), Christie, in *Yellow Iris* (1937), has Poirot contemplate a late phone call that might be "'a millionaire newspaper proprietor, found dead in the library of his country house, with a spotted orchid clasped in his left hand and a page torn from a cookbook pinned to his breast'". The misdirection in *One, Two, Buckle My Shoe* (1940) includes many references to thriller writers, which, in the fashion of so many literary devices, provide more than one outcome. They both offer Christie opportunities for fun and also help to provide echoes that place the action. Reginald Barnes, the former Home Office intelligence link, the sort of individual Christie frequently deploys because they are narrative facilitarors, refers to:

> 'a book with a lurid jacket that lay on a table close at hand: 'I read a lot of these spy yarns. Fantastic, some of them. But curiously enough *they're not any more fantastic than the real thing*. There *are* beautiful adventuresses, and dark sinister men with foreign accents, and gangs and international associations and super crooks! I'd blush to see some of the things I know set down in print – nobody would believe them for a minute!'

Japp, however, is sceptical about Poirot's idea that a missing body has been weighted and is in the Thames:

> 'From a cellar in Limehouse, I suppose! You're talking like a thriller by a lady novelist'.
> 'I know – I know. I blush when I say these things!'

The lady novelist is an ironical reference to Christie, although the most famous of such thriller writers were men. Subsequently, when British espionage comes up, Japp complains, with feeling: "'Shades of Philipps in Oppenheim, Valentine Williams and William le Queux. I think I'm going mad!'" Genres overlap, Alistair Blunt tells Poirot: "'I read a lot of thrillers and detective stories. Do you think any of them are true to life?'" William Le Queux (1864–1927), a onetime journalist, wrote very many spy stories and invasion literature, most successfully *The Invasion of 1910*, an anti-German work which appeared in the *Daily Mail* in 1906 and was a great success. Oppenheim (1866–1946), who was praised by Buchan and worked for the Ministry of Information during the war, focused on easy-to-read accounts of international intrigue, with traitors to the fore. His books, the last of which was published in 1943, were very popular and many were filmed. Germans and radicals were classic villains, a sinister German wartime spy in Oppenheim's *The Great Impersonation* (1920). Christie and Oppenheim could be linked together not only because they wrote thrillers. They could also be sold together. Thus, *The Reader's Library* in 1929 published Christie's 'The Under Dog' and Oppenheim's 'Blackman's Wood' together as *Two New Crime Stories*.

Valentine Williams (1883–1946), a journalist who won the Military Cross in World War I service being seriously wounded, like Captain Hastings, on the Somme in 1916, became a writer of adventures from 1918, making enough that way to give up his career with the *Daily Mail*, for which he had worked at the time of the Zinoviev Letter. His spy stories were made fun of by Christie in *Partners in Crime* (1929). Williams' protagonists included Desmond Okewood and Major Claver, both Secret Service agents. Sinister German agents, notably Doktor Adolph Grundt (Clubfoot), play a role in Williams' novels, as in *The Man with the Clubfoot* (1918), *Clubfoot the Avenger* (1924), *The Crouching Beast* (1928), and *The Gold Comfit Box* (1933). Christie's 'The Adventure of the Sinister Stranger', first published in *The Sketch* on 22 October 1924, parodies these stories, not least with a man with a club foot, and makes reference to the 1918 book. Grundt returns on behalf of Hitler in *Courier to Marrakesh* (1944). In World War II, Williams worked for MI6.[8]

Christie's approach continued after World War II. Thus, in *They Came to Baghdad* (1951), Victoria Jones finds herself plunged in Baghdad into a maelstrom that Edward Goring tells her is: "'So like a thriller – a young man coming in and gasping out one word that doesn't mean anything – and then dying. It just doesn't seem *real*". Baker is also incredulous: "'Phillips Oppenheim, William Le Queux and several distinguished imitators since? Is this real? Are *you* real?"' In *They Do It with Mirrors* (1962), Alex Restarick, responding to Inspector Curry about the murder of Christian Gulbrandsen, says that for someone to be poisoned first and shot afterwards "would be too

---

8   C. Patrick and S. Baister, *William Le Queux, Master of Mystery* (2007).

madly detective story'". In *A Murder is Announced* (1950), Chief Constable Rydesdale is sceptical about what he refers to as "'Quite a best seller plot'".

There are also references in *One, Two, Buckle My Shoe* to the popularity of American-style detective novels. Thus, young Alfred, the pageboy at the dental surgery, is reading "'*Death at 11.45*. It's an American detective story. It's a corker, sir, it really is! All about gunmen'". In *A Murder is Announced*, Marple takes the idea of a fall guy from reading one of Dashiel Hammett's stories. In *Murder Is Easy*, Bridget Conway remarks that heroines are "'abducted, imprisoned, left to die of sewer gas or be drowned in cellars – they are always in danger, but they don't ever die'".

Alfred is not the only youngster shown enjoying detective novels. In *Crooked House* (1949), the twelve-year old Josephine Leonides reads 'masses', and refers to Charles Hayward, the narrator, as Watson, although she is not very keen on Holmes' stories: "'It's awfully old-fashioned. They drive about in dog-carts'". Subsequently, Josephine remarks: "'I should say it's about time for the next murder, wouldn't you … in books there's always a second murder about now. Someone who knows something is bumped off before they can tell what they know'". This proves eerily prophetic in what is in the final event a deeply-troubling novel.

Christie provides somewhat different reflections in other settings. In *Towards Zero* (1944), Mr Treves, a wise elderly solicitor, sets the tone for the novelist's concern with personality and contingency by remarking:

'I like a good detective story. But, you know, they begin in the wrong place! They begin with the murder. But the murder is the *end*. The story begins long before that – years before sometimes – with all the causes and events that bring certain people to a certain place at a certain time on a certain day'.

In the repeatedly flippant *Crooked House*, Charles Hayward reveals that he has got information the police failed to obtain: "'I got it from a private inquiry agent … in accordance with the canons of the best detective stories … has licked the police hollow'".

With her interest in psychology, Christie also ranges to at least imaginary texts on the theory of crime as with Kreuzhammer on *Inferiority and Crime*. Dr Thomas, in *Murder Is Easy*, has a copy of the translation of this invented tome.

Novelists of the period could be wide-ranging, although today there is a tendency to focus on the Modernists, notably Virginia Woolf (1882–1941), who saw themselves as confronting a stale literary tradition. In 'Mr Bennett and Mrs Brown' (1924), Woolf distinguished between what she presented as the false 'realism' of surface description in the successful novels of Arnold Bennett and a 'modernism' that searched for true realism. In place of narrative, Woolf advocated a view of life as a 'luminous halo', and her novels explored such ideas. In *Mrs Dalloway* (1925), she employed interior monologue and stream of consciousness to reveal character and in *To the Lighthouse* (1927) offered a pointillistic meditation on time and fulfilment.

Christie made her views about Modernism readily apparent. In 'Miss Marple Tells a Story', a 1934 radio play first published in 1939, Marple remarks that her novelist nephew, Raymond West, '"writes those very modern books all about rather unpleasant young men and women"'. In 'Greenshaw's Folly' (1960), West, who deals bleakly with the sordid side of life, is described as having a name in literature, but not being a best-seller. Modern literature is mocked in a far more slapstick fashion with the novelist Salome Otterbourne in *Death on the Nile*. In a caricature portrayal, possibly making fun of Lady Ottoline Morrell (1873–1938), this lemonade-drinker offers '"strong meat"' about sex, the alleged pivot of the universe, in her outspoken, unconventional, and realistic *Under the Fig Tree*, a work that is likely to be banned by libraries, before pressing on with the absurd *Snow on the Desert's Face*. On the personal level, the insensitive Otterbourne is a great trial to her daughter, Rosalie, which was the case of Morrell, a major literary hostess who had numerous affairs and was reputedly the model for D.H. Lawrence's Lady Chatterley. Salome may also have been modelled on Elinor Glyn (1864–1943), a writer of daring romantic fiction aimed at women, who in her work and life emphasised personal magnetism and was nearly as prolific in lovers, including Viscount Curzon, as in novels.

Modernism in literature was frequently elitist, had only a limited commercial appeal, compared with many of the 'middle' and 'low' brow writers of the period, and had little airing on the radio. 'Middle' and 'low' brow writers offered a much more authentic reflection of popular culture than anything Modernism could provide. The 'middle' and 'low' brow benefited from the rising disposable income of the period, from the ready availability of inexpensive books, the spread of cheap lending libraries, notably those run by Boots and Smiths, and from increased leisure. Penguin would eventually exploit the new market already developed by railway novels, although commuting lent itself rather to the short story. This was generally provided by magazines, but authors then got a second bite on income through published collections of their short stories. Novelists could be depicted as widely-successful, as with Francis Durbridge's *Send for Paul Temple* (1938), in which the hero writes detective stories for the theatre. Other novelists, however, are depicted in a sorrier state, as with Stephen Carlice in C.H.B. Kitchin's *Birthday Party* (1938).

In Christie's 'The Manhood of Edward Robinson' (1934), the protagonist is reading *When Love is King* on his underground train journey and thinking of the he-men and beautiful women beloved of lady novelists. Women writers were of growing importance, including not simply detective writers, but also, in the inter-war period, Ivy Compton-Burnett, Daphne Du Maurier and Winifred Holtby. In *Evil Under the Sun* (1941), Linda Marshall's hotel room includes:

> A Bible, a battered copy of Shakespeare's plays, *The Marriage of William Ashe*, by Mrs Humphry Ward. *The Young Stepmother*, by Charlotte Yonge. *The Shropshire Lad*. Eliot's *Murder in the Cathedral*. Bernard Shaw's *St Joan*. *Gone with the Wind*, by Margaret Mitchell. *The Burning Court*, by Dickson Carr.

The last was a 1937 locked room mystery, with Carr's frequent, but often unsuccessful, admixture of the occult, as in the horribly over-written *Castle Skull* (1931) and his highly improbable *The Lost Gallows* (1931). 'Greenshaw's Folly' reveals Marple's knowledge of J.M. Barrie (1860–1937) plays, such as *The Admirable Crichton* (1902), a play about social reversal which she thinks very clever, and *What Every Woman Knows* (1908), in which the MP's wife is the source of his success as a speaker. Such writers were not somehow pre-war, for, as with John Galsworthy (1867–1933) and Rudyard Kipling (1865–1936), recognition was also seen subsequently. Barrie received the Order of Merit in 1922, as well as a baronetcy. Galsworthy, who turned down a knighthood in 1917, won the Nobel Prize in Literature in 1932. Kipling, who had done so in 1907, turned down a knighthood and the Poet Laureateship.

In the inter-war years, Modernism had relatively little impact in architecture, despite Giles Gilbert Scott's Battersea Power Station and Charles Holden's House of the University of London, a vast Modernist lump. Liberty's, off Regent Street, a Tudor-revival arts and crafts building, with rambling design and re-used timber, better expressed the widespread desire for a style suggesting continuity. Fashionable architecture comes into play in Christie's works. In idyllic Wychwood-under-Ashe in *Murder Is Easy* (1939), there is 'an anachronism, a large white modern building, austere and irrelevant to the cheerful haphazardness of the rest of the place'. It was built and endowed as an Institute and Boys' Club by Lord Whitfield who smugly remarks: "'Employed the best architect in the country! I must say he's made a bare plain job of it – looks like a workhouse or a prison to me – but they say it's all right, so I suppose it must be'". Modernism is not the sole flaw. Whitfield also rebuilds Ashe Manor into 'an appalling and incongruous castellated mass'. Having rejected the idea of carrying out the original spirit of the building, he replaces the architect, reflecting "'No use living in the past. Those old Georges didn't know much. I didn't want a plain red-brick house'", the last a reference to George I, II, III, and IV, who, in sequence, ruled between 1714 and 1830.

Yet, Christie can also caricature reaction, and frequently so. In 'Death by Drowning' (1932), Colonel Melchett, the splenetic Chief Constable, refers to modern-day young architects who build peculiar houses full of new-fangled stuff of steel and webbing, and are therefore "'Bolshie'" and with no morals. Melchett appears to think it unnecessary to substantiate the links.

Christie mocks modern art in *Murder Is Easy* when Luke considers disguise as an artist but reflects "'I can't draw, let alone paint'", earning the rejoinder "'You could be a modern artist.... Then that wouldn't matter'". In 'Miss Marple Tells a Story', a 1934 radio play, the protagonist has scant time for the remarkable pictures of square people with curious bulges, preferring instead Lawrence Alma-Tadema (1836–1912) and Frederic Leighton (1830–96), both Victorian favourites of types of realist-style exotic. Christie's 'Swan Song' (1934) sees a mocking satire on modern culture in the shape of the ambitious artistic Lady Rustonbury who has a private theatre where there has been 'a play of the ultra new school, all divorce and drugs, also a poetical fantasy with Cubist scenery'.

A classic feature of much writing was a sense of place, as with Bennett and the Potteries, Du Maurier and Cornwall, both Winifred Holtby and Priestley and Yorkshire, and Hugh Walpole and Cumberland. For London, Devon and North Lancashire, the detective writer E.C. Lorac had a fine sense of place, as in *Bats in the Belfry*, *Fire in the Thatch*, and *The Fell Murder*. So also with John Bude and, successively, Cornwall, the Lake District, Sussex and Cheltenham; although his approach to each varied greatly, *The Lake District Murder* (1935) focusing not on the lakes themselves but on petrol garages and the coastal towns. Novelists could be better at depicting settings than making their detectives interesting, as with John Rhode whose *The House on Tollard Ridge* (1929) is good on the relationship between villages and the local big houses.

To an extent, although she ranged widely, Christie could also provide a sense of particular place, notably of London society, the affluent Home Counties, and the rural South. This was not a narrow span, as her areas did include much of the population. The population of Greater London, the area covered by the Metropolitan Police District, grew from about 7,252,000 in 1911, to about 8,203,000 in 1931, and to approximately 8,700,000 in 1939, about a fifth of the nation's population. Ealing, where she had spent much of her childhood, became a much more intensively inhabited suburb. Population growth was no less rapid in places such as Woking, Brentwood, Watford, and Maidenhead, and increased the significance of commuting. Socially, however, Christie's span was less wide. For example, she focused in suburbia not on the new 'semis' or semi-detached houses, but on the suburban villas of the wealthier members of the middle class.

Nevertheless, Christie's geographical references were wider than might readily appear. For example, in *The Murder on the Links*, Hastings and Poirot (as is not shown in the television version) visit not only France but also the variety performance at the Palace in Coventry. As described by Hastings, there is both criticism and a sense of the variety of a cultural milieu that was not his:

'The show was wearisome beyond words – or perhaps it was only my mood that made it so. Japanese families balanced themselves precariously, would-be fashionable men, in greenish evening dress and exquisitely slicked hair, reeled off society patter and danced marvellously. Stout prima donnas sang at the top of the human register, a comic comedian endeavoured to be Mr George Robey and failed signally … the Dulcibella Kids … danced neatly, and did some clever little acrobatic feats. The words of their songs were crisp and catchy'.

The interests of detective novelists were, as a whole, far from formulaic and that diversity extended to individual writers. That Christie did not cover all of English society is a somewhat pointless criticism as she neither sought, nor was expected, to do so. In accordance with the genre, she writes as if determined to disprove the view of Miss Carroll, Lord Edgware's secretary, 'that murders were only committed by drunken members of the lower classes'. That does not make her a better or a worse writer. With Christie, many of the working class who are described are servants. Their presence is often simply transactional, a plot device, although that is also true of many of their more socially-distinguished counterparts. Furthermore, servants were not the major actors in plots or heroes, nor, in accordance with rule eleven of a series of twenty supposed rules drawn up in 1928 by Willard Huntington Wright, under his pseudonym S.S. Van Dine, are they usually villains.[9] However, that was not the case in Herbert Jenkins' 'The Strange Case of Mr Challoner' (1921), nor in Mary Roberts Rinehart's *The Door* (1930), in which the butler was the murderer, although without the phrase 'the butler did it' occurring.

The range with Christie is not generally social but rather that of geographical setting. She presents London, a London somewhat different to that of Doyle. It is more a society than a cityscape, but, within that society, as with Doyle, are a number of milieux. Building on late Victorian concerns and literature, early films also presented London as a setting for crime. Based on a play of the previous year by Charles Bennett, *Blackmail* (1929), directed by Alfred Hitchcock, the first British talkie, featured exteriors of the British Museum where the denouement occurs. A child actor, Bennett (1899–1995) served on the Western Front, being invalided out due to a gas attack.

9   S.S. Van Dine, 'Twenty Rules for Writing Detective Stories', *The American Magazine* (Sept. 1928).

It would be too crude to present Poirot as the metropolitan whose scan includes the wealthy Home Counties. Indeed, *The Murder of Roger Ackroyd* is very much a village Poirot, that of would-be retired contentment. Moreover, he goes for rural relaxation in *The Hollow* (1946). Yet, the cult of rural England and the defence of its order are more properly covered in the Marple novels. An image of the rural provided a centrality to conservative notions of national identity, both in landscape and in civil society.[10] This was an England of the *Shell Guides*, that began in June 1934 with John Betjeman's of Cornwall, and of pastoral music, notably by Ralph Vaughan Williams. There was also a reality of deeper currents on which writers sought to focus or, alternatively, used for context, characterisation, and plot. Christie was more in the latter camp. The deeper currents of rural life, particularly agriculture, are not to the fore in her work.

Criticism of Christie that is more merited would focus on her willingness to continue playing with tired themes of international intrigue, conspiracies, and jewel thieves. Thus, in *The Man in the Brown Suit* (1924), there is the 'Colonel', an arch-criminal who runs a vast but, of course, secret criminal network, ranging from jewel robberies to discreet assassinations, one that bridged the World War. Colonel Race of the Secret Service, a strong and silent man of Empire, is his foe. The same novel glances at the cinema equivalent in the film series *The Perils of Pamela,* in which Pamela repeatedly finds herself up against the 'Master Criminal of the Underworld'. After watching this escape from reality, 'I would get home and find a notice from the Gas Company threatening to cut us off if the outstanding account was not paid'". The heroine in the novel finds herself in just such an adventure. Melodrama is both the content and the tone. Similarly, in 'Jane in Search of a Job', there is reference by the protagonist to 'Guileness Gwendolen, or why girls go wrong'. As with so many writers of the period, Christie went on with secret agents and sinister Russians, as in the Tommy and Tuppence story *Partners in Crime* (1929), and if she added a satirical edge, such plots, while of their time, can pall.

Meanwhile, the nature of detection was changing, as indeed was Intelligence work. The trend to a more scientific pattern of detection was seen

10 J. Marsh, *Back to the Land: The Pastoral Impulse in Victorian England from 1880 to 1914* (1982).

with the development of new ideas and practices in crime scene investigation (CSI). This involved a break from the former practice in which there was a focus on the pathologist in the mortuary, and, instead, the addition of scientific work on the scene. In 1933, the Departmental Committee on Detective Work and Procedure was founded, and, the following year, C.T. Symons became the first salaried scientific advisory to the Home Office. A system of regional laboratories followed, as well as a doctrine and established practice of transferring materials to them.[11]

Expertise was also the theme in the Police College opened at Hendon in 1934. This was intended by Lord Trenchard, Metropolitan Police Commissioner from 1931 to 1935 and former Chief of the Air Staff, in order to provide a form of officer class based on examination and education, rather than on a long-service rise from the ranks. The College included forensic laboratories and training facilities. The College was controversial with the Left, but helped lead to an improvement in police practice and consistency. It also made a mark in novels with characters such as John Rhodes' Jimmy Waghorn, a Hendon graduate. Christie was more critical of such graduates in *The ABC Murders*.

Detection was changing during the Golden Age of Detective Fiction. That was to be a relevant development for many readers and writers alike, as novelists were expected to provide plausibility. At the same time, they were becoming part of the furniture. In P.G. Wodehouse's brilliantly comic *The Code of the Woosters* (1938), possibly the best of the series, Bertie Wooster responds to the presence of Sir Watkyn Bassett and Roderick Spode at Totleigh Towers, by reflecting that it was as if both Holmes and Poirot were there:

'Imagine how some unfortunate Master Criminal would feel, on coming down to do a murder at the old Grange, if he found that not only was Sherlock Holmes putting in the weekend there, but Hercule Poirot as well'.

11 I. Burney and N. Pemberton, *Murder and the Making of English CSI* (Baltimore, MD, 2016); A. Adams, *A History of Forensic Science: British Beginnings in the Twentieth Century* (2016).

4. XENOPHOBIA

Christie's concerns about Bolsheviks, Jews, and others, were not restricted to the immediate international and domestic turmoil of the post-1918 years. Instead, as with other writers, they were important in her novels throughout the decade. This is very obviously the case, as discussed in the last chapter, with *The Big Four* (1927) and its reference to "'the world-wide unrest'", but can also be seen in a novel scarcely seen in that light, *The Mystery of the Blue Train* (1928). The opening scene is again in Paris, and reflected the close links between London and Paris that was frequently a theme in her work and, indeed, in that of many novelists. Thus, in *Lord Edgware Dies* (1933), the peer frequently goes to Paris, where the Duke of Merton also spends much time.

In *The Mystery of the Blue Train*, the opening scene throws forth the standard theme of Bolsheviks and Jews. The rubies, the pursuit of which fire up the plot, are Imperial jewels seized by the Bolsheviks and sold for their nefarious ends, with a Jew being a key player. Jews as villainous were not a new aspect of detective fiction. Aside from Roy Horniman's half-Jewish protagonist in *Israel Rank: The Autobiography of a Criminal* (1907), Erskine Childers and John Buchan among other writers both used anti-Semitic tropes. The foreign origin of many Jews had led to them being positioned in tales of international villainy. Yet this was pushed to the fore due to the association of Jews with Imperial Germany, and then with Bolshevism even more so.

In the Cold War that followed the 1917 revolution, there was a worldwide Intelligence conflict between Britain and the Soviet Union,[1] with relations also intertwined with British politics. In 1924, the Labour government recognised the Soviet Union and organised a trade treaty, only for relations

---

1   V. Madeira, *Britannia and the Bear: The Anglo-Russian Intelligence Wars, 1917–1929* (Woodbridge, 2014).

to cool under its Conservative successor. In 1926, a Soviet role in the unsuccessful General Strike was suspected, although, in practice, this strike was far from revolutionary. In 1927, the Soviet Trade Delegation, accused of espionage, was raided, as were the offices of the All-Russian Co-Operative Society. Alleging Soviet support for subversion, the trade agreement was ended and diplomatic relations broken-off. However, after Labour returned to power in 1929, diplomatic relations were resumed and a trade agreement negotiated.[2] There was also concern about Soviet challenges to British imperial issues, notably in Persia (Iran), Turkey, China, Afghanistan, Iraq, and India. The Soviets supported opposition to Britain in each country.[3] This was a more menacing instance of pre-1917 concerns about Russian expansion, concerns that had helped drive British policy in Asia throughout the nineteenth century and, despite an agreement in 1907, up to World War I.

As earlier in the run-up to World War I, the apparent threat from international conspiracy provides a backdrop to British politics and culture in these years. *Black Coffee* (1930) was Christie's first play; although based on *The Murder of Roger Ackroyd*, Michael Morton had written *Alibi* (1928) in which Charles Laughton acted the part of Poirot, while the production was directed by Gerald du Maurier. Written in 1929, *Black Coffee* proved a relatively unsuccessful play with only short runs in 1930 and 1931 and no transfer to New York. The play was turned into films in 1931 and (in French) 1932, and (by Charles Osborne) into a novel in 1998. The plot has mysterious foreigners in the frame with Lucia Amory, the Italian daughter-in-law of the murdered physicist Sir Claud Amory. Sir Claud is producing a new type of explosive, a theme in a number of works of the period, and the theft of the formula is linked to the murder. Lucia, the daughter of the very foreign-sounding Selma Goetz, an international spy, is being blackmailed into stealing the formula by Dr Carelli, another Italian, who was played by Donald Wolfit. In the event, as deduced by Poirot, the real murderer is Amory's English

2   C. Andrew, 'British Intelligence and the Breach with Russia in 1927', *Historical Journal*, 25 (1982), pp. 457–64.

3   J. Fisher, 'Major Norman Bray and Eastern Unrest in the British Empire in the aftermath of World War I', *Archives*, 27 (2002), p. 5; J. Haslam, The Spectre of War: International Communism and the Origins of World War Two (Princeton, 2021).

secretary, Edward Raynor. Confidential secretaries frequently were villains, not least as they had access to key individuals and their papers. So for example with James Wilder in Doyle's 'The Adventure of the Priory School' (1904).

In Christie's 'The Four Suspects' (1932), Sir Henry Clithering, a reliable figure, refers to the *Schwarze Hand*, a German secret society focused on blackmail and terror, that had begun after the war. In *Lord Edgware Dies* (1933), there is not the Bolshevik theme. Nevertheless, Poirot's politics are made very apparent, Hastings commenting 'there is nothing of the Socialist about Poirot', a remark that is more pertinent given British politics in the period. However, in place of Bolshevism, there appears to be almost an inordinate degree of attention to Jewishness in this novel. At the outset, at a post-show supper at the Savoy, Poirot comments on the talented mimic Carlotta Adams whom he has seen on stage and who is dining separately:

> 'Miss Adams, I think, will succeed. She is shrewd and she is something more. You observed without doubt that she is a Jewess.... It makes for success ... though there is still one avenue of danger ... love of money.... We could weigh the pros and cons. If you care for money too much, it is only the money you see'.

Later in the novel, the new Lord Edgware bases his alibi on going to the opera with the Dortheimers, wealthy Jews:

> 'Into that box they invite young men with prospects.... I was whispering cheerful nothings into the diamond encrusted ears of the fair (I beg her pardon, dark) Rachel in a box at Covent Garden. Her long Jewish nose is quivering with emotion'.

This is a very unattractive use of language. So also for the self-satisfied Sir Montagu Corner in his 'big house' outside London in Chiswick:

> 'He had a distinctly Jewish cast of countenance, very small intelligent black eyes and a carefully-arranged toupee. He was a short man – five foot eight at most, I should say. His manner was affected to the last degree'.

These prejudices are expressed not only by Hastings, in the case of Corner, but also by the new Lord Edgware, although there is not the running forth of the Jewish-Bolshevik trope. Moreover, in later discussing the Dortheimers, the new Lord Edgware notes: "'Marry his daughter I couldn't. She's much too sensible a girl to take me, anyway'". The race theme, furthermore, is not maintained in this novel, but drops away, having served a descriptive purpose when rapidly depicting characters in what is presented as the highly cosmopolitan metropolis.

There is also a degree of homophobia in the novel in the discussion of the murdered Lord Edgware's overly good-looking butler. This, indeed, reads oddly today, suggesting that Christie does not know how to handle the issue. The looks of men were frequently mentioned by thriller writers as an apparent indication of their character, for good or ill. Separately, critics have sometimes discerned a homosexual undercurrent in Holmes and Watson sharing an apartment, but there is no basis for that in the text, and none also for Poirot and Hastings. Possibly the critics know nothing of friendship.

The anti-Semitic theme is present elsewhere in Christie's work. In the spoof 'Mr Eastwood's Adventure', which was first published in 1924 as 'The Mystery of the Second Cucumber', Conrad Fleckman is the name of the supposed murderer of Anna Rosenberg, a German Jewess allegedly living in Britain. In 'The Girl in the Train', published the same year, George Rowland has 'the true-born Briton's prejudice against foreigners', especially for German-looking ones, and the train guard shares his prejudice. In 'The Rajah's Emerald' (1934), Kimpton-on-Sea, a resort of the rich and fashionable, possibly based on Frinton-on-Sea which was popular in the period, has picturesque bungalows belonging to 'rich Jews'. 'Ikey Andrew', the half-Jewish Andrew Leech, who presents himself as Monsieur Antoine, is the mean employer in the hairdressers, *Antoine's*, in *Death in the Clouds* (1935). In that novel, Jane Grey and Norman Gale discover in their courting that they dislike 'loud voices, noisy restaurants and Negroes', as well as Katherine Hepburn, very red nails, fat women and oysters. So also in *The Body in the Library* (1942) in which, in a London party, Dinah Lee allows "'that filthy brute Rosenberg … a disgusting European paw her'", while her companion, Basil Blake, is "'going on with the black-haired Spanish bitch'".

Incessant racism was found in the wider literary culture, and occurred in the depiction of minor as well as major characters, although not invariably so, as with the 'British Israelite' retired Colonel in Anthony Rolls' *Scarweather*. Dorothy L. Sayers' *Have His Carcass* (1932) is replete with racism. In Patricia Wentworth's *The Clock Strikes Twelve* (1945), the very unheroic jewel thief Albert Pearson is in league with 'Izzy', clearly a Jew. John Bude's *Death Makes a Prophet* (1947) has a Jewish villain. So also with Ian Fleming. Thus, in the 1959 novel of that name, Goldfinger is a 'Balt' with possible Jewish blood. In *The Property of a Lady* (1963), the Soviet mole in London is identified as Maria Freudenstein.

Very differently, and later in Christie's career, after of course the Holocaust, in *Hallowe'en Party* (1969), Poirot has a friend, Solomon Levy or Solly, with whom he frequently spends the evening in order to discuss a past murder case about which they had a never ending controversy, the Canning Rd. murder. Like the title of many Holmes cases, this reference goes no further.

There is a sense of change in other respects in *Lord Edgware Dies*. Merton's priggish Anglo-Catholicism appears dated, while Poirot notes a transformative alteration of language, telling Hastings:

> 'You should not use that phrase – playing the game. It is not said any more.... Young people laugh when they hear it. *Mais oui*, young beautiful girls will laugh at you if you say "playing the game" and "not cricket"'.

The reference to the young and women having a different language captures the change in society. So also with the elderly Satterthwaite in *Three Act Tragedy* (1934). He can cite Alfred, Lord Tennyson, the Poet Laureate from 1850 until his death in 1892, who, however, 'was very little thought of nowadays'. Satterthwaite is also discomfited by the young Egg Lytton Gore telling him 'I like men to have affairs. It shows they're not queer or anything'. She also thinks the old simply 'back numbers'. In turn, Satterthwaite, a bachelor, who first appeared with Christie in 1924 and was born in the 1860s, has a Victorian side 'which disapproved of a member of the fairer sex taking the initiative in affairs of the heart'. He sadly notes 'Women don't have hatpins any more'. Like Poirot, Satterthwaite is unmarried. His disappointment in earlier love is mentioned, but he has made no effort to find it again and seems both sexless and without strong emotion. This was also true of Poirot, while Marple is unmarried. This situation is not the same with Doyle's characters: Watson marries as does Professor Challenger.

In *Murder on the Orient Express* (1934), foreignness is again to the fore, with an American, Samuel Ratchett, being both victim and villain, as he is revealed to be Lanfranco Cassetti, a gangster of Italian extraction. Poirot refuses to act for Ratchett. In practice, the 1932 kidnapping and murder of 20-month old Charles Augustus Lindbergh, on which the story is based, led in 1934, many months after the appearance of Christie's novel, to the arrest of Bruno Hauptmann, a German immigrant carpenter, convicted in 1935 and executed in 1936. Although there have been subsequent claims of his innocence, none are particularly convincing. At any rate, Christie was offering in effect a solution before the case was solved, one that found an Italian gangster responsible. This was not a conclusion that would have been unwelcome to British or American readers. With Holmes, Lestrade had referred to the Mafia in 'The Adventure of the Six Napoleons' (1904).

Published late in 1934 in the United States and in January 1935 in Britain, *Three Act Tragedy* deployed the acutely observant Satterthwaite from Christie's *The Mysterious Mr Quin* (1930), an instance of her saving effort, or at least introductions, by means of dipping into her corpus. In 'The Soul of the Croupier' from that collection, Satterthwaite, noting the decline of class at Monte Carlo, observes the Countess Czarnova across the seasons:

> The first time he had seen her she had been in the company of a Grand Duke. On the next occasion she was with an Austrian Baron. On successive years her friends had been of Hebraic extraction, sallow men with hooked noses, wearing rather flamboyant jewellery. For the last year or two she was very much seen with very young men, almost boys.

At this stage, Christie was using a range of characters, as in November 1934, she had published in Britain *Parker Pyne Investigates*, a collection of short stories in which, again in instances of the conservation of character, Ariadne Oliver and Felicity Lemon appear. Moreover, that September, amateur detectives Bobby Jones and Lady Frances Derwent are deployed in the somewhat hectic *Why Didn't They Ask Evans?*.

The conservative attitudes of the 1930s affected the response to immigration in Britain, the United States, and more generally. Ethnic issues were less pronounced politically and socially than they had been in the 1840s-1850s, the period of mass Irish immigration, or than they were to become later in the 1960s. Russian Jews had entered Britain in large numbers from the 1880s until the Aliens Act of 1905. Thanks also to fresh restrictions in 1914 and 1919, immigration declined in the 1920s and 1930s and was not a major social or political controversy in the mainstream. Indeed, Poirot, a Belgian immigrant, shows that 'middle-brow' readers could embrace a degree of cultural diversity. However, immigration had some political purchase from 1933, and there was also a more persistent low-level racism and anti-semitism in Britain. They could at times lead to accounts of violence, as in Raymond Postgate's impressive *Verdict on Twelve* (1940), but were, as with Christie's novels, more commonly a matter of social assumptions and how they affected sociability. Institutional practices also played a role, as in exclusion policies for golf clubs, private schools, or housing. In comparison with the situation today, there was very little racial co-habitation or inter-marriage.

Three Act Tragedy saw a return to Poirot. Foreignness was a theme at the outset, as with the characterisation by Satterthwaite, the narrator, who is a marked contrast with Hastings, not least in being closer to Poirot in personality. Of Oliver Manders, Satterthwaite notes: "'A handsome young fellow, twenty-five at a guess. Something, perhaps, a little sleek about his good looks. Something else – something – was it foreign? Something un-English about him'". Soon after, following a reference by Egg Lytton Gore to Manders as a 'slippery Shylock', Satterthwaite remarks "'Of course, that's it – not foreign – Jew!'" Subsequently Egg notes Manders' wish 'to get rich', but also his Communism. At least, and this is instructive of Christie's use of misdirection, Manders is not the villain. A Jewish moneylender briefly turns up to lend money to *Ambrosine*, the dressmaking company of Cynthia Dacres, although that dimension is not developed.

In *The Body in the Library* (1942), Sir Henry Clithering reflects that the English distrusted any man who danced too well, and he is interested in whether Raymond Starr is really English, finding out that he has an

Argentine grandmother. Soon after, Starr, who in fact turns out to be quite sympathetic and insightful, recalls critically a "'real old Colonel, incredibly ancient, British to the backbone and always talking about Poona'", the British social centre in India, who had disparaged him as a gigolo. Hugh McLean, not inherently an unsympathetic figure, is more critical of Starr: "'Fellow looks like a dago to me'".

Aristide Leonides in *Crooked House*, a Greek from Smyrna (Izmir) who had arrived in London in 1884, is, according to the police, "'crooked … the sort of chap that thought up all the ways you can get round the law'". His county sister-in-law, Edith de Haviland, refers to him as "'a dago … ugly common little foreigner! … those queer spiced rice dishes *he* used to eat'".

Others come within the xenophobic gaze of her characters, although Christie could also clearly differentiate herself from these observers. She does so for example with the socially appallingly prejudicial, as well as xenophobic and racist, old woman whom Poirot meets at the miserable 'Stag' in the somewhat depressing *Taken at the Flood* (1948). Surveying her family, the elderly Emily Arundel in *Dumb Witness* (1937) is displeased with her niece Bella:

> Emily Arundell's people, who were what is known as 'all service people', simply did not marry Greeks.… Not only a foreigner, but a Greek. In Miss Arundell's prejudiced mind a Greek was almost as bad as an Argentine or a Turk.… [the two children]. They had both taken after their father in looks – there was really nothing English about them.

Xenophobic views can be ridiculed, as well as given to villains. Thus, the foolish, if ultimately menacing, Sir Eustace Pedler MP in *The Man in the Brown Suit*, considers it disreputable to have a woman murdered in your house; but even more disreputable if the woman is a foreigner.

Christie, more generally, cuts across xenophobic and prejudiced views with the observation in *A Pocket Full of Rye* (1953) about Jane Marple's village, St Mary Mead: "'There are some nice people living in it and some extremely unpleasant people as well. Very curious things go on there just as in any other village. Human nature is much the same everywhere'".

Christie's interest in human nature was shown in her detective fiction, notably her Quin short-stories which were her favourites, in her interest in many of her novels in saving the innocent from the cruelty of others, and also in her novels as Mary Westmacott. This was especially so in *Unfinished Portrait* (1934), a semi-autobiographical work in which divorce and the idea of suicide play a role. The religious significance of suicide as the defiance of faith and the possibility of redemption, a significance Christie would have felt strongly, makes this work particularly powerful.

Separately, any emphasis on xenophobia can be offset by a potentially rival stress on regionalism and even more localism, as a qualification of nationalism. This was very much the case of Miles Burton's East Anglia in *The Secret of High Eldersham*. At the same time, identities can/could be multiple, so that a localist could also be a xenophobe at the national level, but not necessarily so. Multiple identities were part of the complexity of personality that is significant in Christie, and not least due to the need for misdirection.

The treatment of foreignness in Christie could have depth. Poirot, acting as a moral nemesis, explaining his use of English, draws attention to English xenophobia, and how it can mislead:

> 'It is true that I can speak the exact, the idiomatic English. But, my friend, to speak the broken English is an enormous asset. It leads people to despise you. They say – a foreigner – he can't even speak English properly.... I put people off their guard'.

As with Poirot's boastfulness, again presented as a device and, in the Dickensian fashion, a ready identifier, this provides Christie with a device she can at once use and say to the audience she is doing so deliberately. In *Death in the Clouds* (1935), the xenophobia of the inquest jury foolishly and humorously leads them to decide that Poirot is guilty. In addition, Mrs Mitchell, the wife of one of the aircraft stewards, is certain that the murderer is a foreigner and also that it was wrong that they committed the deed on a British aircraft. She subsequently blames 'Bolshies'. Yet, that is shown to be absurd.

In *The ABC Murders* (1936), Christie makes fun of xenophobia in Andover, when Poirot plays on it, suggesting a Russian murderer in order to get locals talking. Subsequently, the disgusting Albert Riddell calls Poirot and Hastings "'a couple of blarsted [sic] foreigners'", Christie capturing the intonation. In Torquay, Alexander Cust hears conversation to the same end: "'Do you think it was anything to do with the Chinese? Wasn't the waitress in a Chinese café?'" Far more sinister, the murderer in this story has "the partiality for England that had showed itself, very faintly, in the jeer at foreigners'" and enjoys "'scoring off a foreigner'". Poirot gets the upper hand, only to be accused of being an "'unutterable little jackanapes of a foreigner'". In a real putdown, the villain is then told by Poirot, who separates him from true Englishness: "'You are very full of an insular superiority, but for myself I consider your crime not an English crime at all – not above-board – not *sporting*'". That is clearly the view the reader is invited to share, and it compromises the attempt readily to ascribe xenophobia to Christie.

In that novel, indeed, Christie, through Poirot, rebukes xenophobia by remarking: "'The language may be different, but everywhere human nature is the same'", a theme similar to that of 'stereotyped patterns' in 'Triangle at Rhodes' (1937). In *Murder in the Mews* (1937), Christie again rebukes xenophobia by getting the villainous Major Eustace to call Poirot "'some kind of damned dago!'" In *Evil Under the Sun*, the idiotic Horace Blatt disparages Poirot: "'What I say is ... what's wrong with Scotland Yard? Buy British every time for me'". In *Sparkling Cyanide* (1945), there is hostility to foreigners based on their appearance: "'Pedro Morales – nasty bit of goods from Mexico – even the whites of his eyes are yellow'", while Giuseppe Bolsano has 'a rather monkey-like intelligent face', and "'I don't like Dagoes. When they've drunk too much they're not a bit refined any more – a girl never knows what unpleasantness she may be let in for'". Clear-cut, but totally wrong: Morales is a British agent in disguise, and Bolsano is honest.

In *After the Funeral* (1953), the elderly butler Lanscombe's pejorative view of the marriage of a family member to 'A Frenchman ... or nearly a Frenchman – and no good ever came of marrying one of *them*!' is part of his being dated. He also disapproves of the visiting Poirot who 'was attired in an exotic silk dressing-gown with a pattern of triangles and squares. "Foreigners!" thought Lanscombe bitterly. "Foreigners in the house!"' The unacceptable character of racism is captured when the exemplary elderly lawyer Entwhistle is referred to as "'the nigger in the wood pile!'" Colonel

Horace Lacey in *The Adventure of the Christmas Pudding* (1960) dislikes foreigners, while Eve Carpenter is able to castigate Poirot as a foreigner. Ironically, a different form of sensitivity occurs in *Hallowe'en Party* (1969), when Ariadne Oliver organises lunch at The Black Boy pub; a name that was judged objectionable in 2021 by Greene King breweries. Xenophobic remarks were a staple of detective writers. Thus in H.C. Bailey's 'The Missing Husband' (1927), there is reference to 'the abominable Armenian'.

Meanwhile, others at home were matched by Britons abroad. Empire was still a presence, and as a part of a British world that ranged widely, not least with the life and fiction of John Buchan for whom Empire was more authentically British than London. Every year, on Empire Day, which had been launched in 1896, large parades were held in Hyde Park in London. The British Empire Exhibition in 1924–5, for which the first Wembley Stadium was built in 1923, was a major public occasion, prepared for by the 1922 world tour that included the Christies, celebrated in the press and the newsreels, and commemorated by a set of stamps. The assertion of Empire was also seen in architecture, with the new Dominions paying for large buildings in the centre of London, where Australia House, built in 1912–18, was followed by India House, constructed from 1928 to 1930.

Emigration helped strengthen imperial links and there were British communities across the areas of formal and informal Empire. Some communities, such as those in Egypt and, even more, Smyrna (Izmir), were assailed by political crises,[4] but others thrived. Christie's characters have far-flung families and connections. In 'The Under Dog' (1929), West Africa, where Victor Astwell goes to look after company mines, has a bad influence on expatriates as they drink too much. West Africa is elsewhere referred to by Christie as unhealthy. As a separate point, Victor kills a witch doctor who has just slaughtered fifteen children. It possibly does not need mentioning, but the selling of technical information of value to Nazi Germany that is a major part of the plot in the Suchet television version broadcast in 1993 is completely absent in the Christie story, but then we would have a much longer book if we wanted to capture all the differences between Christie and the adaptations, including those during her lifetime. Indeed,

---

4   L. Mak, *The British in Egypt: Community, Crime and Crises 1882–1922* (London, 2012).

she had been displeased by the first Poirot play, *Alibi* (1929), on that basis, not least the original proposal to have a young 'Beau Poirot' who was popular with lots of girls. The Suchet series was particularly egregious, as in 'Yellow Iris' (1993), and very often unnecessarily so.

In *Three Act Tragedy*, Mrs Babbington has three remaining children: 'Edward was in Ceylon, Lloyd was in South Africa, and Stephen was third officer on the Angolia', a ship I have been unable to trace, but possibly a misspelling of the *Angola*, although that was subsequently renamed before it was sunk by a U-boat in 1941. In the *ABC Murders*, Franklin Clarke, a younger son, has pursued his fortune in 'the Malay States', while Mrs Marbury is visited by a brother from Canada. In *Death in the Clouds*, Norman Gale claims to have farmed in South Africa and be thinking of dentistry in Canada, which is labelled a 'Dominion complex'. He also thinks of New Zealand, his interest in British Dominions being referred to as patriotic. In 'The Case of the Caretaker' (1935), the badly-behaved Harry Laxton is sent off to Africa where he makes good. For Christie, the links are many and varied. In *Hercule Poirot's Christmas* (1938), Stephen Farr is homesick in the crowded London grime for the sunshine, blue skies and lush vegetation of South Africa. In *Towards Zero* (1944), Thomas Royle has Malayan plantations. In *One, Two, Buckle My Shoe* (1940), Poirot comes across an 'Anglo-Indian Colonel.... Not at all a bad looking man, Poirot reflected mellowly. Probably a fine shot who had killed many a tiger. A useful man – a regular outpost of Empire'.

In Christie's *Murder Is Easy* (1939), Luke Fitzwilliam is back home from being a policeman in Mayang Straits. There was no such location, and if Mayang suggests Manipur, the Straits suggests the Straits Settlements which were a Crown Colony in Malaya. In the novel, there is reference to another young man joining the Palestine police, while Major Horton had been in India. He presents 'various Indian gods' to the local Museum, which also contains some South Sea curiosities, a Malay head-dress, 'a large and malevolent-looking Buddha, and a case of doubtful-looking Egyptian beads'. In *N or M?* (1941), the retired Major Bletchley provides accounts of his experience on the North-West Frontier before 1914 and in Mesopotamia during World War I, and Tommy Beresford pretends that his wife died a decade earlier in Singapore; while, in *Evil Under the Sun*, the elderly Major Barry has a tendency to tell stories about his time in India, while the nearby lending library has A.E.W. Mason's epic novel of Imperial honour and adventure, *The Four Feathers* (1902). The Boer War (1899–1902) is similarly a point of reference for Christie's characters in the military, also bringing in South Africa. Military service on the bounds of Empire is a theme of detective fiction from Wilkie Collins' *Moonstone* on and was used by Doyle. The killing of Admiral Penistone in the co-authored *The Floating Admiral* (1931) links the South Coast of England to Hong Kong.

Empire is differently in the background in Christie's 'Triangle at Rhodes', in which Commander Chantry implausibly wonders whether there will be a '"general election over this Palestine business"', a reference to the problems the British were facing from the Arab population over Jewish immigration. General Barnes responds '"Whole thing's been badly mismanaged"', and begins telling 'an anecdote of his military career in India'. Military ranks are very much part of male identification of the period.

Empire leaves another legacy in *The Sittaford Mystery* (1931). Set in Devon, there are hunting trophies accumulated by Captain Trevelyan which include 'two or twelve hippopotamus tusks' and 'an elephant's foot stuffed and mounted and a tiger skin'; while the retired Major Burnaby invests unsuccessfully in Empire, with Canadian land, a South African diamond mine, and oil wells. In *Why Didn't They Ask Evans?* (1934), big-game hunting recurs in the case of Alan Carstairs, while Bobby, who receives an unexpected offer of a post in Buenos Aires, gets a marvellous job managing a coffee estate on a big salary in Kenya where 'people' come out on trips and also live, 'people' referring to whites, notably in 'Happy Valley'. In *Sparking Cyanide* (1945), Lucilla complains that the jobs people found for her wastrel son Victor so often seemed to take him out of England. Argentina was a particular destination for those seeking distant opportunities, as with Hastings, though he goes there for very different reasons from Victor.

Setting stories in the Middle East proved a way not only to reflect Christie's interest in archaeology, and experience of the region, but also to capture the continuing success and significance of Britain through her empire. Christie did not, for example, comparably use Ireland as a setting. Yet, these were years in the Middle East of some difficulty for Britain. Mesopotamia (Iraq) had been conquered from the Turks in 1914–18 and became a League of Nations mandate under British administration. An Iraqi revolt in 1920 was suppressed, but Britain eased the situation by devolving powers to an Iraqi government, a process formalised by an Anglo-Iraqi treaty of 1922 that was supported by a supplementary military agreement in 1924. As a result of further agreements in 1930 and 1932, the British retained key air bases, which served as part of its wider network in Asia, crucially providing links to India, and also helped the new state to suppress a Kurdish rising.[5] In 1930, Christie visited the excavations at Ur, which had become famous due to Lionel Woolley's work on the tombs of the Sumerian royal family. His wife Katharine may have been the basis for Louise Leidner in *Murder in Mesopotamia*.

The general situation in Iraq was unstable. Nationalists saw the expansion of the army as a way to integrate the state, and in 1934 conscription was introduced. The previous year, the Assyrians (Nestorian Christian) were defeated, although, looked at differently, this operation largely involved a massacre of unpopular civilians, a massacre staged by the army supported by Kurdish tribes. In 1935, in large part in opposition to conscription, tribal uprisings were suppressed, providing the army with a new source of prestige. In 1936, the Iraqi army staged its first coup and it thereafter played a clearly central role in politics. General Bakr Sidqī, the victor over both the Assyrians and the tribes, was able to force the resignation of the government, but, in turn, in 1937, his government was overthrown by the army.[6] This was not to the forefront in Christie's *Murder in Mesopotamia* (1936), which focused instead on Western visitors to an archaeological dig. There is a strong American presence which would not have hurt with the market: The book was published in both British and American editions.

So also for Egypt. Britain had effectively taken over in 1882, a process given new constitutional form in 1914. Egypt had been successfully defended against Turkish invasion in World War I, but a rebellion in 1919 saw the British overcome resistance, including by dispatching a flotilla up the Nile. However, they did not want to face an onerous insurgency and, in 1922, granted independence while retaining effective military control, notably of the naval base in Alexandria and of the Suez Canal. There was

---

5   W. Dockter, *Churchill and the Islamic World: Orientalism, Empire and Diplomacy in the Middle East* (London, 2015).

6   I. Al-Marashi and S. Salama, *Iraq's Armed Forces: An Analytical History* (Abingdon, 2008).

no further rebellion, but in the 1930s Italy intrigued with Egyptian nationalists as part of a wider challenge to Britain's interests in the Islamic
world.[7]

In Palestine (modern Israel, Gaza Strip, and the West Bank of the Jordan), the British who had conquered the region from the Turks in 1917–
18 had gained a League of Nations mandate, but in 1938–9 faced a major
rising due to Arab opposition to Jewish immigration. *Appointment With
Death* (1938) is set in Jerusalem and Petra, the latter in the Emirate of Tran-
sjordan, which was under British control. In the detective novels of the period, major and minor characters alike often had an imperial background.
Thus, in Anthony Rolls' *Scarweather* (1934), 'Jolly Morgan', the hotel
owner, had 'made money in South Africa' and displayed 'various trophies
of African hunting' from the walls of the dining room.

It is safe to say that *Death on the Nile* was not only not a comment on
the current situation in the Middle East, but also not a fantasy about threats
to Imperial power. The Egyptians who are mentioned are the irritating
crowds who try to sell to tourists. None are developed as characters, let
alone with empathy. That captures the perspective of the tourists that is
being offered. So also with Elspeth Huxley's *Murder on Safari* (1938).

The role of Empire continues for Christie after World War II. In *Taken
at the Flood* (1948), Enoch Arden returns from Cape Town, while Major
Porter of the Royal African Rifles has been in Africa; the King's African Rifles were formed in 1902. In *Hickory Dickory Dock* (1955), Miss Lemon
reveals that her sister had spent much of her life in Singapore where her
husband was in 'the rubber business'. In *A Pocket Full of Rye* (1953), Lance
Percival and his wife, Pat, want to go back to East Africa, Lance deciding
"'I don't take much to this country nowadays'". Instead, he wants "'a different country – a country where there's room to breathe and move about'".
This was a frequent theme among British emigrants of the period, although
one that generally led them toward Australia. In 1953, Britain was the colonial power in Kenya, Uganda, Tanganyika, and Zanzibar, but in 1952 the
Mau Mau uprising had begun in Kenya. In *A Pocket Full of Rye*, the Black-
bird Mine refers to "'some shady transaction.... Something on the West
Coast of Africa'", subsequently East Africa. The fraud there is played on

---

7   N. Arielli, *Fascist Italy and the Middle East, 1933–40* (Basingstoke, 2010).

the co-investor, a frequent theme, and the local population, typically, is not mentioned.

Another crook from East Africa is Robert Orwell in *Third Girl*, who has been prospecting for minerals before trying his hand at impersonation. This is an aspect of overseas as the refuge of scoundrels, as indeed the West Indies is with Tim Kendall in *A Caribbean Mystery* (1964). *The Clocks* (1963) has a Canadian diaspora providing opportunities for impersonation. In *Hallowe'en Party* (1969), the widowed Elspeth McKay has married children in Australia and South Africa.

To a degree, Christie's approach to the Egyptians in *Death on the Nile* matches that of other thriller writers to most murders within Britain, the majority of which were among the poor and therefore ignored in their plots. Yet, whereas with Doyle's Sherlock Holmes stories issues and problems are not only English, both rural and urban, but also often imported from the Empire and America, Christie, through both *The Murder of Roger Ackroyd* and Marple's reiterated insistence on the wickedness of village life, possibly more clearly emphasises a universal character to crime, one that encompasses Englishness. Poirot is in an interesting position. He is both alien and acculturated, and also with his concern about appearance and his vanity has a degree of effeminacy. He is a 'safe' alien whom the reader is supposed to admire, but not too closely.

5. CLASS AND NATION

'Practically all invested incomes have felt the strain'.
Dead Man's Mirror (1937).

'Like everyone else, we had suffered from world depression'. Hastings' comment in the opening paragraph of *The ABC Murders* (1936) set a tone different to that of Christie's recent novels. Indeed, Hastings reveals that he has never been able to afford to hunt. In *Death on the Nile*, Simon Doyle, after five years in the City of London, loses his job because the firm is cutting down, while Pennington complains about the Slump and the impact on share prices. In this novel, these problems make Linnet Ridgeway's money more significant, just as they more generally make issues of inheritance. Capital trumps income in this depression.

The Slump of 1929, followed by the Great Depression of the 1930s, hit the British economy hard. Heavily dependent on exports, they were particularly felt in the heavy industrial sector. These problems led to a marked rise in the number of unemployed: from 1.6 million in 1929 to 3.4 million, about 17 percent of the labour force in 1932. The misery and precariousness of many individuals' lives was captured by some detective novelists, for example Bruce Hamilton in *Hue and Cry* (1931) and Ethel Lina White in *Some Must Watch* (1933). Key characters in other detective novels, such as the seriously flawed Robert Kewdingham in Anthony Rolls' *Family Matters* (1933),[1] were unemployed; but Christie does not pursue that approach.

The Slump, the Depression, and the establishment and success of the National Government, formed the background to Christie's work in the 1930s. Labour was brought down in 1931, as in 1924, through the complex manoeuvres of three-party politics, but that was not the principal issue for the Second Labour government. Instead, it was badly hit by the serious

1   Rolls was the pseudonym of Colwyn Edward Vulliamy.

world economic crisis that began in October 1929, although the economic situation was already grave when Labour came to power, for Stanley Baldwin had left an inheritance of unemployment of 1.16 million, as well as a government deficit, and high interest rates to protect the gold reserves. The impact of the dramatic fall in world trade after the collapse of New York share prices greatly exacerbated the situation. Devaluation was rejected by Montagu Norman, the Governor of the Bank of England, as likely to lead to a collapse of the currency, and, instead, in 1930 the government relied on modest public works schemes to combat unemployment and on an increase in taxation to fund unemployment benefits. Ramsay MacDonald, the Labour Prime Minister, was willing to overturn the maxims of the past, and the Wall Street Crash led him to become an advocate for industrial protectionism.

Nevertheless, the Treasury warned that unemployment benefits threatened national bankruptcy, and the government was under growing pressure from the Conservatives over welfare expenditure and the budget deficit. In early 1931, MacDonald pressed his Cabinet colleagues to support a cut in benefit rates, only to find the majority unwilling to support him, certainly without equivalent sacrifices from other sections of society. While this impasse continued, a European banking crisis gathered pace. The *Kreditanstalt* bank in Vienna collapsed that May and this led to a major run, first on the German banks and then elsewhere, resulting in pressure on British gold reserves. At the same time (31 July), the report of the government-appointed Committee on National Expenditure under Sir George May projected a more serious budget deficit and also urged that the majority of the cuts it deemed necessary should come from unemployment benefits.

Other sections of society were not called upon to make equivalent sacrifices, although to many of them taxation already seemed excessive, which was a theme in Henry Wade's *No Friendly Drop* (1931),[2] a country-house murder. He pursued the theme of country-house crisis in *The Hanging Captain* (1932), in which Captain Sir Herbert Sterron, who can no longer afford to keep up the estate, is found dead.

The Cabinet was opposed both to cutting benefits and to introducing the means-testing of benefits, and this left a rise in taxation as the remedy.

2   Wade was the pseudonym of Sir Henry Lancett Aubrey-Fletcher.

MacDonald, however, found the Conservative and Liberal leaders unwilling to accept this and was pressed by the Bank of England on the threat of national bankruptcy. The government divided over the cuts that were believed necessary to balance the budget in order to restore confidence in sterling. The cut in unemployment benefit, pressed by Philip Snowden, the Chancellor of the Exchequer, and supported by MacDonald, was rejected by the TUC and the bulk of the Labour Party. Trade union loyalty to the Labour government had been tested too much by 1931, but Snowden was not willing to follow alternative strategies, such as introducing tariffs, raising taxes or increasing borrowing. This can be seen as a cautious, but unimaginative, response, yet Labour's lack of a parliamentary majority limited its options.

The Cabinet seemed unable to cope with the crisis and to provide the decisive leadership MacDonald thought necessary. He was worried that financial collapse would hit the working class more than cuts in social expenditure. On 23 August, the Labour Cabinet split over the economy programme recommended by MacDonald. This programme, which was acceptable to the financial markets and the opposition leaders, included a 10 percent cut in unemployment benefit rates. The Cabinet accepted the proposal by eleven to nine, but the nine were not willing to remain part of the government, and on the evening of the 23rd the Cabinet resigned, only to find MacDonald still Prime Minister. Keen to keep a national emergency at bay, George V convened a conference of the party leaders and this led to a cross-party National Government. Unable to rely on his party, MacDonald turned to the opposition and, with a few Labour supporters, joined the Conservatives and the Liberals (though not Lloyd George who was convalescing after an operation) in forming a National Government on 24 August. This was designed to tackle the crisis and push through the necessary changes without destabilising society. A widespread fear of economic collapse and social and political disruption, combined to encourage the formation of such a government, although, unlike Prime Minister Albert Aspinall in Helen Simpson's *Vantage Striker* (1931), MacDonald was not killed.

As with the wartime coalition of 1915–22, the National Government continued beyond the immediate crisis. It remained in power, indeed, until a new wartime coalition was formed in 1940. MacDonald, who was not a great success as the leader, was succeeded as Prime Minister by Baldwin in

June 1935 and he, in turn, as Prime Minister and Conservative leader, by Neville Chamberlain in May 1937. Both Baldwin and Chamberlain saw off criticism from Churchill who did not return to office (and then as First Lord of the Admiralty) until the outbreak of war in 1939.

As with the wartime coalition of 1915–22, the National Government was dominated by the Conservatives, while the opposition was very much Labour, although the Lloyd George Liberals also played a role, and the Samuelite or 'official' Liberals left the government when it introduced tariffs in 1932, although they did not move into opposition until 1933. Mac-Donald's Foreign Secretary in 1929–31, and his predecessor as Labour leader, Arthur Henderson, returned to lead Labour in 1931–2, which became more left wing in opposition, helping underline the clear statement in *Lord Edgware Dies* (1933) that Poirot was not Socialist.

The National Government convincingly won the general elections of 27 October 1931 and 14 November 1935, in large part because it was in tune with majority opinion. Labour lost working-class votes as a result of the economic problems of 1929–31, while the Conservatives benefited from the economic upturn of 1934 and from the consolidation of propertied and business interests into one anti-Socialist bloc. This was a major benefit flowing from the notion of a National Government. As in 1924, many former Liberals voted Conservative. The Liberals had attracted over five million votes in 1929, but they were hit by the Liberal split of 1931, and declined seriously at constituency level. Liberal weakness was to be a condition of Conservative strength.

In 1931, the National Government won 554 seats, the Conservative share rising from 260 in 1929 to 473. Labour won only 52, down from 288. In Christie's *Sad Cypress* (1933), Sir George Kerr, the MP, dies, being replaced by Major Somervell who is returned unopposed, Mrs Bishop remarking there has never been anyone bar a Conservative for Maidensford, a fictional constituency clearly set in the South of England. The new MP is able to afford to purchase at a very advantageous price Hunterbury, a large property. Less impressively, one of Baldwin's MPs is George Lee, a gasbag (as he is correctly described) in *Hercule Poirot's Christmas* (1934). Lee, the MP for Westeringham, is referred to by his father as lacking brains and guts.

In 1935, when the percentage of unemployed insured workers was

16.4, the Conservatives and their allies won 429 seats on 53.3 percent of the vote. Labour, which had just discarded its radical and pacifist leader George Lansbury in favour of Clement Attlee who led the party until 1955, won 154, although the Labour share of the vote was 37.9 percent, a swing to Labour of 9.4 percent. The Liberals took 21 seats with 6.8 percent of the vote. The National Government was represented all over the country, winning all the seats from such industrial towns as Blackburn, Bolton, Derby, Leicester, Newcastle, Oldham, Plymouth, Salford and Sunderland. The Conservatives won at least half the working-class vote, in part due to Anglicanism and the greater tendency of working-class women to vote Conservative, and in part due to a sense that Labour had failed in 1929–31. In *The Young Vanish* (1932) by Francis Everton, an industrialist who was no fan of Socialism or the Liberals, moderate trade union leaders die and another general strike is possible; but that remained simply the plot of a detective novel.

The consolidation of the anti-Socialist vote was democratic, as was the opposition. There was no equivalent to the political polarisation across most of Europe in the 1930s. During the decade, the number of democratic states in Europe fell dramatically. In Britain, in contrast, the extremists did not gain control of the political parties, and their own movements were unsuccessful. There was no crisis of conservatism to generate a powerful radical right. The right-wing extremism of Sir Oswald Mosley's British Union of Fascists (BUF) proved unacceptable, not only to the bulk of public opinion, but also to the Conservative establishment who marginalised the BUF. Mosley saw himself as a second Benito Mussolini, the dictator of Italy from 1922 to 1943, but it proved easier to borrow the latter's blackshirts as a party uniform, than to recreate the political circumstances that had permitted the Fascist seizure of power in Italy. The membership of the BUF, launched as the New Party in 1931 and renamed by Mosley after he visited Italy in 1932, peaked at maybe 50,000 in June 1934, but was below 25,000 thereafter. The BUF won no parliamentary seats, and it did not prove necessary to repress the BUF or to encourage the development of a rival loyalist movement. The BUF was launched late, after the worst was over, and when the economy was beginning to recover. In addition, there were not the same number of 'politically homeless' in Britain as in Germany and, again unlike Germany, no collapse of middle-class centre parties to open a legitimate route to power for extremists. The demagoguery of Mosley and the violence of his supporters helped discredit the BUF. More generally, they revealed the limitations of an extremist movement in a political culture that had little time for those seeking the overthrow of the system.

In response to Mosley, the government in December 1936 passed the Public Order Act banning political uniforms and paramilitary organisations, and controlling marches. Marginalised by its methods, the BUF was unable to benefit from the widespread uncertainties and fears that it sought to tap. Mosley's move into more aggressive anti-semitism in 1936 brought him no benefit, and when, in 1937, the BUF contested East London seats in the London County Council elections, it did badly thanks in part to the absence of any system of proportional representation. Due, however, to Mosley's peace campaign, membership rose in 1939.

Although she was clearly hostile in *One, Two, Buckle My Shoe* (1940), Christie does not address extremist right-wing politics in the pre-war period as some other detective novelists do. They included the critical Ralph Carter Woodthorpe in *Silence of a Purple Shirt* (1934), the prolific Ernest Robertson Pushon in *Dictator's Way* (1938), and the facetious Anthony Rolls with the Britannia League in his *Family Matters* (1933).

Nor was Communism so strong that the Establishment sought to create a counter movement, either by looking to the BUF or by creating a populist movement of its own. The antagonism of many Labour politicians and trade unionists meant that the Communist Party was effectively marginalised. Even the fall of the Labour government in 1931 did not provide an opening for the extreme left. Communist membership rose in the 1930s, but was still no more than 18,000 in 1939. Suffering from the close links of Labour with the trade unions, the Communists were strongest in East London and parts of the industrial zones of South Wales and Central Scotland, and were able to win council seats in their areas of strength. In 1935, the Communists won only one parliamentary seat, the mining constituency of West Fife, while the Independent Labour Party took only four Glasgow seats. Communist attempts to create links through a Popular Front strategy, as in France and Spain, were rejected by Labour. The Communists suffered from often poor leadership and from the deservedly ambivalent reputation of Stalin's murderous Soviet Union.

The Communists did not play a prominent role in detective novels, although a visit to a Communist meeting in London is part of the scenario in Ngaio Marsh and Henry Jellett's *The Nursing Home Murder* (1935). Christopher St John Sprigg, a Communist activist who was killed in 1937 fighting in the Spanish Civil War, produced a series of detective novels from 1933. Another Communist, Bruce Hamilton, a godson of Doyle, took his beliefs into his fiction, as in *Rex v Rhodes: The Brighton Murder Trial* (1937).

Thanks in part to the economic upturn and fall in unemployment from 1933, and to the general prosperity of the metropolitan region, opportunities for extremism were limited. The absence of any tradition of the violent overthrow of authority was also important. Had the General Strike of 1926 led to widespread violence or to a change of government, neither of which was the intention of the trade union leadership or membership, then the situation in the 1930s might have been less propitious. The Communist-led National Unemployed Workers Movement, the 'trade union' of the unemployed, launched marches and demonstrations demanding work, but support was limited – only 700 marching in 1934 – and it was concerned to remain within the bounds of the politically possible. Riots in 1936–7 by striking miners at Harworth in Nottinghamshire were ended by police action.

As well as maintaining stability at a particularly difficult time, nationally and internationally, the National Government was prepared to countenance a greater degree of intervention in the economy than previous governments had believed desirable. Through the adoption of such policies as protectionism, the National Government served as a link between the old world of *laissez-faire* and the new world of peacetime interventionism which came into existence after 1945. Protectionism was enacted in 1932, although it was linked with Imperial Preference.

In comparison with the weaknesses and collapse of democracy over much of continental Europe in the 1930s, the success of the National Government was a triumph, and one that was important to national survival in World War II. In opposition to the Communists and to the BUF, which he presented as un-British, Baldwin, the dominant figure in the National Government until 1937, stressed national identity, continuity, distinctiveness, and solid common sense. Baldwin did so not in order to embrace political reaction, but rather to use images to lessen tensions arising from economic change, particularly rivalry between capital and labour. He was photographed with pigs and five-bar gates, helping to underline an identification with an image of rural values.

Yet, there was also much hardship in the 1930s. 2.96 million people received unemployment benefits in January 1932, 2.25 million in March 1935, and 2.2 million in 1938. Josephine Bell, in *The Port of London Murders* (1938), captured the extent and nature of misery. Writing under that pseudonym, Doris Bell Collier (1897–1987) was a doctor who practised for a while in Greenwich, and her work in this riverside area is the basis for 'the grime and squalor and ugliness', with poverty aplenty, as well as terrible housing. In this world of continued shifts and expedients, sickness is to the fore, as is humanity and individuality. Bell's quickly but finely-etched characters interact with scant sentiment. There was comedy, with June Harvey, the heroine, working in an upmarket lingerie shop, and, very differently, the sickly and malicious Mrs Bowerman. Christie shares some of these comic turns.

Aside from Christie's crucial focus on individual psychology, her imagination located 'Bolshevism' as primarily an urban and cosmopolitan condition, while treating the rural as English and, therefore, more stable. The socio-economic stresses of agrarian society and rural life did not play a significant role in Christie novels. Group murder was seen in the Balkans on the Orient Express, and not in an English village. In contrast, R.C. Woodthorpe's *Death in a Little Town* (1935) sees an unpleasant landowner murdered.

As it is too easy to forget, there was also much prosperity. GNP (Gross National Product) in 1934 returned to its 1929 figure, the economy recovered more quickly than the economies of France and the United States, 2.6 million jobs were created in 1933–8, real wages rose, and prices fell. When, in *Death in the Clouds* (1935), Cicely Bland tells Poirot that there are no millionaires any more for her to marry, Poirot tells her she is wrong even if the man who had three million might now have only two. The economic difficulties of these years affected the characters in Christie novels, although not to the extent of the conscientious but weak industrialist in Freeman Wills Crofts' *The 12.30 From Croydon* (1934) who is driven to murder. His problems and obligations are discussed with a detail Christie never matched. Accepting that, Britain's economic issues are still in the background in her stories. In *Appointment With Death* (1938), Nadine Boynton thinks a job unlikely because 'thousands of men – qualified men – trained men – are out of a job as it is'. Set in an Italian colony, 'Triangle at Rhodes' (1937) has Douglas Gold complain that 'the Italian exchange is so absolutely ruinous at present', a reference to the exchange rate. The same issue recurs in other Poirot novels of the period.

There was a clear geography of prosperity in the 1930s. The heavy industrial sector, such as shipbuilding, declined, badly affecting the North East of England, but the South and Midlands benefited from a demand-led consumer industrialisation with the production of cars, radios and domestic appliances such as cookers and washing machines. The production of cars rose from 116,000 in 1924 to 341,000 in 1938, and private ownership of cars reached nearly two million by September 1938, by when there were 53,000 buses and coaches. In London, the Great West Road became the site of a series of spacious factories that, with their use of electricity, were very distant from the smoke-shrouded world of dockland manufacturing and from the workshops of inner London. Aside from large-scale factories, such as those manufacturing Smith's crisps, Gillette razors, Curry's cycles, and the Hoover factory, there was a host of small modern manufacturing works on the Park Royal Estate and also along the North Circular Road at Colindale and Cricklewood. In East London, Ford's car factory at Dagenham was a major site of activity.

The percentage of British homes wired for electricity rose from 31.8 in 1932 to 65.4 in 1938. In 'Yellow Iris' (1937), Poirot is pleased with his symmetrical electric radiator, preferring it to the shapeless and haphazard character of a coal fire. Poirot repeatedly praises central heating, for example in *Hercule Poirot's Christmas* (1938), where he regrets the torture of a wood fire: roasting the soles of one's feet while a cold draught assailed the back of one's shoulders, which was indeed the case. This new world of devices provided more opportunities for murder plots, as in Christie's 'Wireless' (1933), and more need for explication. The blunt poker was no longer in such need. At the same time, labour-saving devices offered women more time to read detective novels.

Jobs were available in expanding industrial centres in the South East and the Midlands, such as Birmingham, Coventry, Letchworth, Luton, Oxford, Slough, Watford, and Welwyn. Suburbia followed new roads, while new industrial plants could be seen in self-contained industrial estates largely served by road. Indeed, in *The ABC Murders*, there is reference to speculative building on the outskirts of Bexhill on the Sussex coast, as well as change in Christie's birthplace of Torbay:

> Until about ten years ago [Churston] was merely a golf links, and below the links a green sweep of countryside dropping down to the sea with only a farmhouse or two in the way of human occupation. But of late years there have been big building developments between Churston and Paignton and the coastline is now dotted with small houses and bungalows, new roads, etc.

New houses are again a theme in *The Body in the Library*; Braeside, the home of the retired Major Reeves and his wife, being a 'neat little villa, nice garden (1942) of about an acre and a half. The sort of place that had been built fairly freely all over the countryside in the last twenty years'.

In town and cities, the tightly-packed terraces characteristic of the Victorian period, for the middle as well the working class, were supplemented by miles of semi-detached houses with mock-Tudor elevations, red-roofed tiles, and walls of red brick or pebbledash, with a small front and a larger back garden. Each house had a small drive and a separate garage, which was often structurally linked to the house, thus making the site more compact. This housing represented the application of pre-1914 ideas of garden-suburbs, notably with an emphasis on space, calm, and the separateness expressed in individual gardens. The car was an important part of the lifestyle. Suburbs were in part a response to the cult of the outdoors, one captured in new street and suburb names.

D.H. Lawrence, in his 1929 piece 'Nottingham and the Mining Countryside', criticised 'little red rat-traps' and there was certainly a predictability and similarity in the mass produced houses; but there were also subtle variations which were understood by the residents of the new areas. So also with the lives lived. Indeed, true-life murders, such as the Crippen murder in 1910 and the Thompson-Bywaters case in 1922, suggested the variations of your neighbours including the murdering sort. This sense of what might be going on next door encouraged interest in detective stories.

Development was for long largely unrestricted by planning, as the 1909 and 1932 legislation was limited. The Restriction of Ribbon Development Act of 1935 attempted to prevent unsightly and uncontrolled development along new or improved roads. In 1938, a London Green Belt Act followed. However, limiting expansion encouraged greater housing density in towns. This itself had consequences as when H.C. Bailey, in his short story 'The Broken Toad' (1934), refers to the conversion of houses 'by the forces of progress into modern ugliness as blocks of flats offering modern comfort to those who do without babies'.

New housing elsewhere highlights villages that do not change greatly, as in Christie's *Murder Is Easy* (1939), in which the returning Luke Fitzwilliam dislikes the houses 'springing up everywhere'. In contrast, Mrs Pierce, the newsagent's wife, likes the 'lovely lot of new houses' in Ashevale.

Consumerism was related to a marked shift in the world of things, in large part linked to the spread of electricity. Refrigeration had a major impact on food storage and thus on the range of food available in households with fridges. In *Murder in the Mews* (1937), Jane Plenderleith tells Poirot that, bar one coal fire, the others are all gas and that everyone now cooks with gas. Poirot notes that this is much more labour-saving, an instance of Christie's acceptance of change rather than the expression of, in this case, any regrets about the servant problem. In his detective novel *Invisible Weapons* (1938), John Rhode captured change in a cottage: 'Everything here's absolutely up to date … all the latest gadgets – tiled bathroom, latest type of gas cooker, electric refrigerator, coke boiler for constant hot water … a labour-saving house'.

There was a social dimension to these devices. Whereas radios, vacuum cleaners and electric irons were widely owned, in part thanks to the spread of hire purchase, with payments spread out over a long period, electric fridges, cookers, and washing machines were largely restricted to the middle class. These differences were linked to an aspect of the major social divide between those who employed others and the employed. However, as far as the former were concerned, it was increasingly a matter of the occasional daily help, rather than the less numerous full-time domestic servants, the number of whom had fallen from nearly 2.5 million in 1910 to nearly 1.5 million in 1920. In *Sad Cypress*, commenting on the new film with the

American actress Myrna Loy (1905–93), Eileen O'Brien suggests that the lack of a local cinema means that it is impossible to get decent maids in the country. Loy took villainous roles in *Thirteen Women* (1932) and *The Mask of Fu Manchu* (1932), the latter a product of the cinema's strong interest in sensationalist novels.

Alongside contrasts, not least in education, clothing and manners, there were shared experiences. The 'pictures', the cinema, provided one, although there were different prices for the seats. Enormous and lavishly decorated picture palaces were built, while Victorian music halls were transformed into cinemas. Films created and disseminated lifestyles and images. Going to the cinema was a common activity and gave a communal feel to what would later, with television and, even more, the internet, become more individual. By 1939, Birmingham alone had 110 cinemas.

The cinema, in turn, becomes a setting in the plots of Christie's novels, and notably in the tightly written *The ABC Murders* with the Regal at Doncaster where there is an 'all-star, thrilling drama of pathos and beauty' that has an 'emotional and semi-religious end'. In that novel, the film, *Not a Sparrow* is also shown in the Torquay Palladium. The raffish world of the film studio in which Basil Blake works is in the background in *The Body in the Library*, and major film studios were founded in Elstree, Ealing, and Denham near London in the inter-war years. The films also play a role in setting norms, as well as fashions. Thus, Linnet Ridgeway is described by Mr Burnaby, the landlord of the Three Crowns, as like 'the pictures'. In 'The Manhood of Edward Robinson' (1934), the protagonist first meets Maud at the cinema and they continue to go there during their courtship, while, at the end of 'The Rajah's Emerald' (1934), the fashionable young women are going to the cinema for the afternoon. In *The Man in the Brown Suit* (1924), the reference to Colonel Race's '"modern Sheik-cum-Stone-Age love-making"' is one to Rudolph Valentino, the lead in *The Sheik*, a 1921 film sensation based on a 1919 romantic novel of that name.

Christie herself did not have much success in getting Poirot to screen. In February 1934, she granted the Twickenham Film Studios the rights to make and distribute a film of *Lord Edgware Dies* in return for 5 percent of the film receipts (after various exclusions) with the minimum of £300. Following the 1931 Poirot films *Alibi* and *Black Coffee*, the first of which was based on the play of *The Murder of Roger Ackroyd*, this was intended to be part of a series based on the Poirot novels, but the film, directed by Henry Edwards, was weak and unsuccessful. Poirot did not return to the cinema screen until the very different adaptation of *The ABC Murders* in *The Alphabet Murders* (1965) and, far more successfully, and closer to the text, Albert Finney's portrayal in *Murder on the Orient Express* (1974).

Sport was another source of shared experience. There were major social differences among both participants and spectators. At the same time, amateurism was regarded as part of national identity and there were important shared interests for what in *The ABC Murders*, with the St Leger at Doncaster and 'the crowds on the race-course', is referred to as 'the passionate, sport-loving English public'. Major Horton in *Murder Is Easy* goes to the Derby while Mr Abbot, the solicitor, usually takes the day off and gambles on the result. But this process is not socially exclusive. Jim Harvey, the young mechanic, wanted to see the Derby run and, though not being given the time off, gambled on the result.

Playing cricket, being understood as being fair, was a well-recognised phrase, as in *Sparkling Cyanide* (1945), where Colonel Race observes that a '"lot"' of women also play cricket. Criticism of something as too unsporting is described by Poirot, including in 'The Dream' (1937), as a typical English idea. Cricket, however, is the setting for Denzil Batchelor's *The Test Match Murder* (1936).

In *Murder Is Easy*, the newsagent's husband takes '"a great interest in football.... Turns to it first of all in the news"', as he gambles on the results. Football, nevertheless, was not of interest to Christie. In contrast, it plays a role in Bruce Hamilton's *Hue and Cry* (1931) and, more centrally, in Leonard Gribble's *The Arsenal Stadium Mystery* (1939), in which there is a critical comment on mainstream writing – including very much that of Christie: '"Book-writers to the contrary, I don't think there's anything subtle in poisoning a man"'. Gribble offers pockets of poor writing and some clichés, as with both the bad background theme and 'eyes a bit too close together'. Yet, as part of a general psychological reasoning, the idea of proceeding through trying to alter the state of mind of the murderer is well-worked through. The 'strange spiritual strength' of the detective comes into play.

Death on the Nile ends where it begins, not in Egypt, but at the Three Crowns in Malton-under-Wode where the discussion is about who is going to win the Grand National. This provides an ironic counterpart to the idea that it is the future that matters, a proposition very much pushed by Mr Ferguson. He is the political antithesis of the ordered world that is on offer, and not the Egyptian nationalist who does not appear at all, nor Guido Richetti, a very dangerous agitator who has killed more than once and who has long evaded British Intelligence. Pretending to be an archaeologist, Richetti is an undeveloped character whose dastardly context and deeds are not brought out. A villain who is, or pretends to be, an archaeologist is a device also used elsewhere, including in both cases in *Murder in Mesopotamia* and reflected Christie's knowledge of archaeology through her husband.

Ferguson attacks established institutions and capitalism, describes social position as bunk, pretends to be of a low social status, rejects marriage as a legal contract, laughs at education, culture, and death, is not interested in being reliable, repeatedly advocates a focus on the future, refers to some people as parasites or useless fools, and argues that, with the Pyramids, it is necessary to think of the sweated masses that built them, and not the ego-tistical despots for whom they were built. In fact, Ferguson is the very rich young Lord Dawlish, who became a Communist when at Oxford. Cornelia rejects him for the older Austrian Dr Bessner who is kind, knowledgeable, and cares for the sick. Poirot has the last word on Ferguson/Dawlish who replies to the latter's complaint about Cornelia by telling him that she is probably the first woman of an original mind that he has met. To a modern reader, Ferguson's remark that education has "'devitalised the white races'" might be surprising, but ideas and ideologies were fairly jumbled up, in-cluding in Christie's telling, and eugenicist thought was indeed character-istic of the Left as well as the Right.

Communists were generally very different to Ferguson or to Ronnie Carlice of Carlice Abbey in C.H.B. Kitchin's detective novel *Birthday Party* (1938). The case of the Communist paper the *Daily Worker*, launched in 1930, is instructive. It sought to advance Party propaganda, but its circu-lation remained modest until 1935, as part also of a 'Popular Front' ap-proach of uniting the Left, the paper became less explicitly Communist. Instead, cinema reviews, racing tips, murder stories and advertisements re-ceived space, although a political edge was retained, notably with crime linked to social conditions. In turn, an emphasis on the purist approach in the shape of a focus on the class struggle led to the removal of crime reports.[3] Writing in *The Saturday Review* on 7 January 1939, John Strachey, a Communist journalist, presented detective fiction as a form of escapism:

> 'The detective story is the opium of the contemporary British reading public.... The terrors of the detective story world are strictly controlled; they are small, manageable events, such as the murder of an individual; and, above all, they are invariably overcome'.

Strachey's anger in this piece extended to the Prime Minister, Neville Chamberlain, who was a hated figure by the Far Left. Economic improvement helped explain the National Government's overwhelming victory in the general election of 1935, its ability to act as a force for stability, and Britain's success in holding political extremism at bay. Although in *The Division Bell Mystery* (1936) by Ellen Wilkinson, a left-wing Labour MP, the government is in serious difficulties, it both survived crises and maintained firm opposition to public violence. In *One, Two, Buckle My Shoe* (1940), Japp tells Poirot that the Communists and the Fascists are both trying to bring down the government which stands for '"good sound Conservative finance"'. Possibly the name chosen for the dentist, Morley, is designed to remind readers of Mosley, although Morley is no villain. Blunt, a widower whose wife was Jewish, suffers from criticism from the Imperial Shirts who are clearly modelled on Mosley's 'Blackshirts': '"They march with banners and have a ridiculous salute.... They just work up these poor young men ... until they think they are doing something wonderful and patriotic"'. Christie has Poirot hear a sermon from I Samuel 15:23 in which rebellion is presented as a sin. The vulnerability of Britain to extremist conspiracy is laid out to Poirot by Reginald Barnes. Solvency and stability are seen as linked.

Meanwhile, far from Christie retreating from society, the locations chosen in *The ABC Murders* (1936) were not those of St Mary Mead and an ordered, but murder-disrupted, rural life. Instead, the second chapter takes the reader

3   L. Young, 'Internal Party Bulletin or Paper or the Working Class Movement? The Communist Party of Great Britain and the Role of the Daily Worker, 1930–1949', *Media History*, 22 (2016), pp. 123–34.

to the town of Andover, where Hastings' response to the crime is that of disappointment: 'The murder of an old woman who kept a little tobacco shop seemed, somehow, sordid and uninteresting'. Subsequently, Hastings reflects 'The crime attracted very little attention in the Press. It had no popular or spectacular features'. In setting up one of her more incredible plots, and one that is not based on elements of a real case, Christie also played with (some) audience expectations by having Poirot criticise Hastings' desire for 'excitement': 'There are no curiously twisted daggers, no blackmail, no emerald that is the stolen eye of a god, no untraceable Eastern poisons. You have the melodramatic soul'. Hastings, in turn, counters that a second murder in a book makes it more interesting, as it is tedious to follow up everybody's alibi until the end if there is only one. The emerald is a reference to the *Moonstone*.

The murdered woman was poor and from an ordinary background. Her estranged husband was a German 'drunken brute'. Hastings reflects that this is 'the usual type of crime reported in the newspapers'. Instead of this murder launching Hastings and Poirot into a rapid return to milieux of prosperity, considerable attention is devoted to recreating the life, history and lifestyle of the victim. There is an itemisation of her possessions:

> A couple of old worn blankets on the bed – a little stock of well-darned underwear in a drawer – cookery receipts in another – a paper-backed novel entitled *The Green Oasis* – a pair of new stockings – pathetic in their cheap shininess – a couple of china ornaments – a Dresden shepherd much broken, and a blue and yellow spotted dog – a black raincoat and a woolly jumper hanging on pets – such were the worldly possessions of the late Alice Ascher.

The reference to a poor woman reading a paperback (of a title later to be used by novelists) is an instructive guide to the wideness of the market for such works. This is not the only visit to the poor in this or other novels. Poirot seeks information from Albert Riddell, a xenophobic platelayer who is rude to his wife.

The meals of the poor are also captured. Riddell 'was in the act of eating meat-pie, washed down by exceedingly black tea'. Similarly, in *Death in the Clouds*, the steward Henry Mitchell has at home a supper of sausage and mash (mashed potato). At a higher social level, Jane Marple and Diana 'Bunch' Harmon in 'Sanctuary', visiting London, restore themselves from shopping with steak and kidney pudding followed by apple tart and custard. Arriving in the gloomy rural 'Stag' in *Taken at the Flood*, Poirot knows that dinner would be 'Windsor soup, Vienna steak and potatoes, and steamed pudding', with an elderly lady commenting that the steak is in fact chopped-up horse.

In contrast, in *The ABC Murders*, at the Ginger Cat tea-room in Bexhill, there were 'a few sparing lunch dishes for females such as scrambled eggs and shrimps and macaroni au gratin'. Customers come in for 'scrambled eggs and teas' up to 7pm, and sometimes later. At an unprepossessing café in Kimpton-on-Sea, in 'The Rajah's Emerald' (1934), James Bond finds fish and chips and curried beef both sold out and is left the choice of haricot mutton or nothing. Bread and butter pudding, another staple, is not on offer in *A Caribbean Mystery* (1964).

Christie uses food in order to help clarify social position. The meals of Riddell and Mitchell are very different to those, in *The Three Act Tragedy*, which Sir Charles Cartwright, the wealthy retired actor, proposes to offer his house-party guests for dinner 'Melon Cantaloupe, Bortch Soup, Fresh Mackerel, Grouse, Soufflé Surprise, Canape Diane'. Soufflé Surprise involves baking the dish without solidifying the lightly poached eggs that have been placed within the soufflé. It requires skill. Canape Diane provides toast carrying bacon and chicken liver. Subsequently dinner for Sir Bartholomew Strange's house-party offers 'soup, grilled sole, pheasant and chipped potatoes, chocolate soufflé, soft roes on toast'. Ending such a meal with a savoury is an age and class apart. In her foreword to *The Adventures of the Christmas Pudding* (1960), Christie recalls childhood Christmas lunches, with her brother-in-law's family at Abney Hall, of oyster soup, turbot, roast turkey, boiled turkey, sirloin of beef, plum pudding, mince-pies, trifle and every kind of dessert. Accordingly, Poirot receives such a lunch at Kings Lacey, including '"all the old desserts, the Elvas plums and Carlsbad plums, and almonds and raisins, and crystallized fruit and ginger"'. Buffet suppers at Major Rich's in 'The Mystery of the Spanish Chest' (1960), which was based on *The Mystery of the Baghdad Chef* (1932), included *foie gras* and hot toast, smoked salmon, and sometimes, usually in winter, a hot rice dish based on a Near East recipe. In 'The Adventure of the Italian Nobleman' (1923), the meal ordered was soup julienne, fillet de sole normande, tournedos of beef, and a rice soufflé.

The menus preserved at Greenway, Christie's Devon home, reveal that the very wealthy Christie continued to dine splendidly into the post-1945 world, including on lobster. She also has her wealthier subjects eat well. In *A Pocket Full of Rye* (1953), breakfast offered bacon, scrambled eggs, cold ham, cereal, toast and marmalade, coffee, tea and orange juice; and 'there was honey and scones, chocolate cake and Swiss roll and various other plates of things' for tea in the library at the Fortescue household. The same year, the funeral lunch in *After the Funeral* is creamy chicken soup, followed by 'Ham and chicken and tongue and salad. With cold lemon soufflé and apple tart to follow'. There is 'an excellent Chablis'. The cold food is necessary as it is not clear how long it will take to return from the funeral, while the soup can be rapidly heated up.

Later in *After the Funeral*, Timothy and Maude Abernethie, lacking help, offer the visiting Entwhistle clear soup, followed by sole and then a custard pudding. Next day, he dines far better with Poirot, first on *pâté de foie gras* and hot toast by the fire and, then, at the table, on sole veronique, escalope de veau milanaise, and poiré flambée with ice-cream, with a Pouilly Fuissé to drink, followed by a Corton (a type of Burgundy) and, subsequently, for Entwhistle, a very good port and for Poirot a crème de cacao. After that, coffee and then fine brandy. Later in the story, Poirot remarks that beer is horrible, but British; and, instead, has a '*sirop de cassis*'. The health-conscious wealthy are far more cautious, Linda Marshall in *Evil Under the Sun* having for her breakfasts '"Just tea and orange juice and one piece of toast"'.

In 'Four-and-Twenty Blackbirds' (1926), Harry Bollington likes the Gallant Endeavour pub in Chelsea because it offers English food. Turkey stuffed with chestnuts is his favourite dish. He has it after an honest fillet of sole with no messy sauce. Other dishes on offer in the restaurant include thick tomato soup, mulligatawny soup, steak and kidney pudding, mutton, blackberry tart, blackberry and apple pie, sago pudding, and Stilton. In *One, Two, Buckle My Shoe*, Poirot is able to have at Alistair Blunt's home, a well-cooked English meal of clear soup, a grilled sole, saddle of lamb with tiny young garden peas, and strawberries and cream.

Returning from food to *The ABC Murders*, the second setting is also well-etched, with Christie indeed going far from her country houses in order to provide a lower-middle-class setting in Bexhill and what the shrewd

Megan Barnard calls 'our humble little crime'. As with the mention already in the novel by Alice Ascher's niece of London as being 'gayer for a girl', Christie captures a sense of the world of women changing. Betty Barnard is happy to date widely, despite annoying the man whom thinks her his intended, although 'they don't put it as formally as that nowadays'. Her elder sister, Megan, has the 'queer modern angularity', alongside the forcefulness also seen with Egg Lytton Gore in *Three Act Tragedy*. Megan is less developed as a character than the latter but more interesting and impressive.

There were also the gradations that were so important to society and to ideas of class. Megan notes of the two regular waitresses at the tea-room: 'Betty couldn't bear the Higley girl. She thought her common', a frequent phrase in the period. This sense of differentiation is captured throughout the book and has to be set alongside any tendency to refer simply to upper, middle and working classes. Thus, in *The Body in the Library* (1942), in which the chambermaids look down on the hotel dancing professionals, Conway Jefferson explains why he decides to adopt Ruby Keene, who is presented as natural poor, and not the alternatives of either an underclass or a would-be middling class:

> 'She was absolutely natural – completely naïve. She chattered on about her life and her experiences – in pantomime, with touring companies, with Mum and Dad as a child in cheap lodgings. Such a different life from any I've known! Never complaining, never seeing it as sordid. Just a natural, uncomplaining, hard-working child, unspoilt and charming. Not a lady, perhaps, but, thank God, neither vulgar nor – abominable word – "lady-like".… I know character. With education and polishing, Ruby Keene could have taken her place anywhere'.

At the same time, as a reminder of cross-currents, it is possible, in *Crooked House* (1949), for the Assistant Commissioner of Scotland Yard to refer to a marriage in the late nineteenth century as in '"the days before money swept aside all class distinctions"'. Already, in *Murder is Easy* (1939), Honoria Waynflete, who, we are told, is probably still under sixty, comments that, when young, she had been engaged to Gordon Whitfield, then an upwardly-mobile young man of talent, only for her '"people"' to be "'scandalised. Class distinctions in those days were very strong.... My people, I think were wrong'". Her father was a Colonel, though the romance really ended due to callousness toward a canary. The idea of a wider family as the 'people' who define and register norms and provide and guarantee status was one that was strong in country society.

In 'The King of Clubs' (1923), Poirot, who, in *One, Two, Buckle My Shoe* (1940), is to accept that he is essentially bourgeois, grandiloquently remarks that he does not hunt down tramps. However, in *The ABC Murders*, it is all classes of society that are assailed by the murderer, and there is a counterpart, in response, to the depiction, in particular by Baldwin, of a national unity. Party leader of the Conservatives from 1923 to 1937 – a length only since matched, and passed, by Margaret Thatcher (1975–90) – and Prime Minister in 1923–4, 1924–9, and 1933–7. Baldwin was to play a major role in making the Conservatives appear to much of the electorate to be conservative, but not reactionary, consensual, not divisive, and the natural party of government. Baldwin was also adroit at selling a new politics, with the media harnessed to create a political image for a mass electorate. Frequent radio broadcasts helped to cultivate the folksiness that Baldwin sought to project, while Conservative Party propaganda, often geared towards the new female electorate, continued to emphasise the dangers of Socialism to family life and property in general.

The success in overcoming extremism was underpinned by the optimistic emphasis on social cohesion and patriotism offered by films and newsreels. Lord Rothermere's influential *Daily Mail* backed Mosley in 1934, but dropped him as he resorted to violence and increasingly strident anti-Semitism. Conservatism was not just a matter of politics. For example, D.C. Thomson and Mills & Boon, two of the most successful publishers of popular fiction, actively disseminated conservative social and moral standards: sexual energy was restrained, while radicalism, social strain and moral questioning were ignored. Conservatism also rested on a structure of sociability, as with the Primrose League fete, 'in the grounds of the local squire' (in other words, of his home), that Evans, the retired CID Inspector, attends in 'Accident', which was first published in 1929 in the *Sunday Dispatch* under the title 'The Uncrossed Path'. Founded in 1883, the League was a Conservative organisation. In *The Murder at the Vicarage*, the Vicar is an attractive character, and, while Colonel Protheroe, the magistrate, is unattractive, not least in his gleeful harshness to poachers, he does not deserve his fate.

More generally, the success of the National Government made it appear likely that Britain would preserve its political and social system, and the greatest empire in history still seemed stable, strong, and with a secure future. Anti-'socialistic' comments could be given to unappealing figures, such as, in *Murder Is Easy* (1939), Lord Whitfield and the 'fierce-looking colonel' in the train who declaims against '"these damned Communist agitators"'. Nevertheless, Christie reflected these values. Far from being reactionary or restricted to a minority, they were widespread. While happy with electricity and cars, Christie is repeatedly uneasy about some aspects of change. At the start of *Murder Is Easy* (1939), Luke Fitzwilliam, returning from the Tropics, reflects:

> 'Heavens, the people! Crowds of them, all with grey faces like the sky – anxious worried faces. The houses too, springing up everywhere like mushrooms. Nasty little houses! Revolting little houses! Chicken coops in the grandiose manner all over the countryside'.

Similarly, the architect Clough Williams-Ellis, in his *England and the Octopus* (1928), berated builders and planners for their destruction of the countryside and what he called 'the common background of beauty'. A change of values was suggested when All Hallows, Lombard Street, a Great Fire victim rebuilt by Sir Christopher Wren, was closed in 1937 and demolished in 1938–9 to clear the way for the new headquarters for Barclays Bank. The finances of the traditional middle class are also under pressure. Luke is told by the sympathetic Lavinia Pinkerton about the problems of '"servants' wages being so much more"' and '"one's dividends being less"'.

Transport presented a significant area of change. With the Bond films it was sharks, but with the Poirot television stories trains. The love affair is presented with the graphics at the outset which show a powerful train surging forward. Moreover, in story after story, Poirot arrives by train. There are shots of trains, and within trains, and from trains, as well as station shots, and, in all cases, accompanying sounds. There was an element of nostalgia involved, but the 1930s were indeed an age of style related to rail.

The superb hissing (a rather strange description) of large engines in a London terminus is the starting background to *Hercule Poirot's Christmas* (1938). This was the world of rail in which Poirot is depicted on screen. There was a big increase in maximum speeds in the 1930s, especially with the London and North Eastern Railway (LNER)'s *Silver Jubilee* and *Coronation* trains. The *Mallard* set the world steam record of 126 mph in 1938. The attempt to project a modern image including contemporary architectural techniques, for example with Surbiton station and Southern Region (SR) 'glasshouse'-style signal boxes.

The advertising campaigns of rail companies, notably via posters, encouraged travel for pleasure. The Great Western Railway (GWR), which was very much the system used by Christie, helped invent the idea of a Cornish Riviera: the Cornish Riviera train began its service in 1904, running non-stop from London to Plymouth, before pressing on to Penzance. Such advertising campaigns were important not only to the economy of particular areas, but also in creating images of them. Cornwall was seen as a land of romance, rather than of difficult upland farming. Many of the contemporary murder stories set on holiday focus, as with both Christie and Sayers, on Cornwall or Devon, which reflects their place in English tourism, and notably so with Burgh Island, the Devon basis for two Christie novels. These counties brought together opportunities for settings on the coast and on moorland. In starting as a novelist, Christie was helped by Eden Phillpotts (1862–1960), a wide-ranging and active writer who himself wrote a number of detective novels, including the Dartmoor-set *The Red Redmaynes* (1922). They became friends.

In Christie's stories, the railway works as an integrated network, with branch lines feeding into long-range systems, and cross-country lines providing further integration, the whole helping her characters move, but also providing opportunities for plots. Train travel was crucial to the plots of many detective stories, as in Sayers' *Five Red Herrings* (1931) and Miles Burton's very fine *Death in the Tunnel* (1936). Thrillers also used the setting, as in Arnold Ridley's highly successful play *The Ghost Train* (1923), in which a spectral passenger train turns up to be a real one used by revolutionaries to smuggle Soviet arms, with a British agent eventually defeating them. A novel followed in 1927, as did several films, the 1941 version having Nazi sympathisers rather than Communists. Like Hastings, Ridley had been seriously wounded on the Somme in 1916, and then medically discharged from the army. A busy playwright and actor, Ridley, who adapted Christie's *Peril at End House* (1932) into a play that opened in 1940, was to become a familiar figure in his role as Private Godfrey in the popular 1968–77 series *Dad's Army*.

There was a less benign economic situation for the trains, one that the novelists largely ignored. Although the fall in the cost of motoring was a serious competitive problem, some of the difficulties were due to over-ambitious expansion in the nineteenth century, and others to a lack of investment during World War I. Inter-war economic problems were also an issue, especially in the traditional freight markets of coal, metallurgy, and heavy engineering. The General Strike of 1926 proved that the nation could live without railways, and a lot of the lost high-value traffic never returned after the strike. Among the 'Big Four' railway companies compulsorily created in 1923 by the amalgamation of more than 120 companies, the SR was alone in paying a regular dividend to shareholders before nationalisation in 1948. This was the sole company that electrified on a large scale and that did not serve depressed industrial areas, instead catering to London's massive expansion south of the Thames.

The 1923 reorganisation led to a measure of rationalisation, and the standardisation of locomotives and rolling stock cut maintenance costs and helped efficiency. Nevertheless, the railways suffered from under-investment, over-capacity, and a massive wages bill. They were also affected by the impact of the Depression, especially as it hit hard at their traditional freight goods, particularly coal. In contrast, the newer consumer industries tended to have lower freight needs, many of which were met by road transport, which, indeed, provides a basis for the plot in John Bude's *The Lake District Murder* (1935). The 1933 Road and Rail Traffic Act provided inadequate assistance for the railways, while price increases in 1937 hit rail freight. The network became smaller. In the inter-war period, 240 miles of track and 350 stations were closed completely, and another 1,000 miles and 380 stations were closed to passenger traffic. This decline of the system provided opportunities for settings in disused stations which Christie and others ignored.

The railways had often pioneered feeder bus services, and they invested heavily in them after 1928. However, competition from road transport became serious for the railways. Buses were more flexible, could go through villages, the St Mary Meads of the world, and delivered people directly to and from far more places than trains. Also, bus companies were more willing to run late-night services, especially on Saturdays, thus scooping up cinema and pub crowds. Marple often goes by bus, but Poirot far less so; although, in *Mrs McGinty's Dead* (1952), he takes a bus back to Broadhinny, which has a station. In that story, he also uses a hired car.

Very differently, air services developed. Although the Atlantic was crossed non-stop in 1919, commercial services to New York did not begin until 1939, only to be very rapidly stopped by the outbreak of war. In contrast, Imperial Airways had developed services within the Empire. From 1930, the journey to Australia took two weeks. Aircraft held sixteen passengers and stopped each evening for refuelling and for passengers to stay in luxury hotels. The model was clearly leisurely sea voyages, rather than the realisation of swift air travel. In *Sad Cypress* (1933), a witness from New Zealand arrives thanks to 'the quickness of air travel', providing crucial testimony in what is an unusual setting for the Christie reveal, that of a courtroom rather than a house. Detective novelists responded quickly to the possibilities of air travel. Aside from Christie's *Death in the Clouds*, there was a number of other works, both British and American, notably Stuart Palmer's *The Puzzle of the Pepper Tree* (1933), Freeman Wills Crofts' *12.30 from Croydon* (1934), Philip Wylie's *Death Flies East* (1934), and C. Daly King's *Obelists Fly High* (1935).

Such developments had only a limited impact on social norms in England. Looking back, in his 'Decline of the English Murder', a piece published in *Tribune* on 15 February 1946, George Orwell argued that 'the old domestic poisoning dramas' were the 'product of a stable society where the all-prevailing hypocrisy did at least ensure that crimes as serious as murder should have strong emotions behind them'. Christie continued that point in *Crooked House* (1949) by claiming that 'in the name of respectability many murders had been committed'. So also with the means. In *Sparkling Cyanide* (1945), she had Lucilla Drake, an old-fashioned widow, thankful that as yet in England there were no gangsters killing each other with tommy [sub-machine] guns.

An image of Englishness had been presented by her novels written before the war, as, after her detour in setting stories in the Middle East, she returned to England in *Hercule Poirot's Christmas*, *Murder is Easy*, and *And Then There Were None*. In *Murder Is Easy* (1939), when Luke Fitzwilliam returned home, plum pudding on Christmas Day, village cricket, and open fireplaces with wood fires, are all part of the scenario of Englishness. Christie is willing to comment ironically, noting that the scenario could bore people, but she is also able to resonate with its moral convictions. This was a world that was to be tested in World War II, and then by post-war social changes. It is the world most often associated with Christie, not least due to the television and film presentations, but these underrate the range of her writing.

6. WAR

"'Lots of gunpowder everywhere all over Europe. And we weren't ready, damn it!'" The comment of Air Marshal Sir George Carrington in Christie's 'The Incredible Theft' (1937) captured the focusing of the established concern about air vulnerability in light of the newly menacing situation arising from the rise of Hitler – not that he is mentioned. In time-honoured fashion, a seductive female spy is to the fore. The Cabinet minister, who may be the next Prime Minister, refers to himself as 'the man needed to guide England through the days of crisis that I see coming'.

And come they did. So also with other writers, as with Laurence Meynell's 'The Cleverest Clue' (1937), which reflects the period's fear of air attack and the belief in a miracle weapon. The Alfred Hitchcock/Robert Donat 1935 film version of John Buchan's *The Thirty-Nine Steps* had already changed the villains to the Nazis.

Coming to maturity during one world war, Christie was an adult at the height of her powers during the second. Nevertheless, as she has Poirot and Hastings discuss in *Curtain* (1975), which was written in 1940, World War I was their key conflict of memory and reference. *Curtain* and *Sleeping Murder* (1976) can be considered in chapter ten which covers when they appeared, but also in this chapter, as they were written in the early part of World War II in case Christie did not survive it. The latter might appear logical. At the same time, the books were intended as the last works to involve particular characters, and therefore can be assessed from the perspective of the reader and thus of their years of publication. Moreover, there was no explicit reference to the war in either novel.

World War II posed significant challenges to Christie. These included personal challenges, not least the air attacks that motivated her to write these final novels for Poirot and Marple respectively. There was also the question of the content and tone she should adopt for her novels. Furthermore, there was the extent and state of her readership. Indeed, paper rationing dramatically reduced the potential market both for books and the newspaper serials that offered additional profit. Printing and distribution were hit by bomb damage and by the staff shortages arising from conscription. In addition, theatrical audiences were affected by wartime restrictions. At the same time, although far less prosperous, and with other claims on their time, including Home Guard duties and vegetable growing, the reading audience had little else on which to focus their leisure time.

Christie had taken her personal knowledge of archaeology so far as to re-site her murder stories in the archaeological Middle East, and very successfully so. In contrast, there was no comparable re-siting of her fiction during the war. It would not have been expected that Christie should do any wartime re-siting in a military setting, but the wartime crisis for civil society was largely ignored. Published in November 1940, however, *One, Two, Buckle My Shoe* is interesting (as well as effective in plot, characterisation, and pace), not least because of its comments on Englishness and its decrying of radicalism. Being unemotional and 'so very normal' is presented as 'essentially British'. The dentist sees such character as the answer '"to their Hitlers and Mussolinis and all the rest of them.... We don't make a fuss over here. Look how democratic our King and Queen are"'. There is an attempt by an Indian to assassinate the Prime Minister. The novel bridges pre-war and wartime assumptions.

The early stages of the conflict were not ones with the war necessarily to the fore, as, to many, it seemed somehow distant. Indeed, John Dickson Carr's impressive *The Case of the Constant Suicides* (1941) begins in London on 1 September 1940, before the heavy German air attacks on the city had started: 'An air-raid alert meant merely inconvenience, with perhaps one lone raider droning somewhere'. Within a month, the experience was very different.

Wartime social life offered much to detective writers. Plots accordingly about false identities and the resulting murders, were used by Christie in post-war novels: In *Taken at the Flood* (1948), deaths in a wartime bomb blast launch the plot about false identities. A false identity is also significant with the villain in *Dead Man's Folly* (1956), who, in the event, is a deserter, and not a casualty. These themes, however, were not to the fore with the books Christie published during the war. Moreover, the characters do not even read war news in the newspapers as for example does the very rural Constable Mellalieu in George Bellairs' *The Murder of a Quack* (1943).

There is no equivalent with Christie to E.C. Lorac's *The Fell Murder* (1944), set in rural north Lancashire, which reflects her feel for the pressures of a farming family in wartime. The detective, Chief Inspector Macdonald, is deliberative and far from flashy. Lorac's *Murder by Matchlight* and *Checkmate to Murder* are set in wartime London. The latter is scarcely an heroic account, but one of food shortages, blackout, gloom, irritation, an officious and somewhat sinister Special Constable trying to buy up bomb-damaged property, and a young Canadian soldier en route to risk his life in combat. Neither the theme of the book nor the misdirection, however, relates to the war, and Macdonald continues to show his quiet pre-war competence and purposeful determination. The counterplay between the specifics of the plot, essentially played out across neighbouring properties, Macdonald's remorseless search for clarity and the wartime setting, provides a somewhat claustrophobic atmosphere. Raymond Postgate's *Somebody at the Door* (1943) is interesting on wartime conditions, while in George Bellairs' *The Dead Shall Be Raised* (1942) the problems of a rail journey and of arriving at a rail junction during the blackout are ably depicted. The blackout provided a very different context to that of peacetime for streets and houses alike, as in Dorothy Bowers' *Deed Without a Name* (1940) and Lorac's wartime London novels.

Very differently, for Christie, it was classic murder as normality in, for example, *Evil Under the Sun* (1941), *The Body in the Library* (1942), *Five Little Pigs* (1943), and *Towards Zero* (1944). There is no explicit reference to the war in these novels. So also with short stories of the period, although the servant problem is an issue in 'The Case of the Perfect Maid'.

Evil Under the Sun was set on Smugglers' Island, in fact Burgh Island off South Devon, where during the war the fashionable hotel was both used as a recovery centre for wounded RAF personnel and damaged by a German bomb. To pre-empt German attack from Brittany, anti-tank defences and pillboxes were constructed, as was an observation post. Christie had used the island as the inspiration for Soldier Island in *Ten Little Niggers* (1939), which is now referred to by the title of the American edition, *And Then There Were None* (1940). That story, which has both mounting suspense and a well-crafted puzzle, was the best-selling crime novel of all time, with over 100 million copies sold, while Christie adapted it for the stage in 1943. Although published as a book in November 1939, it was not a wartime novel as it had first appeared in a serialisation in the *Daily Express* published from 6 June to 1 July 1939. The novel was adapted for film as *And Then There Were None* (1945), which was an American production. This began a number of film adaptations of the title including in 1965 (the first British version), 1974, and 1989.

Evil Under the Sun, published in June 1941, refers to the improvements of the island hotel carried out in 1934 and how they increased the popularity of holidays there. The novel therefore is another wartime account of pre-war life. It is dated in that sequence to after *Death on the Nile* as the murder of Linnet Ridgeway is mentioned, thus providing a slight degree of linkage between the novels, one that is generally totally absent.

Far from the war being dominant. *The Body in the Library* (1942) begins with Dolly Bantry dreaming of nothing more surprising than the vicar's wife wearing a bathing-suit at a flower show. The early-morning household at Gossington Hall includes three housemaids, a cook, a chauffeur, and a butler. There are presumably also gardeners. Arthur Bantry refers to the influence of the genre in responding to Dolly's news of a body in the library: He sees it as a dream inspired by

> 'that detective story you were reading – *The Clue of the Broken Match*. You know – Lord Edgbaston finds a beautiful blonde dead on the library hearthrug. Bodies are always being found in libraries in books. I've never known a case in real life'.

Dolly also refers to this only happening in books. There was no story of that title.

The politics of the book scarcely relate to the war. Dolly Bantry complains that Basil Blake has "'that silly slighting way of talking that these boys have nowadays – sneering at people sticking up for their school or the Empire or that sort of thing'". Arthur Bantry, an ex-Colonel, county councillor, member of the Conservative Association, active churchman and loyal husband, loathes Basil, a London member of the film industry, who of course has rented a 'ghastly modern bit of building'. This cottage has the ironic name of Chatsworth, which was the palatial seat of the Dukes of

Devonshire. In practice, the cottage sought to fit in, with its half-timbering and sham Tudor, but, to Bantry, any new building was unwelcome. At the end, however, there is both a mention of the war and a wartime reconciliation: Bantry refers disparagingly to Blake as dishonest and, as a member of the younger generation, having no stamina, but Marple responds:

> 'Some of them have been through a bad time.... He did A.R.P. [Air Raid Precautions] work, you know, when he was only eighteen. He went into a burning house and brought out four children, one after another. He went back for a dog, although they told him it wasn't safe. The building fell in on him. They got him out, but his chest was badly crushed and he had to lie in plaster for nearly a year and was ill for a long time after that. He doesn't talk about it'.

Bantry replies "'Quite right. Proper spirit.... Always thought he'd shirked the war'". Marple's description is that of the London Blitz and this is the only reference to the war in the novel.

Five Little Pigs (1943), a Poirot story about sexual tension and jealousy, is a powerful work that offers little hint of the wartime background, for author or reader. Nor is there any real engagement with social developments. Looking back, the elderly Caleb Jonathan comments: "'All the young people were a disappointment to their parents. None of them ran true to type – huntin', shootin', fishin'", but without any more general reflection. The disruption of the previous world war is captured – "'Diana married a fellow who wasn't a gentleman – one of the temporary officers in the war'", of which there were many, including Hastings. There are no reflections on the current one. So also with many novels by other detective writers, such as Sebastian Farr's *Death on the Down Beat* (1941), Patrick Hamilton's *Hangover Square* (1941), Shelley Smith's *Background for Murder* (1942), and Cyril Hare's *Tragedy at Law* (1942). To an extent, a refusal to focus on the war was an aspect of a phlegmatic and fatalistic response, and, more particularly, a stoical emphasis on keeping going whatever the Germans threw at Britain.

Another lawyer in *Five Little Pigs*, Quentin Fogg, does not like having a prosecution case that is easy: "'It's a very English point of view. 'Shooting the sitting bird' describes it best. Is that intelligible to you?'" Without making any wider reference, Poirot replies, "'It is, as you say, a very English point of view, but I think I understand you. In the Central Criminal Court, as on the playing fields of Eton, and in the hunting country, the Englishman likes the victim to have a sporting chance'".

The *Moving Finger* (1943) has its protagonist, Jerry Burton, also recovering, in this case from an aircraft crash, but that reference to the war is not developed. Indeed, we are taken away from the war when Joanna Burton suggests to Emily Barton that she go on a cruise, which was scarcely possible in wartime. Instead, anonymous letters and an erring husband are the means and cause of the murder. The exigencies of wartime play no role, but there is a continuance of the pre-war theme of the financial pressures on the genteel. The angry former parlour-maid, Florence, complains on behalf of Emily, who had been forced to let her house:

> 'Forced to it. And she living so frugal and careful. But even then, the government can't leave her alone! Has to have its pound of flesh just the same.... Shares not bringing in what they used to, so she says, and why not, I should like to know?' 'Practically everyone has been hit that way', I said.

In one reversal of Christie's previous approach, the elderly Emily is not followed up in her brief criticism: "'The schoolmistress here is a most unpleasant young woman. Quite *Red*, I'm afraid'".

Sparkling Cyanide was another wartime novel, in this case the development of the July 1937 short story 'Yellow Iris'. First published in the United States in February 1945, although there under the title *Remembered Death*, the novel offers us only an elliptical view of the war, in the shape of the challenge posed over the last three years by a gang of international saboteurs run from Central Europe who had been gathering secrets, agitating among workmen, and targeting, among others, the tank trials at Lord Dewsbury's works, other prominent British armaments manufacturers, as well as the Ericsen aircraft manufacturers in the United States. Unusually for Christie, this activity is repeated twice in the novel, presumably in an attempt to establish the threat.

As in earlier novels, the British can rely in *Sparkling Cyanide* on Colonel (Johnny) Race, who had once controlled the Counter-Espionage

Department, and is referred to as 'the Empire builder type', and later as 'soldierly'. Race passes muster with the difficult General Lord Woodworth as they had both been at Badderpore in India in 1923, while Empire is again the signifier when Race remembers Mary Rees-Talbot from Allahabad, also in India. Another still-active part of the old Britain is Lord Kidderminster, a key Conservative statesman. He has influence that spans the country, being for example a friend of the Commissioner of the Metropolitan Police, but does not expect the law to overlook his daughter if a murderess. That theme, of no fear or favour, is also offered by Chief Inspector Kemp and is presented as part of Englishness.

Kidderminster's son-in-law, Stephen Farraday, an MP and a coming-man, is a far more troubling figure. Believing in 'the Will', which is twice capitalised, Farraday benefited from the profit his father made by constructing 'a row of jerry-built houses', which is a reference both to what happened and also to the salience of housing as an issue. By predilection a Liberal, Farraday realised that party was dead, and joined Labour, where he did well, only to be thwarted by its lack of openness to new ideas. This is Christie commenting as a Conservative, for reality was otherwise. As a result, Farraday had joined the Conservatives, who were looking for promising young men, contested and won a fairly solid Labour constituency, presumably in 1931 or 1935, and set about marrying into the Kidderminsters, which greatly helped his rise. This is a somewhat unproblematic account of Conservative politics, as rising men who married well, such as Harold Macmillan (1894–1986), who had married Lady Dorothy Cavendish, daughter of Victor, 9th Duke of Devonshire, in 1920 and become an MP in 1924, were not all that common in the Party. Victor was nephew and successor of Spencer, the 8th Duke, upon whom the Duke of Holdernesse in Doyle's 'The Priory School' (1904) was modelled.

Sparkling Cyanide devotes more attention to Christie's interest in inheritance than to Conservative politics. Lord Kidderminster reflects that Farraday had been a disaster as nothing is known of his antecedents or ancestors, and therefore how he will react in a crisis. Subsequently, Race, a source of established knowledge, observes that Victor Drake has bad blood and is not so much weak as positively evil, and that there was a family history of weakness, vice and instability, all predisposing causes to crime. These are very much Christie themes.

In *Towards Zero* (1944), the hero Angus MacWhirter, is introduced in hospital, but as a result of a failed suicide attempt, and not as a battle casualty. This is not a story about the war. Englishness is defined as being good at sport, although the sportsman is the murderous villain. This is the last of five cases with the sensible, well-moustachioed Superintendent Battle.

Poirot does not follow earlier adventures, notably 'The Missing Prime Minister' and *The Big Four*, in opposing international conspiracy. Christie in *N or M?* (1941), in contrast to forgetting war, has instead a wartime thriller that provides Tommy and Tuppence with new relevance, as they had not appeared since *Partners in Crime* (1929). *N or M?* resets Tommy and Tuppence into the new world war as never happened with Poirot or Marple. The war cuts in on the first page of the novel, set in the spring of 1940, with the Germans advancing in France. The plot focuses on the hunt for two murderous top German spies hiding out in Leahampton, in fact Bournemouth. An abridged version was published in *Woman's Pictorial* in April-June 1941 before the November book. Tommy Beresford is given an account of the dire state of the country by Grant, his Secret Service recruiter. Like Race, Grant is another older figure of authority:

> 'This war started in an optimistic spirit. Oh, I don't mean the people who really knew – we've known all along what we were up against – the efficiency of the enemy, his aerial strength, his deadly determination, and the co-ordination of his well-planned war machine. I mean the people as a whole. The good-hearted, muddle-headed democratic fellow who believes what he wants to believe – that Germany will crack up, that she's on the verge of revolution, that her weapons of war are made of tin and that her men are so underfed that they'll fall down if they try to march – all that sort of stuff. Wishful thinking as the saying goes.
>
> Well the war didn't go that way. It started badly and it went on worse. The men were all right – the men on the battleships and in the planes and in the dug-outs. But there was mismanagement and unpreparedness – the defects, perhaps, of our qualities. We don't want war, haven't considered it seriously, weren't good at preparing for it.

The worst of that is over. We've corrected our mistakes, we're slowly getting the right men in the right place. We're beginning to run the war as it should be run – and we can win the war – make no mistake about that – but only if we don't lose it first. And the danger of losing it comes, not from outside – not from the might of Germany's bombers, not from her seizure of neutral countries and fresh vantage points, from which to attack – but from within. Our danger is the danger of Troy – the wooden horse within our walls…. Men and women, obscure, but all believing genuinely in the Nazi aims and the Nazi creed and desiring to substitute that sternly efficient creed for the muddled easy-going liberty of our democratic institutions'.

Subsequently, the German plan is discussed by Commander Haydock, a retired naval officer. It is for a 'new Britain', with self-seeking people replaced by 'brave and resourceful' leaders: '"Between us all we will create a new Europe – a Europe of peace and progress"'. The Germans had gained full details of British military dispositions, and a list of those pledged to assist the invasion included:

'two Chief Constables, an Air Vice-Marshal, two Generals, the Head of an Armaments Works, a Cabinet Minister, many Police Superintendents, Commanders of Local Volunteer Defence Organisations, and various military and naval lesser fry, as well as members of our own Intelligence Force…. These people were ready to betray their country not for money, but in a kind of megalomaniacal pride in what they, *they themselves*, were going to achieve…. It is the Cult of Lucifer'.

This list was far more extensive (and alarmist) than those who did in fact look to Germany. This is a *Thirty-Nine Steps* type of novel, with deceit and subterfuge to the fore. The Lucifer theme helps to provide a moral anchor and looks to other novels in which Christie used it including *Passenger to Frankfurt*. *N or M?* also provides a basis for a later novel involving Tommy and Tuppence, *Postern of Fate* (1973), in which, returning to *N or M?*, Colonel Atkinson refers to highly-placed wartime traitors, a constant theme of this sort of literature, and to the resulting provision of information to Germany and Italy.

N or M? is similar in its approach to the Basil Rathbone film *Sherlock Holmes and the Voice of Terror* (1942), in which Holmes thwarts a German programme of sabotage and an attempted invasion whose mastermind is Sir Evan Barham, the head of the British Intelligence Committee. The overconfident Barham brings Holmes onto the case in order to appear to be doing everything possible to thwart the Germans. Holmes discovered that the real Barham was shot in cold blood while a World War I prisoner and replaced by a German agent, who is cruel, callous, and despises ordinary people. Such films made readers receptive to novels such as *N or M?*. Rathbone himself had starred as the villain in *Love from a Stranger* (1937), which was based on the Frank Vosper 1936 play, in turn based on Christie's 'Philomel Cottage' (1924). Later famous as Jane Marple, Joan Hickson played a minor role in the film. Other wartime conspiracy novels included the prolific John Brandon's effective *A Scream in Soho* (1940) in which London is in blackout, but German spies readily go about their business. Australian-born Brandon (1879–1941) wrote over 120 novels.

Although some novels, such as Edmund Crispin's wittily-conceived *The Moving Toyshop* (1946), made no reference, the war also hangs over into the post-war years, providing plots, as in Douglas Browne's *What Beckoning Ghost?* (1947); a guide to character, as in John Bude's *Death on the Riviera* (1952); as well as a framework for characters, as in Lorac's *Relative to Poison* (1947), in which the heroine has just been demobilised from the ATS (Auxiliary Territorial Service), the women's branch of the army. In a number of novels, for example Christie's *Taken at the Flood* (1948) and Julian Symons' *The Belting Inheritance* (1965), in which a long-dead son allegedly arrives, identity in the shadow of the war plays a role. In *A Murder is Announced* (1950), Jane Marple, as an instance of how one does notice part of a scene with particular sharpness, recalls:

> 'Once, when there was a fly bomb [sic] in London – splinters
> of glass everywhere – and the shock – but what I remember best
> is a woman standing in front of me who had a big hole half-
> way up the leg of her stockings and the stockings didn't match'.

In *Mrs McGinty's Dead* (1952), Superintendent Spence observes "'Our villages, you know, M. [sic] Poirot, aren't friendly. Evacuees found that during the war'". Tied to her mother, Deidre Henderson still does V.A.D. [Voluntary Aid Detachment, nursing help for the military] work and 'some driving for the W.V.S. [Women's Voluntary Service, civil defence]'.

The war also offered Pat Fortescue, in *A Pocket Full of Rye* (1953), an opportunity to consider the particular type of personality suited to the military: her first husband, Don, was shot down and killed in the Battle of Britain: "'He had all the qualities that are needed, wanted in a war. But I don't believe, somehow, peace would have suited him.... He wouldn't have fitted in or settled down'". This theme is a frequent one with Christie, and part of her discussion of different types of masculinity. In the same novel, another reference is to a death at Dunkirk in 1940. In *Destination Unknown* (1954), Boris Glydr is demonstrably good, as he worked for the Resistance, and, after the war, continued by working for the American government in what it is implied is Intelligence work. This continuation reflects Christie's assessment of the Cold War.

In *After the Funeral* (1953), the elderly butler, Lanscombe, a figure of probity and continuity, comments:

> 'We were spared in This Country owing to our Navy and Air Force and our brave young men and being fortunate enough to be an island. If Hitler had landed here we'd all have turned out and given him short shrift. My sight isn't good enough for shooting, but I could have used a pitchfork, and I intended to do so if necessary'.

Somewhat differently, but reflecting Christie's continued interest in mental conditions, one that owed something to her eventually deranged brother Louis 'Monty' Miller (1880–1929), a veteran, Miss Gilchrist, who has to close her café due to the war, recalls:

> 'A woman I know had concussion during the war. A brick or something hit her as she was walking down Tottenham Court Road [in London] – it was during fly bomb time – and she never felt *anything* at all. Just went on with what she was doing

– and collapsed in a train to Liverpool twelve hours later. And would you believe it, she had no recollection at all of going to the station and catching the train or *anything*. She just couldn't understand it when she woke up in hospital. She was there for nearly three weeks!'

Flying bombs, the V1s and V2s of 1944–5, clearly had an impact on Christie, and are mentioned in *Postern of Fate* (1973) as if following a target down a street. This is a gripping image of fear. V-1s were launched at Britain from 13 June 1944, followed from 8 September by V-2s. London was hit by 2,419 and 517 respectively. There were many casualties, and morale was seriously affected.

In *Crooked House* (1949), the Leonides family live together owing to 'the war and blitzes', Roger Leonides being '"bombed out early in the war"', which is later revealed to be London in 1943 when there was in fact relatively little bombing in the city. In addition, the family house in the country loses its gates due to 'patriotism or ruthless requisitioning'. Due to a lack of gardeners, the rock garden is 'somewhat neglected'. Brenda had a fling with Terry '"who was going overseas"', but, as was very much the case with many wartime relationships, he did not stay in touch. William Leonides, a grandson, is killed in Burma. There is a former conscientious objector whom it is assumed no jury will like. The protagonists, Charles and Sophia, met in Cairo during the war. Due to service in the war, Charles does not meet his father for five years.

Indeed, Christie's husband, Max Mallowan, joined the RAF, was sent to Egypt in February 1942, rising eventually to Wing Commander, and did not return to Britain until May 1945. Her Poems published in 1973 include 'To M.E.L.M. in Absence'. Christie's son-in-law, Hubert Pritchard, a Major in the army, was killed in Normandy in 1944.

In *A Murder is Announced* (1950), the war still affects settings. Dayas Hall's kitchen garden has been much reduced due to a lack of staff. Moreover, Detective-Inspector Craddock discusses how the country is full of Continental guns as British soldiers had brought them back from the war.

These wartime links continued in Christie's novels. In *Ordeal by Innocence* (1958), Philip Durrant, a child then, recalls the excitement of the war in London before his evacuation to Devon. In an image from childhood, the fun included bombs, spending nights in the tube stations, and the excitement of a city on fire. Both Luther Crackenthorpe's son Edmond, in *4.50 from Paddington* (1957), and the Laceys' son, in *The Adventures of the Christmas Pudding* (1960), had died in the war. In *The Clocks* (1963), it is a case of 'the death of the first Mrs Bland through enemy action in France, and his second marriage to Hilda Martindale (who was in the NAAFI[1]) also in France'.

By *Third Girl* (1966), wartime links, however were somewhat dated, as in the elderly Sir Roderick Horsefield, a figure, rather like Christie's mem-oires, from 'a bygone day'. He refers to Poirot as '"a chap in Allied Intelli-gence who was out with me at a certain place in France at a certain date"' and, running together the two world wars, comments on the differing po-sitions of Italy, Japan and '"the Russians ... nothing's more difficult nowa-days than the question of allies. They can change overnight"'.

So also for other novelists. Thus, *Death in Captivity. A Second World War Mystery* (1952) by Michael Gilbert (1912–2006) was in part coining experience, Gilbert being close in character to 'Cuckoo' Goyles, a central figure in this story set in 1943 in an Italian-run POW camp in Italy, a closed-community that is ably re-created. Gilbert himself escaped from such a camp in 1943 and, evading murderous German search-parties, made it back to the Allied lines. His *Death Has Deep Roots* (1951) brings together wartime betrayal in France and courtroom drama in Britain. A solicitor, Gilbert wrote his stories in part on his commute by train, a nicely Trollopian touch, one also seen earlier with Buchan on the Oxford-London commute.

The ongoing impact of World War II as a touchstone of value and val-ues is one seen with the generation that went through it, producing a set of assumptions that were as potent as the previous world war. So even more with those, like Christie, who had been through both world wars, working in the second in the pharmacy at University College, London. It is very dif-ficult for modern readers, none of whom in Britain have had that experience of a struggle for national survival, to appreciate its weight, resonance and implications. As a result, this is not only a past that has been lost but also one that it is difficult mentally to recreate. The imaginative strength of that

1   Navy, Army and Air Force Institutes, which in particular ran canteens, clubs, and shops.

experience is further dissipated, not only by the tendency in the visual versions to focus on the material comfort of the period, but also by the interest in 'updating' the plots in order to make them 'relevant', for example by emphasising feminism or lesbianism. Those perspectives may be of interest, but this approach can risk a presentation that directs attention from the timeless quality of the moral dimension that is offered by Christie.

Clearly, that dimension is more to the fore in some of her stories than others, but throughout there is a sense of the sanctity of life, one captured best in the Quin short stories, but also in Poirot's strong hostility to murder, including of the murder of difficult individuals. Deaths are not casual in Christie. This remained the case in her wartime novels, and helps to explain the shock of *Curtain* (1975). The plots of her wartime stories, as of the others, are ingenious, and that ingenuity has led to her stories as a whole being dismissed as little more than elaborate puzzles. While there was not always with Christie the sinuous moral weight of the writing of P.D. James, this approach is misleading and has distracted attention from the extent to which the stories rest in a moral framework that provides an ethical force that is closely related to the plot and gives it a point greater than that of providing a puzzle. To Christie and her readers, the war itself was a moral struggle, and thus her stories of killers defying the norms, killing, and being brought to justice, had further weight.

7. RECESSIONAL, 1945-51

It was not only state and empire that were under pressure in the aftermath of World War II. So also with the social code that was so important to continuity. The Mass Observation Project carried out in 1949 the British Sex Survey which revealed changing moral values and clear evidence of sexual dissatisfaction: A quarter of the husbands and a fifth of the wives admitted to being unfaithful, and a quarter of the men had slept with a prostitute. In a period of austerity, life more generally was lacking in stability, certainty, and creature comforts – if not altogether grim. Extended to include bread in 1946, and coal and potatoes in 1947, rationing continued into the mid-1950s. There were serious shortages of coal, the basic source of energy and fuel, and life appeared miserable as well as cold. The political and trade union situation was unsettled. The Labour governments of 1945–51 claimed that Communist conspiracies were behind the strikes, most prominently the London dock strike of 1949. Strikes were an aspect of the malaise, although they receive only occasional attention from Christie. Reading the *Times* on the train in *A Pocket Full of Rye* (1953), Inspector Neele notes 'the imminent strike among the dockers', an occupation that had proved highly militant leading the Labour government in 1949 to declare a state of emergency and deploy troops.

Labour emphasised its pragmatism, but also had a strong ideological thrust compounded of ethical Socialism, Fabianism, a belief in planning, and a measure of Marxism. There was a massive extension of the power of the state, with a series of nationalisations, including railways (1948), hospitals (1948), the electricity supply (1948), gas (1949), and steel (1949). The creation of the National Health Service in 1948 was a major extension of control and direction.

Christie was less than sympathetic about this policy and tone. The ghastly, highly-intellectual David Angkatell in *The Hollow* (1946) never reads the *News of the World*, but says that in the future there will be communal heating laid on from a central supply and that every working-class house will be completely labour-saving. The reference to central supply captures an authoritarian dimension. A theme of fair shares for all is offered by the snooping pretend-electrician in *Mrs McGinty's Dead* (1952).

In practice, there was no hegemony, for Labour's ideas of an egalitarian national community. Criticism of government regulations was growing greatly by 1947, and a different sense developed of the fairness of evading controls by means of illicit and illegal practices, whether 'black' or 'grey' market.[1] An elliptical hit at ideas of social reform is offered by Christie in *They do it with Mirrors* (1952). The danger of visionaries who want to be God, forgetting that man is only the humble instrument of God's will, was spelt-out by Dr Galbraith, Bishop of Cromer, at the close of the novel. The educational philosophy of Stonygates is shown to be a total fraud and a killer. This philosophy, indeed, is the source of malignity in a novel in which traditional xenophobia, as with 'the unEnglish Mongolian type of face' and "the Italian in you that makes you turn to *poison*", is also revealed to be misplaced. Stonygates is not the same as the educational reforms being pressed by the Labour government, notably the comprehensive principle advocated in 1945–7 by Ellen Wilkinson, the very left-wing Minister of Education, but there was a shared drive for change in both.

In cultural and social terms, the late 1940s and 1950s also saw a revival of pre-war patterns, and as part of a society that very much sought such continuity after the trauma of war. The ruralism of much 1930s' culture was revived, as in continued interest in landscapes,[2] and the appearance in 1950 of Ralph Vaughan Williams' *Folk Songs for the Four Seasons*. The classics were celebrated, notably on film, as in David Lean's 1946 version of Dickens' novel *Great Expectations*. Audiences in London flocked to see plays by Noel Coward, both old (*Private Lives*, 1930) and new (*Look After Lulu*, 1959) alike, as well as plays by Terence Rattigan (*The Winslow Boy*, 1946) and William Douglas-Home (*The Chiltern Hundreds*, 1947; *The Manor of Northstead*, 1954).

1   M. Roodhouse, *Black Market Britain, 1939–1955* (Oxford, 2013).
2   *Landscape in Britain 1850–1950*, Hayward Gallery, London, 1983, exhibition.

In addition to continued ruralism and suburbanism, there was more of an engagement with the urban experience under the Labour governments, and especially with the welcome to modernity seen in the 1951 Festival of Britain which was centred on buildings, notably the Royal Festival Hall, constructed on a site on the war-bombed South Bank of the Thames in London. The Modernist architect Basil Spence made his name with the Sea and Ships Pavilion there, as well as with his prize-winning design for Coventry Cathedral which was built in 1956–62. Offering a Labour vision of progress, the Festival of Britain was very different to the 1924–5 British Empire Exhibition to which Christie had contributed. This represented a major change during her life. The 1951 Exhibition, which included exhibitions outside London, was visited by close to 8.5 million people. The Festival reflected confidence, or at least interest, in new solutions.[3] The rocket-like, cable-tensioned, Skylon presided over the London site. Boldness was designed to replace the drab dullness of the 1940s. Nevertheless, most people were less confident than at the time of the Great Exhibition in London in 1851.

Modernism was also seen in projects and buildings that were aspects of a planned environment, a key theme in the politics and public culture of the period.[4] More bluntly, W.H. Auden began his poem 'The Chimeras' with the line 'Absence of heart – as in public buildings'. There was also the particular culture of the Labour years (1945–51), satirised in *Crooked House* (1949) as '"that dreary play in verse about miners"'. In what might have been a satire on approaches to presenting Poirot, Ariadne Oliver, one of Christie's better characters, rejects a proposed staging of one of her novels that makes her protagonist Sven Hjerson young, a wartime Norwegian Resistance member, a meateater and keen on women; only to be told by Robin Upward that, for a play centring on adventure, you cannot have a hero who is a '"*Pansy*"', a pejorative term then used to describe male homosexuals. Christie mocked Social Realist fiction, in *A Murder is Announced* (1950), in the person of Edmund Swetenham who had begun to write a novel about a smelly unshaven man, a horrible old woman, and a vicious young

3   H. Atkinson, *The Festival of Britain: A Land and Its People* (London, 2012).
4   I.B. Whyte (ed.), *Man-Made Future: Planning, Education and Design in Mid-Twentieth-Century Britain* (London, 2007).

prostitute, interminably discussing the state of the world and the purpose of life. However, he abandons that for a roaring farce in the style of 'What the Butler Saw'.

In *Crooked House*, Clemency Leonides, a research scientist, represented the modern and is an unattractive figure. She eats functionally and is described as "'really likes being uncomfortable and having only one utility tea-cup to drink out of. Modern, I suppose. She's no sense of the past, no sense of beauty'". There is also no real attempt by Christie to give her depth.

The theme of modernity proved challenging, for example in the film *Seven Days to Noon* (1951) which deals with a scientist threatening to set off an atomic bomb in London as a warning about the dangers of nuclear destruction. Modernity was also vulnerable. In 1952, Churchill, a critic of the Festival of Britain as Socialist, had the Skylon taken down. He had become Prime Minister in October 1951, as the result of a significant Conservative revival after the disastrous showing in the 1945 election, a revival that had already nearly led to Conservative success, notably in South-East England, in a general election held in February 1950. Christie's nephew Jack stood then for Manchester-Gorton, but was defeated. Labour had won it in 1906, holding it until the Conservatives took it in 1931, only for the latter to lose it in 1935. In 1950, William Oldfield, the Labour candidate, was re-elected with 55 percent of the vote. The election was very different from the canvassing in Sanford Angelorum when Edmund Crispin has Gervase Fen stand as an Independent in *Buried for Pleasure* (1948). Crispin's humour was more to the fore in his novels than that of Christie in hers.

The Labour years were very harsh for the traditional middle class, especially those living on savings. Dividends were low and taxation high under the Labour governments of these years, the "'blood-suckers'" to the lively and perceptive Ariadne Oliver in *Mrs McGinty's Dead* (1952). Taxation was notably high on dividends. The black market is mentioned in *Crooked House* when the selfish Magda Leonides needs a new outfit for the inquest, telling her husband: "'I simply haven't got a coupon left – I've lost the address of that dreadful man who sells them to me – you know, the garage somewhere near Shaftesbury Avenue'". Her understanding husband, Philip, refers to income tax as "'somewhat heavy'" and death duties on his father's estate as "'very heavy'".

The world of service had been far more disrupted than by World War I. Indeed, in the fictional *North Benham News and Chipping Cleghorn Gazette*, the staple local newspaper in *A Murder is Announced*, there are 'frenzied appeals for Domestic Help'. Having observed 'I really don't know how people manage to feed big dogs nowadays', Mrs Swettenham, like Colonel Easterbrook, returned from Empire, comments of one issue: 'Selina Lawrence is advertising for a cook again.... Just a waste of time advertising.... Nowadays unless one has an old Nannie in the family, who will go into the kitchen and do everything, one is simply *sunk*'. Laura and Robin Upward in *Mrs McGinty's Dead* have 'no proper servants. Only old Janet. And we have to spare her all the time', although the wealthy Carpenters have 'an imperturbable manservant'. The servant issue is also mentioned in *A Pocket Full of Rye*. Edith de Haviland, in *Crooked House*, remarks: '"Don't know what we'd all do without nannies. Nearly everybody's got an old nannie. They come back and wash and iron and cook and do housework. Faithful"'. That is a reflection of Magda's ability to anger servants. In *Mrs McGinty's Dead*, Ariadne Oliver jokes that a charwoman would be the obvious murder victim, which in part reflected the difficulty of dealing with their obduracy. The very serious shortage of any kind of skilled domestic labour readily gets Lucy Eyelesbarrow work in *4.50 from Paddington* (1957). In contrast, in *Crooked House*, the wealthy Aristide '"had a cook, housemaid, parlour maid, and valet-attendant. He liked servants. He paid them the earth, of course, and he got them"'.

In *After the Funeral* (1953), the ever complaining Maude says of Stansfield Grange:

> 'We had to let this go to seed during the war. Both gardeners called up. And now we've only got one old man – and he's not much good. Wages have gone up so terribly.... No servants. Just a couple of women who come in. We had a resident maid until a month ago – slightly hunchbacked and terribly adenoidal and in many ways not too bright, but she was *there* which was such a comfort – and quite good at plain cooking'.

There is also reference back in *A Murder is Announced* to the pre-war world:

'I suppose there was once heaps of coke and coal for everybody?' said Julia with the interest of one hearing about an unknown country.

'Yes, and cheap, too'.

'And anyone could go and buy as much as they wanted, without filling in anything, and there wasn't any shortage? There was lots of it there?'

'All kinds and qualities – and *not* all stones and slate like what we get nowadays'.

'It must have been a wonderful world', said Julia, with awe in her voice.

Christie's radio play, 'Three Blind Mice', broadcast in 1947, was adapted into a 1948 short story, a 1950 CBS television film, and the play *The Mousetrap* (1952). Set in 'the present', in Monkswell Manor, which has recently been converted into a guesthouse, it presents broken-down folk, drifting here and there, with class boundaries broken down and nothing quite what it was before. Everyone tries to make do and mend, as Christie accurately evokes the world of rationing, dowdiness, carrying on, and bankruptcy, that characterised so much of post-war English life. Indeed, she reached the height of her powers in depicting social change in the post-war era. The crises, despair and expedients, including murder, of many on small private incomes between the 1930s and the 1950s, due to taxation, inflation, and lower dividends, was captured very well by Christie, as in *A Murder is Announced* (1950), *Mrs McGinty's Dead* (1952), and *Hickory Dickory Dock* (1955). A play about murder is discussed in *Crooked House* where not only Magda, an actress, but also some of the scenes, notably those involving her, are presented as theatrical. Based on a 1925 short story, 'Traitor's Hands', that in 1933 was published as 'Witness for the Prosecution' in *The Hound of Death*, Christie's play *Witness for the Prosecution* (1953) was a brilliant and successful courtroom roller-coaster that became a 1957 film with Marlene Dietrich, Charles Laughton and Tyrone Power, directed by Billy Wilder.

While the Angkatells, former representatives of the British Raj in India, live in some splendour at The Hollow in the 1946 novel of that name, Monkswell Manor is similar to the Guest House in Broadhinny in *Mrs*

McGinty's Dead (1952): 'a rather decrepit country house where the young people who own it take in paying guests'. The husband in that novel had been a Major in India, Major being the general rank for also-rans, as opposed to those who succeed as Colonels. In an image of much of England, Poirot finds faded armchairs, chair-covers, and wallpaper, a sofa with broken springs, a carpet with holes, tables without castors, and a hotel without even 'a *daily*' as no domestics were available. The cooking is atrocious, for example under-stewed oxtail, rather different from the ducks and caramel custard at The Hollow. The decrepit character of Monkswell Manor is due not only to recent circumstances but also to the owner's parents who had lived there having had no money. Other detective writers also noted the crisis of country-house living, for example the underrated Francis Duncan in *Murder for Christmas* (1949) and Henry Wade in *Too Soon to Die* (1953).

Plain food itself did not have to be bad. In *The Hollow*, Inspector Grange is able to look forward to his oldest pipe, a pint of ale, and a good steak and chips, which he feels both plain and objective. Later in the novel, Lady Angkatell feels that her proposed lunch of partridges au Choux and Soufflé Surprise, would not work for Grange, for whom she would propose a really good steak followed by an old-fashioned apple tart or apple dumplings.

Christie's *Mrs McGinty's Dead* sees references to the housing shortage, Mrs Kiddle explaining to Poirot that she, her plasterer husband Bert, and three young children had moved into a house where Mrs McGinty had been murdered because they had been living with Bert's mother where they had had only 'a back sitting-room and sleeping on two chairs'. No wonder Bessie Burch and her husband Joe were very proud of their 'small modern council house of their own' and had not wanted, instead, to take over the rent of Mrs McGinty's cottage. Housebuilding had been identified by the Conservatives as a way to challenge Labour. They had pledged in 1950 an increase from the Labour target of 200,000 new houses a year, to one of 300,000. Harold Macmillan, Minister of Housing and Local Government in 1951–4, oversaw the programme and reached this target at the end of 1953, a year ahead of schedule. He made his reputation as a result.

A sharper look back on change is offered in *A Pocket Full of Rye* when Inspector Neele considered his upbringing at the gates of Hartington Park, a vast mansion given to the National Trust. He mentions the damp and insanitary nature of the lodge, and the absence of running water, as well as electricity, but also notes: 'They were a healthy family and a happy one, all thoroughly behind the times'. Conversely, the name Yewbree Lodge is criticised by Neele as not matching his idea of the country, with both the architecture and gardens being 'highly artificial'.

Murder meanwhile appeared to some commentators to have become cruder. That was the complaint of the distinguished novelist George Orwell, no less, although his short essay, *The Decline of the English Murder*, is best for its title and drew on the scrappiest of data. Orwell's theme was expressed by Poirot in *Mrs McGinty's Dead*, in which he reflects:

> He recalled vaguely a small paragraph in the papers. It had not been an interesting murder. Some wretched old woman knocked on the head for a few pounds. All part of the senseless crude brutality of these days.

Indeed, the self-interested journalist Pamela Horsefall of the sensationalist *Sunday Comet* complains 'no sex appeal about it'. In *Hallowe'en Party* (1969), the complacent and snobbish Rowena Drake refers to the (fictional) two murders in Woodleigh Common, neither of them recent:

> 'I think there was a lorry driver who killed a pal of his – something like that – and a little girl whom they found buried in a gravel pit.... They were both rather sordid and uninteresting crimes. Mainly the result of drink, I think'.

Christie, however, adopts a different approach, not least presenting many of those in the working class sympathetically, for example Ted Bigland in *Sad Cypress* (1933). Her approach, indeed, is that of a shared morality, with flaws across society, as when Miss Peabody in *Dumb Witness* (1937) remarks 'Queer kinks people get', an observation linking the affluent Bella Tanios and a plain kitchen-maid.

Christie continued to write in her range of genres, but she reset her thrillers. *They Came to Baghdad* (1951) was very different in content and tone to the pre-war stories Christie had set in the Middle East. Then, with her focus on archaeology, the Middle East had offered an opportunity for a more scenic and differently specific form of murder story. An archaeological dig provided another version of a country-house murder.

Now, instead, in a much underrated novel, one of her better thrillers, the Middle East became a place for her earlier genre of thriller detection stories, one with the Cold War providing a location in a distinctive here-and-now that drew on her sense of Baghdad, and one that easily held up with others of the late 1940s and early 1950s. Otto Morganthal's "'All the world is mad'" provides a very different context to that of evil intentions over inheritance. Moreover, there was the unwelcome overhang of the war, with Edward Goring, who had won a DFC as a wartime fighter pilot, being unable to find his 'appointed place in the world of 1950'. Meanwhile, Anna Scheele has no problems in being welcomed in the Savoy because she 'represented DOLLARS', which is an indication of the repeated sterling crises and exchange problems of the late 1940s, notably that of April 1949. Anna is told by Mr Bolford of Savile Row that the country is in a mess with no-one taking pride in their work and a loss of quality. Henry Carmichael, who has that quality, is a son of the 'Great Game' against Russia, whose father had been a British official in Kashgar, a centre for that rivalry, and who in turn had become a British agent able to pass himself off as a Arab. Indeed, as Carmichael approached Baghdad, his love of the East led him to long intensely for the calmness of its fatalism. That is an element that fascinated Christie.

Meanwhile, Britain still has an Imperial system, one about which the British had become more familiar due to the war. Ernest Bevin, the Labour Foreign Secretary from July 1945 until March 1951, hoped to use Imperial resources to make Britain a less unequal partner in the Anglo-American alliance, and did not see the withdrawals of 1947–8 from India, Pakistan, Ceylon (Sri Lanka), Burma (Myanmar), and Palestine (Israel), as the end of Empire. Indeed, there was a particular determination to remain a key power in the Middle East, one that looked toward the Suez Crisis, an unsuccessful military intervention in Egypt in 1956.

In *They Came to Baghdad*, which was dedicated 'to all my friends in Baghdad', there is much British influence in Iraq, including the Iraqi Iranian Oil Co. (which was modelled on the Iraq Petroleum Company), a Consul-General at Basra, hotels that specialise in British visitors, and British archaeologists. Christie knew Iraq as her husband Max Mallowan was Director of

the British School of Archaeology in Iraq from 1947 to 1961.[5] More generally, Iraq was part not only of the sterling area, but also of Britain's system
of continuing influence, and a key element in anti-Soviet Cold War geopol-
itics, notably with the 1955 Baghdad Pact, until the coup of 1958 led to the
killing of Faisal II. En route to Iraq by air, in Libya at the airport in Tripoli,
Sir Rupert Crofton Lee, a distinguished British visitor, is 'met by an officer
in uniform with red tabs, and hurried off in a staff car to some dwelling of
the mighty in Tripolitania'. Britain indeed had such a presence. Carmichael
appears an exotic part of this imperial system, but, after its conquest from
the German-backed Italians, the British Military Administration of Libya
was in control of the key sections of the country from 1943 until 1950, followed by the British Civil Administration in 1950–1.

In *They Came to Baghdad*, Richard Baker is another Christie character
who takes forward World War II, its memories providing him with the
'smell of *fear*' when in Baghdad:

> One occasion in particular when he, and two others, had been
> parachuted from a plane, and had waited in the small cold hours
> of dawn for the moment to do their stuff. A moment when
> morale was low, when the full hazards of the undertaking were
> clearly perceived, a moment of dread lest one might not be ad-
> equate, a shrinking of the flesh. The same acrid, almost imper-
> ceptible tang in the air.

The casting enables Christie to have full play with ideas. Thus, the perceptive Mrs Cardew Trench in Baghdad is very dubious about the idea of
world brotherhood: "'All nonsense if you ask me. The more you try to get
people together, the more suspicious they get of each other'". She is also
very clear in her prejudices: "'young women in slacks with unwashed necks
and spectacles'".

Just short of halfway through the book, after the murder of a British
agent in Baghdad, the young Victoria Jones, the well-realised central character, is given an explanation by Dakin from the embassy, yet another wise
figure with which Christie peoples the British world:

5   M. Mallowan, *Twenty-five Years of Mesopotamian Discovery* (1956).

'The only hope for the future lies in peace, in production, in constructive activities and not destructive ones. Therefore, everything depends on those who hold those two divergent viewpoints, either agreeing to differ and each contenting themselves with their respective spheres of activity, or else finding a mutual basis for agreement, or at least toleration.... The opposite is happening ... a third party or group working under cover ... enormous sums of money.... In every country there are agents of this group, some established there many years ago ... the delusion that by force you can impose the Millennium ... the belief in a superstratum of human beings – in supermen to rule the rest of the decadent world ... nobody knows what goes on in the interior of China ... the whole system is penetrated and infiltrated with their agents'.

In the end, a villain explains, in terms that can be seen later in *Passenger to Frankfurt* (1970), although, by then, no imperial setting is viable any more:

'The old bad things must destroy each other. The fat old men grasping at their profits, impeding progress. The bigoted stupid Communists, trying to establish their Marxian heaven. There must be total war – total destruction. And then – the new Heaven and the new Earth. The small chosen band of higher beings, the scientists, the agricultural experts, the administrators ... the young Siegfrieds of the New World. All young, all believing in their destiny as supermen.... When destruction had run its course, *they* would step in and take over'.

The Siegfrieds was a Wagner reference. Considering all the people who would be killed first, Goring presses on to say that it did not matter. Victoria Jones offers the counterpoint of normality and value:

'Those *were* the things that mattered – the little everyday things, the family to be cooked for, the four walls that enclosed the home, the one of two cherished possessions. All the thousands of ordinary people on the earth, minding their own business, and tilling that earth, and making pots and bringing up families and laughing and crying, and getting up in the morning and going to bed at night.... *They* were the people who mattered, not these Angels with wicked faces who wanted to make a new world and who didn't care whom they hurt to do it'.

The religious message was driven home by referring to the principal villain as Lucifer (a frequent Christie comparison), and later as Judas, and by seeing 'a religious flavour' in the evil project, that of a self-created God. Martyrdom is another aspect of this dimension.

The rushed, fantastical denouement, in classic thriller style, reveals 'vast installations and underground laboratories functioning in a remote valley beyond the bounds of civilisation'. There is reference to 'Antichrist', while, on the positive side, Carmichael's microfilms are preserved and presented by Sheikh Hussein el Ziyara of Kerbela, a Muslim Holy Man.

They Came to Baghdad can be better understood in the light of the success of *Dick Barton – Special Agent*, of which 711 episodes were broadcast on BBC Radio between 1946 and 1951, with a peak audience of 15 million. The fictional Barton was an ex-Commando and had a VC. There were also three Dick Barton films in 1948–50.[6] Separately, the theme of the traitor within, which was used by Christie in *They Came to Baghdad* and in other works, was from the outset a significant staple of the thriller genre, but this theme was greatly encouraged in 1951 by the defections of Guy Burgess and Donald Maclean. Moreover, the Americans firmly and correctly believed that Kim Philby, the Secret Service's liaison officer in Washington, was a traitor and in 1952 the Director of the CIA insisted that he not return to Washington.

Meanwhile, the public was assumed to be becoming more educated about crime as a result of reading detective novels. That leads Sir Henry Angkatell in *The Hollow* to suggest that many would know what guns could be identified from the marks on the rifling. In that novel, Christie has one

6   J. Chapman, '"Honest British Violence": Critical Responses to Dick Barton – Special Agent (1946–1951)', *Historical Journal of Film, Radio and Television*, 26 (2006), pp. 537–59.

of the characters, the bright and dynamic doctor John Christow, reading *The Clue of the Dripping Fountain*, a made-up title.

In *Mrs McGinty's Dead*, Ariadne Oliver, who is to a degree a gentle caricature of Christie, finds at the Post Office Penguin versions of three of her highly popular detective novels: *The Affair of the Second Goldfish*, *The Cat It Was Who Died*, for which she was criticised for an overly short blowpipe, and *Death of a Débutante*, which she reflects is wildly impossible, has at least six murders, and has sulphonal wrongly soluble in water. This is Christie being facetious, and the blowpipe is presumably a reference to *Death in the Clouds*. Deirdre Henderson enjoys Ariadne's books, though telling her that Deidre's sensitive mother does not as they keep her awake at night. The significance of distribution systems is revealed by the Hendersons getting their books via the Times Book Club. Another middle-aged woman who does not like detective stories is Mrs Allerton in *Death on the Nile*.

Crooked House itself, although, in an arresting reveal, it has a troubling murderer, includes an unusually positive account of possible murders, one somewhat different to the standard emphasis on sin in the Marple and Poirot novels. Speaking of murderers, the thoughtful Assistant-Commissioner Sir Arthur Hayward tells his son Charles that:

> 'Some of them ... have been thoroughly nice chaps ... nice ordinary fellows like you and me.... Murder, you see, is an amateur crime... I'm speaking of course of the kind of murder you have in mind – not gangster stuff. One feels very often, as though these nice ordinary chaps have been overtaken, as it were, by murder almost accidentally. They've been in a tight place ... The brake that operates with us doesn't operate with them.... morally immature ... I don't think, in my experience, that any murderer has really felt remorse ... they are 'different' ... for them it is necessary ... it was "the only way"'.

Meanwhile, Christie was selling extremely well. The Labour years, indeed, proved very good for her. In 1948, a million copies of her works were issued simultaneously by Penguin and made publishing history. 100,000 copies each of ten titles were issued, and all of these titles were rapidly and frequently reprinted. This procedure was followed in Penguin for Ngaio Marsh, Margery Allingham, Carter Dickson, and Simenon. The Penguins mentioned in *Mrs McGinty's Dead* were a reference to this process.

Like Fleming in James Bond novels which appeared from 1953, Christie appealed across the political spectrum. However, if her work is regarded as particularly conducive to a Conservative mindset, it is worth remembering that, although the 1945 electoral result was the most miserable one for the Conservatives since 1906, they still took 39.8 percent of the vote (Labour 47.8 percent; Liberals 9.1 percent).

The war and the Labour governments might appear to have been the major reasons for change, but Christie presents a more profound cause and sense in *A Murder is Announced* (1950), one that matches the disruption that is important to so many Sherlock Holmes stories. She claims that fifteen years earlier, everyone in rural England knew who everybody was, with people living where past family members had done, and new people bringing letters of introduction or having links, such that anyone really new stood out and was the subject of discussion, as with the society discussed by Jane Austen. In contrast, now, in an example of Christie's perceptive and ably-expressed grasp of changes in society, Marple states that every village and small market town is full of people who come without any ties, come from all over the world, including the Empire. The big houses are sold. No-one is known, and people are taken at their own valuation. As a result, the subtle links of English social rural life had collapsed, not least as urban norms become more common. The war has also helped people to copy identities as they reinvent themselves to often sinister ends.

In this, and other respects, there was a strong sense of flux. Detective novels provided both a genre focused on the resulting instability and also a degree of protection from it, in the form of a resolution as order was restored. By playing fair in their clues with the readers, the authors enabled the latter to be part of the search for a solution, and thus gave them agency as well as entertainment and safety.

8. THE NEW ELIZABETHAN AGE, 1952–63

In Patricia Wentworth's detective novel *The Listening Eye* (1957), Ethel Burkett writes about her sister to her aunt Maud Silver, a Marple-like figure

> who had taken the unjustifiable step of leaving an excellent husband whom she complained of finding dull. 'As if anyone in their senses expects their husband to be exciting!' wrote Mrs Burkett. 'And she doesn't say where she is, or what she is doing, so all we can hope and trust is that she is alone, and that she hasn't done anything which Andrew would find impossible to forgive. Because what is she going to live on!'

In such norms and more generally, it was continuity that was apparent, mostly from the pre-war era, but in part also from the war years. Many of the wartime changes continued by the post-war Labour governments, notably identity cards and rationing, were axed by the Conservative government elected in 1951 in a deliberate return to the pre-war era. Much of life showed considerable continuity. Clothes were more similar to those of the 1930s than those of the 1970s and reflected hierarchies of class, gender and age. Collectivism also still had a strongly moral dimension.

Public morals and popular culture had for long been policed, but this policing had been accentuated in the mid-twentieth century, because, alongside the immediate requirements of wartime controls, fears of subversion and the disruptive consequences of individualism influenced attitudes to practices that were not in the accepted social mainstream. In addition, the emphasis on the collective effort and provision led to a hostile attitude towards those who did not accept norms: not filling in forms or not having a fixed address was a defiance of bureaucracy. There was also a longstanding moral policing that criminalised habits judged unacceptable, such as drug-taking. Abortion, homosexuality, prostitution, and suicide were criminal

137

offences, and consenting adults had therefore no privacy. Restrictive divorce laws affected marriage, childcare, and sexuality. Censorship affected what could be read, seen, and listened to. Literary merit was no defence against charges of pornography.

The leisure activities of the many were regulated, whether drinking, gambling, or watching television. There were permitted hours for drinking in pubs and, in the case of gambling, no off-course cash betting. Such restrictions made criminals out of the large numbers who broke them. Corporal punishment (beating with the cane, slipper, or, in Scotland, tawse) remained common in schools. Young men were brought under the sway of the state through conscription. Continued after World War II, this was not phased out until 1957–63. The first of the popular 'Carry On' comedy films, *Carry On Sergeant* (1958),[1] focused on this universal obligation. Although capital punishment – hanging – was limited to murder, the ability of the legal system to deliver such a verdict, the consequence, indeed, of most murder stories, contributed to the sense of a powerful state, with moral codes that it was determined to enforce.

Change was slow to come. In July 1956, the House of Lords rejected the abolition of capital punishment. Sexual policing continued, with homosexual acts illegal. In 1960, the House of Commons rejected the recommendations of the Wolfenden Commission for the liberalisation of the laws on homosexuality. Moreover, entertainment went on being regulated. In a process that included making cuts and changes, as well as self-censorship, the Lord Chamberlain, through the Examiner of Plays, had to give a licence before any public performances on the stage, while cinema censorship and film classification to determine audience composition had started in 1912. When permitted, erotic entertainment had to fit into the hierarchies of control and regulation.[2]

Social norms continued to play out largely through life as experienced in families and localities. The press of Christie's favoured Devon recorded familiar items. Thus, the *Western Times* on 4 January 1952 published a photo of a family reunion dinner, another of four generations at a party, a

1   *Carry on Admiral* (1957) is not part of the series.
2   F. Mort, 'Striptease: the erotic female body and live sexual entertainment in mid-twentieth-century London', *Social History*, 32 (2007), pp. 27–53.

call from a Justice of the Peace for heavier fines on motorists, criticism of the drowning of a valley in order to construct a reservoir, and an attack on the secrecy of local authorities towards the press.

Continuity with the pre-war world continued to be clearly seen in the theatre, with the production of new or revived plays by established play-wrights such as Terence Rattigan and Noel Coward, as well as Christie's *Mousetrap*, a play very much located in a world of conventional social dis-tinctions, which unexpectedly became the world's longest-running play, only closing in 2020 as a result of the Covid-19 Pandemic. In Christie's novel *After the Funeral* (1953), there is discussion of a revival of *The Baronet's Progress*, an imagined play with a very traditional title. Nicholas Blake, the pseudonym of the Poet Laureate, Cecil Day-Lewis, in his detective novel, *The Worm of Death* (1961), satirised conventional approaches, as of a West End play in which a young man sets out to supplant an elderly husband in his wife's affections:

A hand comes out from a secret panel while the husband's back is turned, shakes a powder into the young man's glass. He dies, down-stage right. The husband is suspected. But the poisoner turns out to be their faithful old housekeeper, whose daughter has been seduced by the young man.

Yet, Blake himself employed, both in this novel and elsewhere, the very hackneyed bad-blood/chip-on-shoulder theme beloved by Christie. This theme was crucial to her debate about the roles of genetics, upbringing, predestination and free will, on which see the opening chapter.

Although hit by the greater role of television, which increased with the launching of commercial television in 1955 and the purchase of many sets, the cinema continued to be important. It offered established themes, in-cluding film versions of certain Christie novels and plays. The successful Christie films for this period were *Witness for the Prosecution* (1957); *Murder, She Said* (1961), which was a version of *4.50 from Paddington*; and *Murder at the Gallop* (1963), the last a version of *After the Funeral*, although with Marple replacing Poirot. Altering the text is scarcely a modern feature, al-though changing the tone is more so. In addition, as with other detective writers, Christie's novels made reference to the world of the cinema, as in

Ordeal by Innocence (1958), where there is a reference to cinema usherettes walking round selling lemonade and ice-cream, while Philip and his mother, though poor, had sometimes gone to the cinema in London: 'the pictures'.

Cultural continuity was more generally the theme. In contrast to established approaches, the works of *avant-garde* playwrights, such as Samuel Beckett, scarcely appeared on the stage. There was also much continuity in music, alongside an engagement by some with difficult works such as the operas of Benjamin Britten and the music of Michael Tippett and Harrison Birtwhistle. Looking at the music alongside the piano for the performance at Stonygates in *They Do It with Mirrors* (1952), Inspector Curry finds works by Hindemith and Shostakovich. He has never heard of them and is surprised by the foreign names. In contrast, inside the old-fashioned music stool is the '"old-fashioned stuff"' including Handel's Largo, Czerny's Exercises, Chopin's preludes, and the 1930 song 'I know a lovely Garden' by Guy d'Hardelot and Edward Teskemacher, a song the vicar's wife used to sing when Curry was young. That is very much an image of tradition, as is the Christmas chapel performance of Handel's *Messiah* in George Bellairs' *The Dead Shall Be Raised* (1942).

In books, there was also much continuity with inter-war authorship, notably with Christie in detective fiction and P.G. Wodehouse in light satire. He continued to publish as if there had been only limited change in British society, and certainly so for a readership that wanted to think accordingly. Although there was more social realism from some detective writers, Christie in part echoed the experiences and values of an earlier age, while also arguing, correctly, that they continued to have validity. Thus, in *A Pocket Full of Rye* (1953), repeating Luke Fitzwilliam's return to England in *Murder Is* Easy (1939), Pat tells Jane Marple:

> 'With the fire and the lamps and you knitting things for babies.
> It all seems cosy and homely and like England ought to be'.
> 'It's like England is', said Miss Marple.

Also in 1953, in *After the Funeral*, there was reassurance about the police and after that an admonition not to belittle them: '"They are a very shrewd and patient body of men – persistent too"'. Yet, the selfish and desperately unimpressive Timothy Abernethie launches a rant: '"This country's full of gangsters nowadays.... Nobody's got the guts to put these things down – to take a strong hand. What's the country coming to...?"' Entwhistle, the elderly lawyer, reflects: 'It was a question almost invariably asked sooner or later by his clients for the last twenty years', in other words including the pre-war National Government. Timothy, using an argument about the Conservative Party, that Fleming was to have James Bond employ in 1953, goes on to attack the Conservatives elected in 1951:

> 'It all began with that damned Labour Government. Sending
> the whole country to blazes. And the Government we've got now
> is no better. Mealy-mouthed, milk-and-water socialists! Look at
> the state *we're* in! Can't get a decent gardener, can't get servants'.

This remark was a critique of what was known, from 1954, as Butskellism, with reference to successive Labour and Conservative Chancellors of the Exchequer, Hugh Gaitskell (Chancellor, 1950–1, Shadow Chancellor 1951–5) and Rab Butler (Chancellor, 1951–5). However, the remark is undercut by a full depiction of the consistently unsympathetic Timothy's selfishness. This again becomes the context for his claim that there is '"No loyalty any more in the lower classes"', as well as his remark that '"the Chief Constables aren't the right type"'. By this he meant not former military officers with whom he felt it comfortable to communicate. A more sympathetic character, Mr Goby, has a less selfish response. He complains that it is no longer easy to recruit for his intelligence system:

> 'They don't come that way nowadays. Not willing to learn, that's
> what it is. Think they know everything after they've only been
> a couple of years on the job. And they work to time. Shocking
> the way they work to time.... It's the Government. And all this
> education racket. It gives them ideas. They come back and tell
> us what they think. They *can't* think, most of them, anyway. All
> they know is things out of books.... Government snooping is
> god's gift to investigators'.

Poirot later reflects: '"There is no proper education nowadays. Apparently one learns nothing but economics – and how to sit Intelligence Tests!"'

Indeed, IQ tests and the 11-plus examination on which they were based had become important with the 1944 Education Act, and IQ testing became significant in the 1950s.

Political comments varied. In *Mrs McGinty's Dead*, Robin Upward remarks that he is a Liberal because he adores lost causes and that the Party is small and select. The 1950s were a time when the two-party system swept all before it, with each of Labour and the Conservatives receiving more than 40 percent of the vote. The Liberals obtained 9.1 percent of the vote in 1950, but only 2.6 percent in 1951, their fall helping the Conservatives to win an overall majority of seats in that election. Nevertheless, the Liberals rejected Conservative advances and remained a separate party.

Christie was far from alone in her moral politics, even if some of her stablemates were somewhat different. *Casino Royale*, the first of Fleming's Bond novels, was published in 1953. It depicted a hero who was a comfortably-off gentleman, unworried about his income, and at home in Continental casinos and eating *pâté de foie gras*. Like most heroes in British fiction and films of the period, he had had a 'good war', as indeed had Fleming. The war, indeed, helped define that generation of British males, as World War I had defined their predecessors. Moreover, Bond, like Christie's protagonists, is given purpose by the morality of the wider struggle in which he figures, one that calls on all whatever their profession or status. Like Christie, Fleming offered a Manichean world. Evil was afoot, and while the sense of sulphur was not as close as in Dennis Wheatley's black magic novels, notably *The Devil Rides Out* (1934) and *They Used Dark Forces* (1964), it was more atmospheric than in the subsequent novels. Wheatley (1897–1977), a veteran of the Western Front who played a role in planning in World War II, was a conservative who opposed what he saw as the oppressive Socialism of the post-war Labour governments.[3]

The hubris and callousness of evil was present with both Christie and Fleming, but there were major differences, not only in context but also in novelistic structure. In her detective novels, Christie delayed the denouement to the close, springing the surprise then as the conclusion to the story and the culmination of its staging. Indeed, her novels to a degree offered

3   P. Baker, *The Devil is a Gentleman: The Life and Times of Dennis Wheatley* (Sawtry, 2009).

stage-sets as if they were plays. Fleming, in contrast, relied on providing in his narrative a capture of Bond which offered the opportunity for the apparently victorious villain to reveal and gloat over his dastardly schemes. This was a common device with thrillers, as earlier with the Fu-Manchu stories and the Buchan and Christie versions. The escape of the hero then leads to a conclusion of action in every sense.

Despite contrasts between detective novels and thrillers, there was a common theme: The weaknesses inherent in evil, notably deceit, self-deceit, arrogance, over-confidence, cruelty, and instrumentalism, help ensure its flaws. In part these weaknesses do so by providing opportunities for the bravery and integrity of the thriller hero and for the moral bravery and intelligence of the detecting hero. There was an overlap with the many occasions in which Christie had her protagonists, in both thrillers and detective novels, exposed to the risk of death at the hands of villains, notably, but not only, by poison.

Referring back to Elizabeth I of England (r. 1558–1603), a 'New Elizabethan Age' was confidently forecast at the time of the accession of Elizabeth II in 1952 and her coronation in 1953. The latter was a highly traditional occasion, albeit with the addition of deferential television coverage, broadcast live and watched by just over twenty million people, 56 percent of the population. The approach infuriated Evelyn Waugh, a militant Catholic, and thus opponent of Elizabeth I,[4] but was widely popular.

Christianity and the pinnacles of the class system were much in evidence in the ceremony. Moreover, the Christianity of the period was mostly establishment in tone, as well as being a matter of old, white men telling others what to do. A standard heading or subheading in the popular press, notably in the *News of the World*, still then a Sunday shocker, and a paper that only ceased publication in 2011, was 'Bishop Speaks Out', usually in response to reported moral outrages that challenged the established moral code.

Christie's novels scarcely appeared anachronistic in this context. In the psychologically-tense *Ordeal by Innocence* (1958), Arthur Calgary, near the close, refers to a phrase in the latest translation of the *Book of Job* from the Bible, while the book ends with the traditional good news of a proposal

---

4   M. Amory (ed.), *The Letters of Evelyn Waugh* (1980; London, 1982 edn), p. 369.

and acceptance. There is a discussion of whether Jacko Argyle, a key figure, was an invalid because of environment or, in what readers are told is the old Calvinistic doctrine, because he was a wicked vessel doomed to destruction and born to go wrong. Agreement is reached on the latter.

There was also with Christie a continuation of Cold War themes and spy stories, as in *Destination Unknown* (1954) in which crucial British and French scientists disappear. In this novel, Christie repeatedly warns about the dream of an ideal world, a warning that has moral as well as political force. Most of the action is set in Morocco. The exotic comes in an old Fez, the Leper Colony, and the garden that is like an Arabian Nights fairy tale. As with the 1930s' novels set in Egypt, Iraq, and Jordan, the foreigners, despite in this case the role of French officialdom, are able to act with singularly little control.

The conspiracy is revealed by the 'Herr Director': to create a scientific power, the Unit, that will dominate world affairs and provide a *Pax Scientifica*. This is a false religion headed by a megalomaniac God-like figure, but with the 'Master', Aristide, a cosmopolitan Greek plutocrat, the real motive power of the world economy, directing the action and using brain surgery and experimenting with humans to that end. Hilary Craven tries without success to convince him to be good by reference to the Bible. The novel was written in the aftermath of the Klaus Fuchs/Bruno Pontecorvo affair of 1950 concerning the leakage of atomic secrets to the Soviet Union, and reflected persistent Cold War concerns about missing scientists. In Britain, the novel was first serialised in the magazine *John Bull*. Alongside *Death Comes as the End*, *They Came to Baghdad*, *Passenger to Frankfurt*, and *Postern of Fate*, this weak novel has not been adapted. Aside from the brilliant first, which is set in ancient Egypt and would be very difficult to adapt for that reason, the others are all thrillers. They would all be costly to adapt.

A different source of danger, but again with the theme of a villainous plutocrat appeared in Fleming's *Moonraker* (1955), in which the villain, Sir Hugo Drax, was a Nazi working for the Soviets who had been able to disguise his origins and become a tycoon, cornering the market in colombite, a metal crucial for the manufacture of jet engines. Drax was very different from Aristide, but also showed the vulnerability of society to tycoons. A vulgarian, Drax was nevertheless a public hero thanks to his financing of a British nuclear rocket. Goldfinger is also a villain who is an insider.

At a more mundane level than the atomic warhead attack on London planned by Drax, *After the Funeral* (1953) repeatedly provided Christie with an opportunity to consider the change that had already occurred. The large, but dated, stately home, Enderby Hall, was based on the money made from corn-plasters. Its aged butler, Lanscombe, deliberately provides an opening setting from the past. For Lanscombe, rejecting the 'gimcrack' of the new, it was the last twenty years or so that were blurred and confused, whereas he could remember more clearly the period before; in other words the 1920s. There is an elderly housemaid; and also a young cook who does not respect Lanscombe or the house, but likes the money. In an earlier age, the staff had included a kitchen-maid and a second gardener. Entwhistle, the lawyer, thinks 'No such thing as old-fashioned service nowadays. Household helps and baby sitters, God help us all!' He also reflects on 'these days of taxation' and how it had been necessary to retrench the 'scale of living' accordingly. 72 years old, Entwhistle is presented as having the views of the past, as when thinking about Rosamund's husband: 'Really, a chemist's assistant! In Mr Entwhistle's creed, girls did not marry young men who served behind a counter. But now of course, they married *anybody!*' Helen Abernethie also reflects on taxation, and on how the house might be pulled down and the entire estate built over.

Women are very important to the plot of *After the Funeral*, but far more central in *4.50 from Paddington* (1957) where the case is entirely solved by impressive women, notably the young and skilful Lucy Eylesbarrow, and the men, in contrast, are somewhat weak. More generally, there is an adventurousness in the depiction of Marple as a female, if not feminist, heroine, disadvantaged by gender, age, and an absence of wealth and social status, and having to put up with repeated male condescension. She was repeatedly far more perceptive than the male policemen.[5] Marple was an important character in Christie's later detective novels. Leaving aside the short stories, there was one Marple novel in the 1930s, two in the 1940s, four in the 1950s, three in the 1960s and two in the 1970s, which meant that from 1950 the Marple novels were close in number to the Poirot ones of the period.

A very different tone was offered by Margot Bennett in *The Man Who*

5   M. Shaw and S. Vanacker, *Reflecting on Miss Marple* (1991).

Didn't Fly (1955). Bennett (1912–80), a left-winger who had been injured while a nurse on the Republican side in the Spanish Civil War (1936–9), was a successful thriller writer who turned to television scriptwriting and to science fiction. In *The Man Who Didn't Fly*, the lost wreckage of a light aircraft that crashes into the Irish Sea en route to Dublin includes the pilot and three men who boarded the aircraft, but four were due to be on the flight. The identity of the last and the reason for his disappearance is the basis for a plot much of which is set in an impoverished, downwardly-mobile, middle-class household. Unsure about the source of their meals and cloths, and with their finances a matter of shifts and expedients, the characters are prey to delusions, illusions, and schemings for a fast buck:

> 'I wanted to be an old-fashioned remittance man, but she wouldn't send me the remittance…. I like cigarette cases and watches – they give a man something to pawn in time of need…. She saw herself less brutally than the observer, not for a moment imagining that the pool was already drying up and that the thirsty traveller would pass it without a glance. She knew that soon she might have to rise from the pool and clutch the traveller and hold him while his eyes turned away'.

The writing is very different from that of Christie, who would not have offered 'He sat on a low stool, his great, yellow, rectangular face hanging over the bar like a disfigured moon'.

The Conservatives did very well in the general elections held in 1955 and 1959, winning more than 49 percent of the vote in each case. One of those first elected in 1959 was Christie's only nephew, James 'Jack' Watts (1903–61), whom she praised in her autobiography, and to whom she had dedicated *The Secret of Chimneys* (1925). He served in World War II. Watts had been very active in Manchester Conservative politics from the early 1930s and was in favour of limiting immigration and building housing for the workers. He was elected, with 62.3 percent of the vote, in 1959 for Manchester Moss Side, a seat the Conservatives had won off Labour in 1950, and a safe one that was only lost in February 1974, and then after significant boundary changes. Watts died aged 57 in 1961 and his Belgravia house was bequeathed to his aunt. Christie herself was doing well. Agatha

Christie Ltd was founded in 1955, while in 1956 she became a Commander of the Order of the British Empire.

At the same time as signs of continuity, change in British politics, society, and culture, gathered pace in the late 1950s, notably with the 'bolt from Empire', the attempt to join the European Economic Community, the forerunner of the European Union, and, very differently, the 'Angry Young Men' and 'kitchen-sink drama'. After the debacle of the Suez intervention in 1956, the British government abandoned Imperial rule at a rate that had not been anticipated. Moreover, there was a move toward the new European Economic Community, although an application to join made in 1961 was vetoed by France's President Charles de Gaulle.

'Kitchen-sink' drama saw an engagement with contentious issues and in a difficult tone. John Osborne, Harold Pinter, Alan Sillitoe, Arnold Wesker, and other playwrights of 'kitchen-sink drama' deliberately rejected earlier conventions in a determined effort to shock, as with Osborne's bitter *Look Back in Anger* (1956). This literature was an aspect both of the 1950s as a decade of change and of the 1950s as the anticipation of the 1960s; both elements that it is overly easy to neglect because of the focus on the 1960s as the decade of change, a focus that directs attention to the young of that period who now comprise many of the commentators.

This aspect of the 1950s was seen in the popularity of American 'Rock and Roll' music, which very much was a rejection of established British popular entertainment, and also in the degree to which the women in the Bond novels did not seek matrimony or motherhood. With 'Rock and Roll', Bill Haley and the Comets proved popular in Britain, as did Buddy Holly. Bob Dylan first performed in London in 1962. As an aspect of protectionism, the Musicians Union opposed the entry of American pop stars.[6]

'Kitchen-sink drama', however, was different (as well as deliberately difficult) as it had a clear social and, often, regional placing. These were not plays depicting the lives and mores of the social elite, as with the plays of Coward and Rattigan. Instead, 'kitchen-sink drama' sought both to reject the previous world of the well-made play, which Christie exemplified, and also to be socially gritty. There was an attempt to deal with people in serious

6   S. Frith, M. Brennan, M. Cloonan and E. Webster, *The History of Live Music in Britain. I: 1950–1967: From Dance Hall to the 100 Club* (Farnham, 2013).

economic difficulties, and in commonplace milieux, as with Wesker's *The Kitchen* (1957); and to focus on the North of England, which was understood as a tough environment, or on the world of London bedsits. The net effect was a new 'Condition of England' literature, one that looked back to the inter-war writing of Orwell. Christie appeared anachronistic.

Separately, there was criticism of the entire genre of recent detective fiction, notably in Edmund Wilson's condescending 1944 *New Yorker* essay 'Who Cares Who Killed Roger Ackroyd'. Wilson began with Rex Stout's Nero Wolfe, before criticising the 'puzzle mystery' in the shape of *Death Comes as the End*, which was highly atypical of Christie's work then, as remains the case. The novel is presented as 'a sleight-of-hand trick'. In contrast, despite the title, *The Murder of Roger Ackroyd* was not discussed. This essay reflected intellectual snobbery toward what was seen as 'low' or 'middle' brow and also social criticism.[7] So also with Paul Johnson's attack, in the *New Statesman* of 5 April 1958, on the James Bond novels, specifically *Dr No*, under the title 'Sex, Snobbery and Sadism'.

The critique of Christie as anachronistic appeared even stronger from the perspective of the new 'Condition of England' novels. In *A Caribbean Mystery* (1964), Marple dislikes the modern novels sent by her very successful novelist nephew Raymond West in his attempt to bring her up-to-date. She complains that they are about very unpleasant people, doing very odd things, and not apparently even enjoying them. In Christie's characteristic judgment by inversion, she has Marple consider that 'sex' was enjoyed far more in her young days, although usually labelled Sin, than nowadays when it seemed to be regarded as a kind of Duty.

Immigration was one increasingly significant theme of both continuity and change with pre-war circumstances. Meanwhile, Christie continued her placing of foreignness, although without the associated 1920s' connotations with Communism. In *A Pocket Full of Rye* (1953), the unappealing City figure is revealed accordingly: '"His father's name wasn't Fortescue. Fontescu – and he came from somewhere in Central Europe. I suppose this

---

7   J.L. Horschild, '"Who Cares Who Killed Roger Ackroyd?" Narrowing the Enduring Divisions of Race', in J. Rieder and S. Steinlight (eds), *The Fractious Nation? Unity and Division in Contemporary American Life* (Berkeley, Califf., 2003), pp. 155–69.

man thought Fortescue sounded better"'. He is also placed in terms of those who did not help during the war and had remained undesirable since: 'certain connections with the Black Market … a twister'. Fortescue can afford a butler, a cook and a parlourmaid. Very differently, the book has the elderly acerbic Miss Ramsbottom comment '"Had a young clergyman here last week. Black as your hat. But a true Christian"'.

In *Hickory Dickory Dock* (1955), Miss Lemon's sensible sister, Mrs Hubbard, becomes warden of a London student hostel at Hickory Road:

> '…Having lived in the East so long she understands racial differences and people's susceptibilities. Because these students at the hostel are of all nationalities; mostly English, but some of them actually *black*, I believe'.
> 'Naturally', said Hercule Poirot.
> 'Half the nurses in our hospitals seem to be black nowadays', said Miss Lemon doubtfully, 'and I understand much pleasanter and more attentive than the English ones'.

Soon after, Colin MacInnes focused on the increasingly numerous and prominent West Indian community in London[8] and on race relations in his novel *City of Spades* (1957), going on, in *Absolute Beginners* (1959), not only to discuss youth culture, but also the anti-black Notting Hill race riot of 1958 in London. The content, tone, and language were scarcely conventional: 'His chief exploit … had been to wreck the Classic cinema in the Ladbroke basin, and, with some of his four hundred, drop the law's coach-and-four into a bomb site, while others engaged the cowboys [police] in pitched battle with milk bottles and dustbin lids'.[9]

In *The Worm of Death* (1961), 'Nicholas Blake' (Cecil Day-Lewis) arrived at a conclusion of sorts like that of Miss Lemon in 1955, However, this is through a very different but also positively presented character, Nelly, a former Docklands prostitute who takes in lodgers:

8   A. Bidnall, *The West Indian Generation. Remaking British Culture in London, 1945–1965* (Liverpool, 2017).

9   C. Macinnes, *Absolute Beginners* in *The Colin Macinnes Omnibus* (London, 1985), p. 139.

'...They're nice boys, most of them – don't give any trouble –
particularly the spades'.
'I'm glad you don't have a colour-ban'.
'Not me'. She chuckled comfortably.
'Nelly the Ever-Open Door – that's me. We're all the same un-
derneath the skin, I always say'.

The contrast was the racial prejudice seen for example in the *Daily
Sketch*, a London newspaper, in its issue of 14 September 1953, which pro-
claimed 'Gunmen at Large: Dope, Daggars and Terror in the Streets. The
Facts'. This title introduced an exaggerated account of the problems of Tiger
Bay in Cardiff and a misleading attempt to link them to the black popula-
tion of Butetown, another part of Cardiff where there was much poverty.

'Kitchen-sink drama' and its equivalent spanned the late 1950s and
early 1960s. It was often iconoclastic in tone and it clearly sought to question, even subvert, existing genres. For example, in spy fiction, Fleming's
Bond was joined in 1962, with *The IPCRESS File*, by Len Deighton's Harry
Palmer, a working-class spy who had to cope with betrayal from within the
Secret Service by a social and professional 'superior'. While betrayal was in-
evitably a Christie theme given the emphasis on subterfuge and the use of
misdirection, it was certainly not a Bond one. Nevertheless, such betrayal
was an aspect of the real history of the post-war Secret Service, notably with
the spy Kim Philby, an establishment figure who was revealed as a Soviet
spy.

In a less iconoclastic fashion, Alan Hunter, in his 1957 novel *Landed
Gently*, referred to jingoism as doomed alongside other aspects of the Old
World, especially the satanic mills and social injustice, the former a reference to traditional factories. Instead, money is now made through service
industries, as by Mr Rafiel in Christie's *A Caribbean Mystery* (1964), with
an enormous chain of supermarkets, in his case in the North of England.

Yet, alongside the emphasis on change, it is important to note that this
did not mean that Britain was clearly moving against the Conservatives
who, in practice, instead, were responsible for much of the change they
were overseeing, particularly granting independence to most of the Empire.
Meanwhile, thanks to the state provision of free or subsidised health care,
education, council housing, pensions, and unemployment pay, rising real

incomes fed through into consumption, helped by the major cut in 1953 of the purchase tax on consumer durables. The percentage of households owning a washing machine rose from 25 in 1958 to 50 in 1964; with the relevant dates for 25 and 50 percent of cars being 1956 and 1965, and for fridges 1962 and 1968. Electric-powered devices such as tin-openers are seen as desirable in *Postern of Fate* (1973).

This was a period of economic growth, successful capitalism, and a government that responded to consumerism. These years continued to provide Poirot with the cases that are briefly mentioned but not discussed by Christie. Thus, in 'The Mystery of the Spanish Chest' (1960),[10] reference is made to his involvement in a delicate and complex mission for a major oil company concerning a questionable transaction by a senior employee. Very lucrative, sophisticated, and bloodless, this is presented as crime and detection at the highest levels. The implication is that Poirot makes his money by this means.

Moreover, Christie continued to sell well. Having, in 1948, had ten books published simultaneously by Penguin, in 1953 they brought out a second 'ten'. These were Christie's choice as the favourites she felt should represent her in the Penguin list, and for each she wrote what Penguin claimed was a special introduction in which she would give a background to the story, explain how she came to write it, and defend her inclusion of it among her ten favourite novels. In practice, the readers were somewhat sold short by the brief introductions. At any rate, readers might like to pause here and guess what they think the list would have been, or indeed what their list would be. In the event, it was:

The Murder of Roger Ackroyd
The Body in the Library
Death Comes as the End
Death on the Nile
The Labours of Hercules
Miss Marple and the 13 Problems
The Moving Finger
The Mysterious Mr Quin

10   Although based on a 1932 story.

Parker Pyne Investigates
Crooked House.

At the same time, it is instructive to note the nature of popular interest. Commercially the most successful film of 1959 in Britain was the smutty comedy *Carry on Nurse*, part of a long-running sequence of *Carry On* films which remained successful until the 1970s. Commercially the most successful film of 1962 was the Cliff Richard musical *The Young Ones*, a vehicle for a very conventional English type of pop singer, while in George Bellairs' *Surfeit of Suspects*, Inspector Tattersall is 'enjoying a Western with his wife in the local cinema' when he is called out to deal with three bodies.

While still selling very well, Christie's novels had a mixed relationship with this popular world, and she was being left behind a bit in changing times. 'The truth is, I am not in tune with the modern world', Poirot's reflection in the well-sketched post-prandial opening chapter of *Mrs McGinty's Dead* (1952), might as well refer to the author as to her elderly protagonist. One can see them both reflecting on the cinema:

> The looseness of its plots – the lack of logical continuity in the argument ... the photography ... seemed often no more than the portrayal of scenes and objects so as to make them appear totally different from what they were in reality.

With Old Etonians, Eden, Macmillan, and Home, as Prime Ministers from 1955 to 1964 (and other ex-Public Schoolboys before that), Meadowbank, the exclusive girls' school in *Cat Among the Pigeons* (1959), might not seem to be out-of-date. However, from a later perspective, it appears very dated. The school was mentioned by Christie a decade later in *Hallowe'en Party*:

> 'It has changed a little nowadays. Different aims, different methods, but it still holds its own as a school of distinction, of progress, and also of tradition. Ah well, we must not live too much in the past'.

In *Cat Among the Pigeons*, Christie noted British vulnerability: 'Governments are in such a difficult position. Vulnerable, so to speak. What with oil, and steel, and uranium, and cobalt and all the rest of it, foreign relations are a matter of the utmost delicacy'. This view was expressed by Mr Robinson, one of 'the Arrangers behind the scenes' whom Christie frequently deployed in her novels, especially the thrillers. In a continuation of her inter-war style, Christie presents Robinson as cosmopolitan:

> The man who came into the room did not look as though his name was, or could ever have been, Robinson. It might have been Demetrius, or Isaacstein, or Perenna – though not one or the other in particular. He was not definitely Jewish, nor definitely Greek nor Portuguese nor Spanish, nor South American. What did seem highly unlikely was that he was an Englishman called Robinson. He was fat and well dressed, with a yellow face.

Nevertheless, the language and settings of her novels are very different than those of many of the detective novels of the period. Thus, in *The Christmas Egg* (1958) by Mary Theresa Coolcan (1927–2017), an able writer who wrote as Mary Kelly: 'One of the three was buying the round which had fallen due to him; a small man with a face like a battered nut, in which blue eyes glittered like chips of glass'. So also with the Sergeant Cluff novels of Gil North, the pseudonym of Geoffrey Horne (1916–88), a Yorkshire-born Cambridge graduate who was in the Colonial Service from 1938 to 1955 before returning home and producing novels from 1957. Set in bleak moorland landscape, and even more in the invented hard and poor mill town of Gunnarshaw, with its inadequate housing and poverty-stricken people, North did not offer illusions in novels such as *Sergeant Cluff Stands Firm* (1960) and *The Methods of Sergeant Cluff* (1961). The descriptions could be harsh: 'Her eyes were red with lack of sleep, black, sunken half-circles under them. Her clothes kept her flesh together and Cluff guessed that undressed, she would be shapeless'. As with Christie's protagonists, Cluff, who echoed the *Moonstone*'s Sergeant Cuff, was a watchful figure and an indomitable protagonist, but, like Simenon's Maigret, his integrity had a cragginess very different to those of her protagonists.

In contrast to Christie, Julian Symons' *The Progress of a Crime* (1960) presented police brutality as commonplace. Like her, there was the ridiculous

London press, not least in the person of the catarrhal proprietor Lord Brack-man – "'Got a lot of stomach trouble, Edgar. Bowel trouble'". However, un-like most works by Christie, Symons' impressive book, which indeed had a background in a real life killing and case, was not an encouraging read.

Christie's politics continued to be apparent. At the outset of *Cat Among the Pigeons*, Prince Ali Yusuf, the Sheikh of wealthy Ramat, is shown as naïve in his confidence in popular approval of the welfare state he had funded. The more sensible Bob Rawlinson is sceptical about democracy:

> 'If they boot you out of here, some spouting hot air merchant will take over, yelling his own praises, building himself up into God Almighty, and stringing up, or cutting off the heads of anyone who dares to disagree with him in any way. And mark you, he'll *say* it's a Democratic Government – of the people and for the people'.

These tensions are also present, in *The Adventures of the Christmas Pud-ding* (1960) in the unnamed, Commonwealth-linked 'rich and important native state' that had been passing through a period of restlessness and dis-content, where the betrothed of the new ruler, a cousin, wants democracy, progress, and education. Kuwait and Oman were the most obvious candi-dates. The Middle East continued to turn up thereafter, not least in James Elroy Flecker's haunting poem 'The Gates of Damascus' providing the title and foreword for Christie's *Postern of Fate* (1973). Flecker (1884–1915), a member of the Aesthetic movement, was a romantic for Asia notably in his poem *The Golden Journey to Samarkand* (1913). This choice of poet and subject reflected both an engagement with the poetry of that period and the particular quest of the poet, and Christie's interest in moral choice that is central to 'The Gates of Damascus'. That poem is also quoted twice in her short story 'The Gate of Baghdad' (1934). Meanwhile, the imperial links of the British diaspora still played a role in her novels.

For another instance of a traditional setting and arrival in Christie's work in this period, there is the 'big white Georgian house' with butler and chauffeur in *Dead Man's Folly* (1956). In contrast, by the publication of *Endless Night* in 1967, one character complains "'big unwieldy country houses are a drag in the market'" because of taxation and the difficulty of finding domestic help in the country. Already, in *4.50 from Paddington*

(1957), there is change focused on Rutherford Hill. It was built in 1884 by a Crackenthorpe, who made his money in 'fancies': small cakes. He had two sons that he brought up as gentlemen but neither wanted to go into the business. The elder one spends a lot of time in Italy buying Classical statues, while the younger marries an actress and dies in a car crash while drunk driving. A miser, the elder son complains about taxation and says he expects the '"socialists"' will get the house off his heir and turn it into '"a Welfare Centre or something"'.

The Laceys in *The Adventure of the Christmas Pudding* (1960) can only update their mansion Kings Lacey by selling land for development. They have to rely on a retired cook and a retired butler, as well as women who come in from the village. Mr Jesmond notes that '"the real old-fashioned type of Christmas"' was dying out as people now spent it at hotels, while Mrs Lacey complains that her granddaughter Sarah won't go to dances, or come out properly, or be a debutante, but instead is in a coffee-bar set with an undesirable young man. This was Christie observing her world. Such a coffee-bar world was particularly prominent in Soho and was to be one of the forcing houses of 'The Sixties'.

The driving home of change comes in *The Mirror Crack'd from Side to Side* (1962), with the clear-eyed Marple observing in the opening chapter that St Mary Mead had greatly altered. The old core was still there, albeit with much money spent on plumbing, electric cookers, dishwashers, and additional bathrooms, while, moving to the East Lodge, Dolly Bantry, now a widower, had added a modern kitchen, a bathroom, electricity, and a new mains water supply. Meanwhile, the shopping in St Mary Mead had changed greatly, not least with a new supermarket, although in practice supermarkets were largely urban. Miss Hartnell complains about the inconvenient methods of shopping in the supermarket, including the inappropriate sizes of prepared portions. The Development, a repeatedly offered capitalisation, provides houses in place of meadows, but also, in this 'brave new world', a lifestyle including hire purchase. The same year, Christie's birthplace, Ashfield, a two-acre property in Torquay she had sold in 1940, was demolished and replaced by a new 'estate' that she subsequently visited and thought 'the meanest, shoddiest little houses I had ever seen'.[11] Such houses were increasingly common.

11 A. Christie, *An Autobiography* (London, 1977), p. 550.

The nightmarish quality of a London smog was not used by Christie, but was captured in Patricia Wentworth's *Ladies' Bane* (1954):

> It was rather like a slow motion picture. That was the fog of course. Nothing could really move in a fog like this. The buses would be stopped – and the cars – and the people who were abroad would crawl like beetles and wish to be home again – and the watches and clocks would all slow down and time too.

Christie herself in her author notes of the period referred to disliking living in cities. The London smog of 1952 killed more than 4,000 people and led to the Clean Air Act of 1956. Air pollution was an aspect of a traditional environment that was under attack. About 750 Londoners died in another smog in 1962, one that I can remember.

Meanwhile, Christie's London was being rebuilt. Hyde Park and Mayfair residences had long played roles in her stories, and those of other detective novelists; but social change was registered as aristocrats sold their town houses. One of the grandest, Londonderry House in Park Lane, the site of numerous fashionable inter-war parties, was sold in 1962 and demolished to be replaced by the Londonderry House Hotel. Lady Eardsley 'queening it in Park Lane', as envisaged in *The Man in the Brown Suit* (1924), was now very much a figure of the past. In 1956, a Regency terrace looking onto Hyde Park was purchased by Charles Clore, a Christie-style plutocrat, who constructed the 28-storey London Hilton on the site. A traffic underpass was built below the new fire-lane roundabout at Hyde Park Corner, and Park Lane became a major through-route. The ugly modernist Bowater Building was thrown up in Knightsbridge.

Much town-changing was a matter of brutal rebuilding. Set in the Potteries, *The Spoilt Kill* (1961) by Mary Kelly captures the major changes arising from the shift from coal and the Industrial Revolution:

> Town halls, valiant parks, grim black churches, isolated and rearing, heaps of eroded slag, micaceous rocks and new colleges, factories, offices, thrusting sheer above surrounding waves of low slate roofs that dipped and sagged with age. Progress and consciousness were gradually but ineluctably

sponging down the past. An improvement, of course; but it was impossible not to murmur occasionally, from the deep forgetful rosy well of sentiment, a sad farewell to the old bottle ovens and the soot.

Completed in 1963, the Engineering Building at Leicester University, which was designed by the Scottish architects James Gowan and James Stirling, was deliberately futurist, and was proclaimed as Britain's first postmodernist piece of architecture. The Engineering Building was actually rather a bolder modernism than that of Le Corbusier, and was influential in using industrially-produced materials. The auditoria in the building were topped by protruding cuboid skylights.

Bold architectural schemes responded to the cult of the new, leading to much 'New Brutalism' in architecture. Seven greenfield, plate-glass universities were opened, beginning with Sussex in 1961 (for which Sir Basil Spence did much of the architectural work), and ending with Kent and Warwick in 1965. The new universities offered new initiatives in teaching and organisation, notably with interdisciplinary curricula. Meeting in 1961–3, the Committee on Higher Education chaired by Lord Robbins recommended a marked increase in the number of students. The thesis of the committee report, which was presented to Parliament by Macmillan, the Prime Minister, in October 1963, was that every child with the potential for higher education should receive it, and, if not at state expense, then with a significant state subsidy.

There was a relationship between cultural changes and the rise, under Harold Wilson, of Labour to power in October 1964. A sense that a distinct and anachronistic 'old order' existed and needed replacing by a new meritocracy able to use planning[12] provided a clear way to stir up opposition to the Conservatives as well as, less prominently but also significantly, to encourage the latter to show increased interest in reform policies. These themes were very much part of the public culture of these years. They helped fuel the 'satire boom' that became significant in the early 1960s, with clubs such as The Establishment Club in London, live shows, and radio and television

12   G. Ortolano, *The Two Cultures Controversy: Science, Literature and Cultural Politics in Postwar Britain* (Cambridge, 2009).

programmes. Programmes such as 'That Was The Week That Was' on television, 'The Goon Show' on the radio, and the new satirical periodical *Private Eye* made existing class distinctions and social conventions appear ridiculous as well as dated. Failure in government, economy, and society could thus be traced to the alleged incompetence of British arrangements. Like Lord Dawlish in *Death on the Nile* (1937), the satirists were largely well-educated young men, often from an affluent background, and were scarcely representative of society as a whole; but that did not lessen the force of the charge. There were particularly strong attacks on the last years of the Macmillan government and on its aristocratic character.

Change in a very different form came with the Mini, designed in 1959 for the British Motor Corporation by Alec Issigonis. This was a car contrasting in design to those earlier in the decade, and it reflected an inventive engagement with the possibilities of the new. Indeed, design was to become a major theme and language, one that deliberately focused on new and newly-presented products.

Consumerism was also apparent in the development of Sunday newspaper colour supplements. These began on 4 February 1962 with the first *Sunday Times* colour supplement. Entitled 'A Sharp Look at the Mood of Britain', this depicted what was allegedly a new sense of national purpose and classlessness, and included photographs of Jean Shrimpton wearing a Mary Quant dress, and a new James Bond story.

Christie was scarcely in the forefront of such change. Instead, in her novels there were both the practices and values of the past, and aspects of continuity that now appear part of history. Thus, in 1964, in *A Caribbean Mystery*, Miss Marple makes a reference to a conductress on the Market Basing bus who helped the passengers on. That was the age before driver-only buses.

Yet change is certainly present in her stories, including in opportunities for murderers. Thus, in *4.50 from Paddington*, reflecting on the disposal of corpses, the sensible Elspeth McGillicuddy notes that, whereas in the past it was possible to put bodies into trunks, now suitcases were used by passengers instead, and there was no space in them for a body. So also with victims changing. Major Palgrave, the victim in *A Caribbean Mystery* (1964), is one of the cadre of elderly retired officers, usually having served in India, but, in this case, after India in East Africa, that are dying out.

Certainly they are part of a past that Marple regrets at the start of that book. Indeed Palgrave had shot elephants.

Meanwhile, there were fewer trains from Paddington, and elsewhere, from which to throw corpses, or possibly be observed doing so. The railway system had been hit badly by World War II, and the immediate post-war situation was even more serious. A government-imposed ban on fare and freight price increases led to a serious fall in net earnings in 1945–7. Nationalised in 1948, the railways were placed under the British Transport Commission, which was also made responsible both for London Transport and for a large amount of road transport. The Commission was supposed to integrate the transport system and rebuild it after wartime damage and lack of investment. However, such integration was not pursued, not least because road haulage was denationalised in 1953. The loss of money from 1953 undercut the positive changes that did occur as a consequence of the Railway Modernisation Plan of 1955 although the number of passengers was roughly stable in the 1950s.

Arriving at the fictional Market Kindle station in *They Do It with Mirrors* (1952), Marple finds a large, empty, windswept station with six platforms and a bay but hardly any passengers or railway staff. Poirot, nevertheless, is not the only one who remains devoted to rail travel. In *Mrs McGinty's Dead* (1952), he waits on a crowded platform at Kilchester waiting for his train to Broadhinny, with more crowds coming in due to it being market day, and is nearly pushed onto the line.

In *A Murder is Announced* (1950), Mitzi is referred to as "'screaming like a steam engine'"; but steam was to be replaced by diesel and electricity. Thus, the West Coast Main Line from London to Glasgow was electrified between 1959 and 1974. Nevertheless, there was no investment to match that being spent on roads including the beginning of the motorway system. The M6 Preston bypass was opened by Macmillan in December 1958, and the M1 punched through the Midlands from Watford to Birmingham in 1959. Private car ownership rose from 2.26 million in 1950 to 5.53 in 1960.

The Beeching Report of 1963 by Dr Richard Beeching, the Chairman of British Rail, led to dramatic cuts in the network that very much altered the local world of Christie's Britain. The report had positive aspects in that it urged a concentration on fast intercity services and bulk freight flows, for example to power stations, and foresaw the container revolution before anyone else did. Beeching, however, was specifically excluded by his brief from the Minister of Transport from considering the social and economic consequences of rail closures; his remit was simply to make the railways pay their way. As a result of the report, freight and passenger services were greatly curtailed, the workforce cut, lines were taken up, and many stations became unmanned halts, or were converted to other uses. Cross-country lines, such as the Oxford to Cambridge (now scheduled for eventual re-opening) and the Somerset and Dorset (Bath to Bournemouth), were shut, as well as numerous branches. Railway buildings became homes, offices, workshops and shops. Thus, in Berkshire, the Abingdon and Farringdon branches both closed to passengers in 1963, while in 1964 the Didcot to Newbury line was hit, this being the last link in a line to Winchester already shut in 1961. A branch line to Lambourn closed in 1973.

The relative decline of rail travel did not end its grip on the popular imagination, but that focused on the now-discarded system of steam trains which were only retained by enthusiast-run private lines or on main lines for rare special excursions. The Poirot television series was an aspect of this nostalgia, which definitely contributed to the appeal of the series. The television was to focus on the train far more than Christie herself did.

However, in her lifetime, her characters and works were already being greatly changed. 1962 saw Poirot's television debut with *Hercule Poirot: The Disappearance of Mr Davenheim*, which had originally appeared in 1923. Martin Gabel who played Poirot was to be Moriarty in the Broadway production of *Baker Street*. In contrast, the film *Murder Ahoy!* (1964), the last of the four Marple films made by Metro-Goldwyn-Mayer starring Margaret Rutherford, had a screenplay not based on any of Christie's stories. This was scarcely new, but very much suggested the porosity of Christie's creations.

9. THE 'SIXTIES', 1964-9

Poirot had come a long way from Styles in *The Alphabet Murders* (1965), which had him in a comic story based on *The ABC Murders*. Indeed, the first victim, Albert Aachen, is a clown, and Tony Randall's Poirot has a buffoonish character in a film with a definite slapstick feel. Britain also seemed to be changing: "'From what you read and hear nowadays, it seems that murder under certain aspects is slowly but surely being made acceptable to a large section of the community'", remarked Miss Emlyn, the headmistress in *Hallowe'en Party* (1969). *At Bertram's Hotel* (1965) was all about change precisely because the grand London hotel presented itself as unchanged:

> By 1955 it looked precisely as it had looked in 1939 – dignified, unostentatious, and quietly expensive.... There had of course been many other hotels on the model of Bertram's. Some still existed, but nearly all had felt the wind of change. They had had necessarily to modernise themselves, to cater for a different clientele.... Bertram's ... a vanished world.... You were in Edwardian England once more.

The point, however, of the story is that Bertram's can only do this because it is a base for crime, and profits from it. This is very much Christie dealing with an altered social world, and, if the response in this case was fantastical, it is as one with the extent to which fraud or speculation served to keep at least part of the Establishment going. Indeed, Christie was prescient in observing the degree to which the overlap of old and new provided opportunities for crime. In this story, Marple, who very much offered an authorial perspective, also recognised that it was unhealthy as well as potentially dangerous to want time to stand still.

The 1960s were already offering less establishment and more radical models in novels and on the stage before what is generally understood as 'the Sixties' began, a process variously dated to 1963–6. The sense of 'the Sixties' owed much to the impact of popular music. This was an impact that emanated from every transistor radio, thus linking culture, technological provision, and entrepreneurial ability. Initially, the key change was the response to the Beatles, a Northern popular group who, with their debut single 'Love Me Do', released in October 1962, set the 'Mersey beat' (Liverpool, their home city, was on the River Mersey), and who offered working-class experiences prominence and sound.[1] Pop music, which did not appeal to Christie, challenged the 'received pronunciation' of the English language, providing a regional difference that was taken up by the BBC where the importance of conformity in diction, style and tone declined from the 1960s. The film director Guy Hamilton later noted:

> The combination of angry young men, Michael Caine and the Beatles killed the leading men who all spoke with Oxford accents.... Unless you had a Brummy [Birmingham] accent, forget it. I think the Beatles and the pop scene in general had a major influence on the cinema at this time.[2]

Other groups and performers also came from Liverpool, including Cilla Black. Indeed, popular music lent itself to female as well as male performers. If the bands, with their emphasis on electric guitars, were very-much male preserves, many singers were women. This was very different to the alternative Liverpool cult, football. Interest in Liverpool, which was very much not part of Christie's world, was also shown by the popularity of *The Liver Birds*, a television sit-com set there that began in 1969.

In practice, in the context of 'Beatlemania' in 1963–4, the Beatles went south, to London, and became a global as well as a national product. It set the sound of the Sixties. Their broadcast of 'All You Need Is Love' in 1967, transmitted to 26 countries, was seen by about 400 million people. Thanks largely to the Beatles, popular music became a British industry, replacing

1   D. McKinney, *Magic Circles: The Beatles in Dream and History* (Cambridge, Mass., 2003); K. Gildart, *Images of England Through Popular Music* (Basingstoke, 2013).
2   A. Turner, *Goldfinger* (London, 1998), p. 89.

the American 'rock and roll' of the 1950s. This was to be a major export industry.

The Beatles contributed powerfully to the idea of a 'New Britain', an idea that was very powerful in the mid-1960s, and one to which the now older Christie did not respond so successfully as she had done to the disruption wrought by its precursor in 1945–51. The idea of a 'New Britain' was again linked to the policies advocated by the Labour Party, which, under Wilson, governed the country from 1964 to 1970 and 1974 to 1976,[3] and which entitled its 1964 general election manifesto 'The New Britain'. This idea was related to a variety of cultural and product developments, including the new clothes fashions pioneered in Carnaby Street in London and the modern design themes often related to new technology, such as the supersonic Concorde aircraft and the Post Office Tower in London (1964). Wilson, a northerner who cultivated his image as a northerner and also went south, ensured that the Beatles were given honours, although this proved controversial.

Appearances changed in the mid- and late 1960s. Male hair became longer, while the dress code changed from shirt, tie and sports jacket for males to jeans and sweaters. Women wore miniskirts, showing an expanse of flesh that would have amazed their predecessors, corsets were out, and tights replaced stockings, suspenders, and garter belts. Christie has both George, Poirot's poorly-sketched valet, and an apparently ageless Poirot disapprove in *Third Girl* (1966). In an indication of concern about the attendant impact on social differentiation, George, 'a delicate social recorder', notes that '"it is not always easy to tell nowadays"' whether dealing with a young lady or a young man. Adopting an approach to which Christie was to return, Poirot's visitor is described:

> Long straggly hair of indeterminate colour strayed over her shoulders. Her eyes, which were large, bore a vacant expression.... She wore what were presumably the chosen clothes of her generation. Black high leather boots, white open-work woollen stockings of doubtful cleanliness, a skimpy skirt, and a

3   Wilson resigned on 5 April 1976, and was replaced as Prime Minister and Labour leader by James Callaghan.

long and sloppy pullover of heavy wool. Anyone of Poirot's age and generation would have had only one desire. To drop the girl into a bath as soon as possible. He had often felt this same reaction walking along the streets. There were hundreds of girls looking exactly the same. They all looked dirty.

Even Ariadne Oliver has a newly inappropriate hairstyle. Mr Goby, the private investigator, adds: "'Trouble is nowadays they [women] won't look twice at a nice hard-working lad. They prefer the bad lots – the scroungers. They usually say 'he hasn't had a *chance*, poor boy'''".

Labour introduced a range of social legislation including on abortion, homosexuality, capital punishment, censorship, and divorce. Separately, birth control was transformed with the contraceptive pill, with its ready availability, which in part was a matter of public policy, and with the sexual revolution, which in a way was repeatedly criticised in Christie's comments on appearance. Working-class talent provided a powerful infusion of energy in a world in which pop stars, hairdressers and photographers were celebrities. In a very different fashion to 'kitchen-sink drama', the working class emerged into the light of day. In *Third Girl*, Goby complained: "'Good boys aren't as easy to get as they used to be. Think too much of themselves nowadays. They know it all before they've started to learn'''".

At the end of his poem 'The Clothes Pit', published in his *Terry Street* (1969), Douglas Dunn captured the impact of music:

Three girls go down the street with the summer wind,
The litter of pop rhetoric blows down Terry Street,
Bounces past their feet, into their lives.

Beat-music drove the rhythm, Oliver grumbling in *Third Girl*: "'the only people whose names they know are pop singers, or Groups, or disc jockeys'''". The mid-1960s saw a cycle of 'Swinging London' films, including *Darling* (1965) and *Blow-Up* (1965), both of which examined the morals and mores of a permissive society[4] in which the role of family values and of the churches were largely redundant. For Alfie, the protagonist, played by

4   R. Murphy, *Sixties British Cinema* (London, 1992).

Michael Caine in the 1966 film of that name set in London, women, clothes and cars were commodities that proved one could get on in the world without the privileges of birth and education. Supermarkets provided new, anonymous shopping experiences and spaces. And new foodstuffs and drinks, such as the decaffeinated coffee Poirot describes as 'an abomination' in *Third Girl*.

Change accelerated. By 1967, the Beatles had become hippies and drugs were in the air. The Beatles changed music in a number of respects. With *Sergeant Pepper's Lonely Heart Club Band*, the lyrics were printed on the back of the album for the first time, and the meaning was a long way from their earlier 'She Loves You, Yeah, Yeah, Yeah'. Half a million people attended an open-air pop festival on the Isle of Wight.

The young were not the only ones to the fore. A focus on change also affected the built environment, with much torn down in the 1960s by a well-meaning, but often misguided, and sometimes corrupt, combination of developers, planners and city councils, who were convinced that the past should be discarded. They embarked on a rebuilding that was very different in style and tone. As a result, cities such as Newcastle saw major damage to their centres. The needs of road transport played a central role, with major roads driven through the cityscape, as with London (with the Westway), Birmingham, Exeter, Glasgow, Newcastle, and Wolverhampton.

Modernist functionalism drove the pace of architectural development, as with Richard Seifert's uncompromising slab-like Centre Point (1967) skyscraper in central London. This modernism was seen in hospitals, schools, and other buildings, as well as housing. And so also in Christie's work *Third Girl* with Borodene Mansions 'that great block that looks rather like Wormwood Scrubs prison',[5] or 'the old-fashioned market town' assailed by 'Progress' in the shape of the new supermarket, the Gifte Shoppe, Margary's Boutique, Peg's Café, and a 'palatial new bank'.

Third Girl also sees criticism of the here-and-now, and, notably, on a longstanding theme for Christie, that of modern art. The anti-modernism Christie offers is indeed familiar. Visiting the Wedderburn Gallery in London, Poirot finds

5   *Third Girl*, 2.

a picture which depicted three aggressive looking cows with vastly elongated bodies overshadowed by a colossal and complicated design of windmills. The two seemed to have nothing to do with each other or the very curious purple colouring.

The Claude Raphael show includes the ironic counterpoint suggested by '"one of Raphael's masterpieces"': 'an orange lopsided diamond with two human eyes depending from it by what looked like a spidery thread'.

Miss Battersby, the Headmistress who has retired as a result of growing impatience with parents, tells Poirot that the latter nowadays lack the strength of character to save their daughters from unsuitable young men.

Far more explicitly than with Christie, there was resistance to, or, at least, criticism of, many of the cultural changes of the period. For example, alongside novels pressing for new experiences and for the experience of the new came the anti-sixties novel, such as A.S. Byatt's *The Game* (1967) and Kingsley Amis' *I Want It Now* (1968).[6]

Ironically, modernism was often far from functional, not least as a result of a misguided preference for flat roofs – a mistaken design in a rainy climate. Concrete cladding also frequently proved a problem. Erno Goldfinger, after whom Fleming named a villain, was responsible for modernist horrors including Trellick Tower in West London. This is very different from many of the interior shots in the David Suchet Poirot series on television which were filmed in Highpoint, the Lubetkin blocks of flats on North Road.

There was also continuity. The *Carry On* films continued as before with works such as *Carry On Screaming* (1966), a spoof on horror films. Not that the comparison would have pleased her, so also with continuity in Christie's novels. This include a degree of self-referencing as part of a genre. Thus, in *Third Girl*, Poirot begins at breakfast-time with chocolate and a *brioche*, having

> finished his *Magnum Opus*, an analysis of great writers of detective fiction. He had dared to speak scathingly of Edgar Allen Poe, he had complained of the lack of method or order in the

6   S. Groes, *British Fictions of the Sixties. The Making of the Swinging Decade* (London, 2016).

romantic outpourings of Wilkie Collins, had lauded to the skies two American authors who were practically unknown.

Christie offered a killer in her established manner in the Tommy and Tuppence story *By the Pricking of My Thumbs* (1968). This is a totally unsatisfactory novel, with its 'mumbo-jumbo' conspiracy, including a secret room, ideas of child murder as salvation, and 'a killer of the Lord'. Nevertheless, flawed as it is, not least revealing Christie's difficulty in extending her range, the novel introduces care home murder as a theme, which hardly lacked, or indeed lacks, topicality.

Hallowe'en Party (1969) provided Christie with an opportunity to address popular views on murder stories. Oliver's novel *The Dying Goldfish* is criticised by Joyce:

> 'I didn't like that one', said Joyce. 'There wasn't enough blood in it. I like murders to have lots of blood'.
> 'A bit messy', said Mrs Oliver, 'don't you think?'
> 'But exciting', said Joyce.
> 'Not necessarily', said Mrs Oliver.

In *Hallowe'en Party*, Poirot and the retired Inspector Spence contemplate the current age, Spence claiming:

> 'More girls nowadays marry wrong 'uns than they ever used to.... Nowadays ... Mother doesn't know who the girl's out with, father's not told who the girl is out with, brothers know who the girl is out with but they think 'more fool her'. If the parents refuse the couple go before a magistrate and manage to get permission to marry"'.

The extent to which the 'mentally disturbed' are no longer kept in care, for their safety and the safety of others, is condemned. Separately, there is criticism of:

> 'The nasty bit of goods, or the poor afflicted fellow, whichever way you like to look at it, gets the urge again and another young

woman goes out walking and is found in a gravel pit ... there's a lot of that nowadays'.

Rowena Drake later adds to the gloom:

'Mothers and families generally are not looking after their children properly, as they used to do. Children are sent home from school alone, on dark evenings, go alone on dark early mornings ... lead very permissive lives. Have their own choice of friends'.

She subsequently adds: '"Even the people who wreck telephone boxes, or who slash the tyres of cars, do all sorts of things just to hurt people, just because they hate – not anyone in particular, but the whole world. It's a sort of symptom of this age"'.

Dr Ferguson brings in change with the police, referring to the retired Spence: '"Bull-dog breed. Good honest police officer of the old type. No graft. No violence. Not stupid either. Straight as a die"'. The unstated implication was that the modern police, as Julian Symons would certainly have argued, were very different. The doctor also repeated the earlier point about there being too many murdered children of late and, linked to that, too many mentally ill individuals who ought to be sectioned (detained) but are left free to attack. At the same time, there is a distaste by the doctor for a turn to psychiatry:

'There are times when I get tired of hearing those words: "Remanded for a psychiatrist's report", after a lad has broken in somewhere, smashed the looking-glasses, pinched bottles of whisky, stolen the silver, knocked an old woman on the head. Doesn't much matter what it is now. Remand them for the psychiatrist's report'.

Also elderly, Jeremy Fullerton, the local lawyer, regards the end of hanging, which he terms 'the full penalty', as a mistake: 'The young thugs nowadays thought they didn't risk much by prolonging assault to the point where it became mortal. Once your man was dead, there'd be no witness to identity you'. He also thinks about 'innumerable school children' murdered after accepting lifts from strangers and separately comments "'there's a lot of corruption about these days. It's been on the increase for the last ten years"'. In addition, Fullerton

> 'was contemptuous of many of the magistrates of today with their weak sentences ... the students who stole books, the young married women who denuded the supermarkets, the girls who filched money from their employers, the boys who wrecked tele- phone boxes, none of them in real need ... most of them had known nothing but over-indulgence in bringing-up and a fer- vent belief that anything they could not afford to buy was theirs to take'.

This situation was contrasted with the arbitrary harshness of the 'police state' in Eastern Europe, although that was not what Christie wanted.

Much of the novel is about the nature of justice in a time of social change. Poirot provides an absolute standard:

> He was a man who thought first always of justice. He was sus- picious, had always been suspicious, of mercy – too much mercy, that is to say. Too much mercy, as he knew from former experience both in Belgium and this country, often resulted in further crimes which were fatal to innocent victims who need not have been victims if justice had been put first and mercy second.

Rejecting Rowena Drake's support for proper remedial treatment for criminals and allowances for broken homes, Poirot instead argued the need to understand the role of genetic make-up. This led anew to the theme of "'A Satan young and beautiful as Lucifer can appear to mortals.... Michael Garfield, the follower of Lucifer the beautiful, was evil, and your daughter was innocence and wisdom, and there is no evil in her"'.

Just as Fleming's later novels had a tone and sometimes content of de- spair and depression, so, with Christie's commentary, you can grasp a dark- ening of mood and the sense of the 1960s destroying a cultural continuity that had lasted from the Victorian age. This destruction reflected the impact of social and ideological trends, including the rise of new forms and a new agenda moulded by shifts in the understanding of gender, youth, class, place and race, as well as by secularisation. London was both a stage for change and a moulder of it, in particular for the 'Swinging Sixties', the idea of new lifestyles and fashions that were presented to the world from a series of London settings, such as the clothes boutiques of Carnaby Street and the Abbey Road recording studios. Permissiveness was a matter, as in *Third Girl*, not only of the activities of the newly prominent but also of the former social elite, many of whose members became what would previously have been regarded as decadents. There was an overlap between the milieux of both groups.

In *Endless Night* (1967), a somewhat disturbing novel but with a skilful misdirection, there was a move away from Englishness, in that Americans played a significant role. Moreover, there was a willingness to engage with the modern. Major Phillpot is a conservative magistrate and local landowner who is a self-proclaimed "'bit of an old square'", who likes old buildings. Nevertheless, he still likes the new house built for Ellie and Mike (Fenella and Michael): "'It's got shape and light. And when you look out from it you see things – well, in a different way from the way you've seen them before.... Very interesting'". The critically very well-received novel was a very powerful piece of writing, told, in a reprise of an earlier method, from the perspective of the murderer. In some respects, the novel was a tribute to Patricia Highsmith's *Ripley* stories, but with the insanity of 'endless night' the consequence of a wrong moral choice. A religious dimension is there at the close.

The churches, meanwhile, found it difficult to minister to the population as a whole. There were calls for 'relevance'. In the widely-read *Honest to God* (1963), John Robinson, Anglican Bishop of Woolwich, sought to address the inability of the Church of England to reach out to many, especially in run-down urban areas, by pressing the need for a determination to respond that would include a new liturgy. In practice, older and rural congregants were more significant. There had been a widespread and protracted decline in attendance at Easter by Church of England congregations. In 1931, there had been 2.2 million communicants, but, by 1951, the number had fallen to 1.9 million and by 1966 to 1.8 million. When taken as a proportion of the total population, the overall percentage attending church became even smaller. Faith became less important, not only to the fabric of life but also to many of the turning points of individual lives, especially dying. Baptism and confirmation became less common while more Christians did not marry in church. In addition, the beliefs of Christians changed, with traditional doctrine neglected by many, notably belief in the Resurrection.

The churches retained a role in education, with many state schools Protestant or Catholic foundations, and with the churches playing a modest role in their governance. However, as a consequence of the formation of the National Health Service in 1948, the major roles of the churches in charitable functions and the provision of social welfare were both largely replaced by the state. The last state-backed national day of prayer was in 1947, and a proposal for another in 1957 was rejected. Christianity declined as the glue and purpose of society.[7]

While the Church of England increasingly fought shy of mentioning Evil, Christie went on with the assault. In *The Pale Horse* (1961), a title taken from Revelations 6:8, where Death rides on a pale horse, Detective-Inspector Lejeune rejected the idea that the murderous Zachariah Osborne '"was all due to some gland in his spleen or his sweetbread or something either over-functioning or under-producing"'. Instead, Lejeune presented him as a '"wrong 'un.... Evil is not something superhuman, it's something *less* than human. Your criminal ... never will be important, because he'd always be less than a man"'. The villain murders the good Father Gorman.

Christie, as ever, was clear and open in her values. *The Pale Horse* and *Endless Night* evoked the turn into the 1960s in an impressive way, one possibly remarkable for a writer of Christie's age. While the ageing Christie lamented the changing times, she was still capable of crafting impressive detective stories that delivered suspense and surprise.

---

7   H. McLeod, *The Religious Crisis of the 1960s* (Oxford, 2007); A. Chandler and D. Hein, *Archbishop Fisher, 1945–1961: Church, State, and World* (Farnham, 2012).

10. TO THE END, 1970-6

Passenger to Frankfurt (1970), written to mark her 80th birthday, is not Christie's best novel. As opposed to her detective novels, such as *Nemesis* (1971), her spy thrillers do not age well, but the later they were written, the worse they became, in part because they appeared more anachronistic. This was a matter not only of style but also of changes in politics and society. Both Fleming and John le Carré had the same problem. The *Evening Standard* praised this novel as 'Vintage Christie', which to some might have been part of the problem. Instead, however, it was the plot that was the difficulty, for there was no hold on reality. Christie herself explains it in an 'Introduction' in which 'The Author speaks'. She notes that the author produces the ideas and the characters, but insists that the setting has to be real. For today, she refers to the evidence of eyes and ears, but also the way in which the press holds up a mirror:

> 'Look at that front page every day for a month, make notes, consider and classify.
> Every day there is a killing.
> A girl strangled....
> Fear is awakening – fear of what may be ... the possible causes behind them'.

She then turns on to foreign news:

> Hi-jacking of planes
> Kidnapping
> Violence
> Hate
> Anarchy – all growing stronger.

This is a theme also seen in *Postern of Fate* (1973). And then she adds her imagination:

> A fantastic cause. A secret Campaign for Power…. This story is in essence a fantasy. It pretends to be nothing more. But most of the things that happen in it are happening, or giving promise of happening in the world of today. It is not an impossible story, it is only a fantastic one.

The story, more a thriller to use Christie's terms, has a number of characters who cannot really confront modern times. They include Christie, in her opener, introducing Sir Stafford Nye, 'of excellent family … dreaming very happily of fishing an English river'. Soon answer comes, his aunt, Lady Matilda Cleckheaton, now living in only part of the family Georgian manor house, who, having warned him that trains 'very often did not run, or changed their plans', asked him to bring with him, from London, Camembert and Stilton, adding:

> 'Impossible to get anything down here now. Our own grocer – such a nice man, so thoughtful and such good taste in what we all liked – turned suddenly into a supermarket, six times the size, all rebuilt, baskets and wire trays to carry round and try to fill up with things you don't want and mothers always losing their babies, and crying and having hysterics. Most exhausting'.

Henry Horsham, from 'Security', soon provides a warning of a world in turmoil:

> 'What with the Chinese and the Russkies and the rather queer crowd that's behind all the student troubles and the new Mafia and the rather odd lot in South America. And the nice little nest of financiers who seem to have got something funny up their sleeves…. Everyone's playing a double game or a treble or a quadruple one…. Things are going badly in this country. Can you wonder?'

The last was the argument voiced by those such as Cecil King, the press lord, who had looked in 1968 for the replacement, even overthrow, of the Wilson governments of 1964–70. The general air in the novel is one of social malaise, as in the personal advertisements:

> 'Young man who objects to hard work and who would like an easy life would be glad to undertake a job that would suit him'. 'Girl wants to travel to Cambodia. Refuses to look after children'.

Lady Matilda presents the politics:

> 'All those awful, awful Labour people…. Why, when I was a girl there wasn't such a thing as a *Labour* Party. Nobody would have known what you meant by it. They'd have said "nonsense"…. And then there's the Liberals, of course, but they're terribly wet…. Conservatives…. Too many earnest women'.

Instead, Lady Matilda warns of international revolutionaries using the deluded, destructive young, as she claims Hitler had done. Subsequently, there is a comment about '"the insidious cult of permissiveness … the cult of drugs"'. The idea of a cult is at the fore, an idea frequently employed by Christie and not always helpfully so as far as the quality of the plotting is concerned. Drawing in part on cyclical notions of history, the anxiety level in this novel is then ratcheted up in Germany with a Nazi throwback, an international Aryan movement, and someone pretending to be Hitler's son. The risk of a Nazi return was handled far better in John Le Carré's novel *A Small Town in Germany* (1968). There is also discussion in *Passenger to Frankfurt* of atomic weaponry, and gas comes in, with young scientists '"dedicated to the cause of anarchy"'.

The nuclear superpowers are presented as vulnerable. The theme of science and scientists as a form of power takes forward *The Big Four* (1927) and also *Destination Unknown* (1954). Virtue, in contrast, appears to be represented by such as Colonel Pikeaway, a chain-smoker of cigars who also praises Churchill and is sceptical about current politicians:

'The heads of some of our young firebrands. Stuffed full they are of German philosophy, Black Power philosophy, dead French writers' philosophy… our judicial courts here saying we must be very careful not to do anything to damage a young man's ego because he *might* have to earn his living'.

Pikeaway, who is in the Colonel Race tradition although more relaxed, is to return in *Postern of Fate* (1973). The consistently ridiculous *Passenger to Frankfurt* ends in a particularly ludicrous fashion with the forces of good turning to Project Benvo, a gas which makes people benevolent, the unmasking of the conspirators, and a deadly fight in which they are thwarted. This, in effect, is *The Big Four* in a new setting, with 'The Ring', of five organisers of chaos, the equivalent, although less to the fore, of the four in the earlier novel. The Neo-Nazi theme really does not work. In addition, Christie exaggerated the degree of linkage between what she disliked. There were conspiracies in this period linked to the Soviet Union, but Christie failed to focus on them. Moreover, in a characteristic weakness of her thriller plots, her account of a conspiracy outside the Cold War was far less successful than Fleming's SPECTRE, which had been introduced in *Thunderball* (1961), and also far more wordy.

In marked contrast to some other of her later works, *Passenger to Frankfurt* is not a successful novel, but it is very significant as an introduction to Christie's thought late in her life. Far from overcoming or dropping the somewhat crude anti-Bolshevik themes of her 1920s' novels, she repurposes them, but not terribly well. Light is thrown on the political assumptions behind at least some of her other work.

Edward Heath won the 1970 elections for the Conservatives. Under them, Christie received the Order of Dame of the British Empire in 1971; her earlier honour of CBE in 1956 had also come from a Conservative government. The 1970s, however, were to be a decade in Britain in which optimism was increasingly shadowed by economic recession and political tension, and novels repeatedly registered problems. The 'social revolution' became for some novelists self-deception, adultery and a fraud, as in Iris Murdoch's *The Sacred and Profane Love Machine* (1974).

Yet, it can be too simple to present a unitary account of change. If the 1960s was a period of pop concerts and drugs, it also saw a burst of Christian evangelism, notably centred on the American Billy Graham and his revivalist missions to Britain. Moreover, trainspotting and making jam remained popular hobbies, and the 1970 and 1974 elections saw considerable votes for the Conservatives. Christie can be located in this context.

In *A Caribbean Mystery* (1964), there is an emphasis on Marple having been brought up to have a proper regard for truth, and, as throughout Christie, this truth has a moral force. One of the last chapters of *A Caribbean Mystery* is entitled 'The Last Day', and Marple is quoting from the Bible about the moral effect of truth at the start of the chapter before later finding a parallel with *Hamlet*. Entitled 'Nemesis', the penultimate chapter of *A Caribbean Mystery* sees Marple seek to discharge that role, which gives a link to the book of that title, which again had Marple as the protagonist. *Nemesis* (1971), a powerful and thoughtful book about guilt and retribution, is one that still grips and also shows that the weakly-fanciful *Passenger to Frankfurt* was far from typical. Produced shortly before the last novel she wrote, *Nemesis* also includes the powerful Biblical quote that expresses so much of Christie's perspective:

Let justice roll down like waters
and righteousness like an everlasting stream.

There is no politics in the sense of the previous book, but, instead, a broader politics of good and evil, and of the need for responsibility for guilt, captured in an exchange half-way through between Marple and the perceptive Home Office advisor, Professor Wanstead. The first observes:

'If you expect me to feel sympathy, regret, urge an unhappy childhood, blame bad environment; if you expect me in fact to weep over him, this young murderer of yours, I do not feel inclined so to do. I do not like evil beings who do evil things'.
'I am delighted to hear it', said Professor Wanstead. 'What I suffer in the course of my profession from people weeping and gnashing their teeth, and blaming everything on some happening in the past, you would hardly believe. If people knew the bad environments that people have had, the unkindness, the difficulties of their lives and the fact that nevertheless they can

come through unscathed, I don't think they would so often take the opposite point of view. The misfits are to be pitied, yes, they are to be pitied if I may say so for the genes with which they are born and over which they have no control themselves'.

The book is full of morality and the search for justice. Elizabeth Temple says from her death-bed:

'It may be dangerous for you – but you'll find out, won't you?'
'With God's help, I will', said Miss Marple. It was a vow.

Before dying, Elizabeth Temple returned to the theme: '"Another name for truth, verity"', while Miss Marple refers later to her '"guardian angel"'. In each case, the reference is to a human, but the term is still suggestive. This was very much Christie's moral politics, as seen in much of her writing, for example *Curtain*. *Nemesis* introduces another elderly moral figure, Archdeacon Brabazon, one of the most sympathetic clerics in the Christie corpus. He urges the acceptance of humans as affected by the '"genetic make-up which gives them the characters they have"', and offers a very clear take on sex:

'Sex cannot take the place of love, it goes *with* love, but it cannot succeed by itself. To love means the words of the marriage service'.

The murderer is referred to by Miss Marple as a '"poor lost soul"' because '"malignant evil … brings suffering"'. The moral force of the novel is potent and purposed, much more so than the type of novel that Christie has Marple dislike when she sees one in a rural shop-cum-post office:

Miss Marple looked with distaste at the jacket of the book, a naked girl with blood-stained markings on her face and a sinister-looking killer bending over her with a blood-stained knife in his hand.
'Really', she said, 'I don't like these horrors nowadays'.
'Gone a bit too far with some of their jackets, haven't they', said

Mrs Vinegar. 'Not everyone as likes them. Too fond of violence in every way, I'd say nowadays'.

On a lighter tone, the book ends with Marple turning down the idea of putting her £20,000 payment into savings as "'The only thing I shall want for a rainy day will be my umbrella"'. She decides instead to spend the money on having fun. Earlier in the book, her luxuries are revealed as a taste for partridges and (separately) *marrons glacés*, and a trip to Covent Garden. Despite being very different from Poirot, they are linked by charity, justice, and good food.

Elephants Can Remember (1972), a tour through the past in terms of plot, 'Old sins have long shadows', cast, and atmosphere, brings back Poirot, as well as other related established cast members, notably the novelist Ariadne Oliver, the confidential agent Mr Goby, and the rather featureless, but dependable, Superintendent Spence. There are plentiful references to previous novels, but the mood is scarcely that of the early ones. Thus, Empire plays a role as a faded presence of mementoes and memories. One woman had been long ago 'to Malaya or some place like that, with her soldier husband'. Kipling is praised by one of the retired policemen. Ariadne can remember 'listening to a story of India and Egypt from an attendant Nanny'. There is a sense of value in that world:

> The pictures of girls, of schoolboys, of children and various middle-aged people, all mainly photographed in their best clothes and sent in nice frames or other things because they hadn't forgotten Nanny. Because of them, probably, Nanny was having a reasonably comfortable old age with money supplied. Mrs Oliver felt a sudden desire to burst out crying. This was so unlike her that she was able to stop herself by an effort of will, 'an instance of self-discipline very different to the demonstrative sentiment of the present day'.

Elephants Can Remember saw a decline in the range of vocabulary used, more repeated phrases, and more indefinite word usage, which suggests a decline in mental dexterity. There were also some meandering conversations, although they contributed to the tone of recollection in the novel. Moreover, it had an ingenious puzzle and sustains interest until the denouement.

Empire was certainly past. In the short story 'The Harlequin Tea Set' (1971), mention is made of World War II veterans going to Kenya '"as so many did"' and settling there. After independence (which was in December 1963), we are told some stayed on, some returned home, and some went to Western Australia.

Postern of Fate (1973), the last novel to be written, brings up another echo of the past, with Tommy Beresford, once alerted by Colonel Atkinson to an after-echo wartime treason, wondering whether there were younger members of traitorous families who might be a threat, either in response to the revival of old creeds or with regard to new ones. There is a critical reference to Mosley; and earlier to 'Common Market ideas' as if they are part of the troubling 'new ideas' affecting an England which is now in '"a funny state"'. Espionage is central, there is reference to Phillips Oppenheim, and Colonel Pikeaway, who is still around, says there is '"funny stuff"' going on with the Common Market: '"you know, behind things"'.

This anxiety is subsequently explained in terms of the real Common Market being good, but, in contrast, the world being affected by materialism, violence, rebellion by the young, and Fascism. The novel is all a bit of a jumble, and the writing suffered from repetition and more limited vocabulary, suggesting mental decline. The philosophy recommended is clear – philanthropy rather than egalitarianism; but not the means. Secret developments are thrown forward, there are references to the *Passenger to Frankfurt* plot, and this is linked to 'new fascists' and to the violence of the young, notably against the old, with a comment back to the vanity of the Children's Crusade, a reference to delusion. The history is drawn of a Fifth Column that goes back to before World War I, with Communism, Fascism and pacifism all part of the equation, and, moreover, still active. As an attempt to locate in the current world, there is reference to the new motorways. Published in October 1973, this was the last novel Christie wrote (as opposed to the last two to be published), being accompanied into print by her *Poems*.

1973 saw increasing problems for Britain, although the crisis of the OPEC oil price hike and the ungovernability linked to the coal miners' strike did not follow until the winter immediately after the novel's appearance. The Heath government was unable to control an increasingly difficult domestic situation, with mounting violence in Northern Ireland the most acute sign of a widespread failure of existing institutions and practices. Alongside that, the attempt, as under the earlier Labour Wilson governments, to innovate the way out of crisis had not worked, and had had the additional consequence of a disorientation for many, notably among the elderly, as transformation was implemented: from the coinage and traditional local government identities to Britain's international position.

Meeting Christie in this period at a matinée of *The Mousetrap*, the young Donald Sturrock remembers being taken into her box:

> She looked quite scary – much thinner in the face than some of the earlier photographs when she looks quite plump. And she wore those pointy framed glasses that added to her rather forbidding appearance.... I had read a vast amount of her books, so I think she was rather touched when this child started citing chapter and verse to her. She was very nice. I remember she then asked me who I thought had dunnit in the show. She must have been pleased that I got it wrong.[1]

Written during World War II, to which reference is made, but not published until 1975, *Curtain* takes up anew the theme of old crimes and, again, with old faces. With a real sense of closure, Hastings, a widower returned from Argentina, is the narrator and Styles the setting. It is now a guest house, which captures the changes of the 1920s and 1930s, and would have been even more the case by the 1970s. At the start, the returnee notes changes: 'Styles St Mary was altered out of all recognition. Petrol stations, a cinema, two more inns and rows of council houses'. Run by the retired Colonel Luttrell (the name that of a longstanding West Country landed family), Styles, the guest house, has many echoes of the past. Arriving, Hastings meets:

> the type of man that is becoming more and more rare, an Englishman of the old school, straightforward, fond of out-of-doors life, and the kind of man who can command.

1   Donald Sturrock to Jeremy Black, 28 Jan. 2021.

I was hardly surprised when Colonel Luttrell introduced him as Sir William Boyd Carrington.[2] He had been, I knew, Governor of a province in India, where he had been a signal success. He was also renowned as a first-class shot and big game hunter. The sort of man, I reflected sadly, that we no longer seemed to breed in these degenerate days.

Hastings is disappointed that his room is 'furnished in a cheap modern style.... I should have preferred a style more neatly approximately to the architecture of the house itself'. Christie, however, as ever, focuses on Hastings' values, notably when he refuses to listen through keyholes, which leads Poirot to respond '"You will remain the English gentleman and someone will be killed. It does not matter, that. Honour comes first with an Englishman"'. As is Christie's norm, this is a matter of English and not British. This was the last of her novels in which Poirot appeared. He had done so in 33 of her novels and 54 short stories, and his death was to be followed by an obituary on the front page of the *New York Times*.

Christie allows her characters in *Curtain* a detour to reflect on divorce. This was a contemporary topic for readers, when the book appeared, not least because the Divorce Reform Act in 1971 had encouraged a further increase in the rate. Already, in 1971, there had been 74,437 divorces in England and Wales. An emphasis on female satisfaction and self-expression encouraged the trend, and most divorces were initiated by women. At Styles, where the reference, when Christie was writing, was to the 1937 Act, the question was:

> Were men and women actually happier by reason of the greater facilities afforded for divorces, or was it often the case that a temporary period of irritation and estrangement – or trouble over a third person – gave way after a while to a resumption of attention and friendliness?

2 The name recalls Sir Archibald Boyd-Carpenter (1873–1937), who had served in the army before becoming a Conservative politician, although with no links to India.

Christie provides a diversity of views indicating her awareness of 'how much at variance people's ideas are with their own personal experience'. Hastings, 'essentially an old-fashioned person' who had been happily married, believed in letting people start afresh. Boyd Carrington, who had been unhappily married, was opposed to divorce as he saw marriage as '"the foundation of the state"'. And so on. For example: 'Franklin, the modern scientific thinker, was, strangely enough, resolutely opposed to divorce. It offended, apparently his idea of clear-cut thinking ... anything else resulted in what he called a mess'. Franklin is similar to Clemency in *Endless Night* (1967). Both lack appeal and charisma.

The brilliant solution in *Curtain* reveals that Christie wanted to be still as ingenious at the close as in her most famous novels, notably *The Murder of Roger Ackroyd*; and a gripping conclusion is brought by letter. The last words bring up the theme of Biblical judgment, Hastings reflecting, in connection with a symmetrical bullet hole, 'The mark on Norton's forehead – it was like the brand of Cain'. The frequent references to Shakespeare toward the close provide a direct clue, in the case of Iago from *Othello*, but also a form of moral measure and closure. Referred to in *The Man in the Brown Suit* and in 'Four-and-Twenty Blackbirds', *Othello* is also the point of reference in the villainy in 'The Mystery of the Spanish Chest', while such a chest is central to the legend of the 'Mistletoe Bough' which first appeared in print in the poem *Ginevra* (1822), and reference is made to Iachimo hiding in a chest in Shakespeare's *Cymbeline*.

More generally, there are many Shakespeare references in Christie. *Sparkling Cyanide* sees references to *Othello*, *Romeo and Juliet*, *Macbeth*, and the story of Agamemnon and Clytemnestra. The play, *Twelfth Night*, is not acknowledged because the quote 'Journey's end in lovers meeting' is assumed to be well-known, but *Destination Unknown* ends with Jessop commenting on Hilary Craven: her '"journey's end is the usual one after all"' and Leblanc being able to spot this as Shakespeare. *Sad Cypress* takes its title from *Twelfth Night*. 'And we are for the dark' from *Antony and Cleopatra* is quoted in *They Came to Baghdad*, while Macbeth is quoted at the start of *Hercule Poirot's Christmas*, and the quotation is repeated in the text. So also for the 'tide in the affairs of men' with *Taken at the Flood*. Shakespearean murder provides more than just a reference. It helps capture a tone and reflect a living culture. Quotation from Shakespeare was also used by other detective novelists, for example Dorothy Bowers in *Deed Without a Name* (1940). Christie's works reflect a wideranging knowledge of literature. Thus, *Endless Night* (1967) comes from William Blake's account of courses open to humans.

Sleeping Murder, Marple's last case to reach publication, followed *Curtain* in 1976. It was published posthumously, although it had been written in 1940 during World War II when, in an understandable response to German bombing, she thought she might not survive the conflict. Indeed, 58 Sheffield Terrace in Holland Park, Kensington, where she lived from 1934 to 1941, was near an area of significant bomb damage. Originally entitled *Murder in Retrospect*, the book itself deals in part with a period earlier than the action. In *Sleeping Murder*, Christie again is clear in the moral setting. At the close:

'Wicked', said Gwenda. 'Wicked-wicked-wicked'.
'Yes', said Miss Marple. 'There isn't really any other word....
It was real evil that was in the air that night'.

The power of theatre is also to the fore in this novel with the repeated reference in the last chapter to John Webster's play *The Duchess of Malfi*, in which lines 'Cover her face; mine eyes dazzle; she died young', and plot '"were really the clue to the whole thing"'. Play and novel included a brother killing a sister. The strong plot avoided Christie's reputation going out on one of her weak thrillers, as would have been the case had she concluded with *Postern of Fate*. As such, she had staged her publication sequence brilliantly.

11. RETROSPECTIVES, 1971-2021

As with Fleming and Bond, harsh comments were there in Christie's lifetime, notably from Edmund Wilson in 1944. In addition, later authors could be unsparing of Christie's type of fiction, in part possibly driven to contempt by anger at her sales which by 2016 exceeded two billion books in over 100 languages, including about 100 million copies for *And Then There Were None*. There have been over 7,000 translations of her work, while, released in November 2017, a film version of *Murder on the Orient Express* starring Kenneth Branagh, cost $55 million and took in $352.8 million. The reputation is worldwide. Thus, 1.1 million West Germans saw *Murder on the Orient Express* when it was shown in West German cinema in 1975, while the film *Death on the Nile* (1984) was shown 54 times between 2015 and 2020 on German, Austrian and Swiss television.

In his denunciation of the genre, *Snobbery with Violence: English Crime Stories and their Audience* (1971), revised and reprinted in 1979, Colin Watson, himself an author of detective novels, devoted a chapter to Christie. It was far from one of his most critical, and offered some good points, not least that Poirot was acceptable because his foreignness was familiar. However, there is also criticism of both author and audience. The detective story is presented as playing an increasingly important part in the attempts by the middle class to maintain its status, and Christie as providing not the world of adventure and opulence offered by Phillips Oppenheim, Anthony Hope and William Le Queux (one of 'maître d'hôtel and millionaires') but instead 'familiar homeliness' and 'stock characters observing approved rules of behaviour according to station, and isolated utterly from all such anxieties and unpleasantness as were not responsive to religion, medicine and the law'.

This approach reflected a failure to engage with the range of Christie's writing, not least in her treatment of crime and related human drives, but it was a commonplace view. Indeed, while subsequent changing presentation of her stories and plays throw a light on English culture, there were already contradictory views during her lifetime. Christie responded to criticism of this type in her *A Caribbean Mystery* (1964). She has Marple have to put up with being criticised by Raymond West for not leaving her 'idyllic rural life' in order to focus on real life. Marple considers this criticism very ignorant, as the facts of rural life were far from idyllic. Moreover, there was always something going on in St Mary Mead.

As with Watson, so also with Julian Symons in his *Crime Omnibus* (1984), a work that reflected his general disdain for Golden Age fiction. This was pretty harsh on Christie: 'the never-never land of her imagination where it seems always to be tea-time in some Edwardian year. The colonels, doctors, lawyers and others who inhabit this world are no more real than Cluedo figures'.[1] The plots, settings, and characterisation were certainly different from Symons' novels, but there were the shared artificiality and instrumentality of both genre and fiction.

P.D. James, in her *Talking about Detective Fiction* (2009), offered a more subtle account than Watson or Symons and in particular praised Marple 'who is not only unique in working entirely alone without the help of a Watson, but in being invariably cleverer than the police detectives she encounters'. However, James' view that Golden Age novels were a genre of escape in which there is no real pity, empathy or sympathy, but instead a 'confident morality',[2] can be questioned. There was not only less confidence than morality, but, more particularly, a marked degree of complexity in some of the writings.

In *The Story of Classic Crime in 100 Books* (2018), a compendium as concise as it is comprehensive, Martin Edwards focuses instead on an unprecedented skill in misdirection and consistency in ingenious whodunnits, while noting that her focus on a surprise solution took precedence over other elements.[3] Interestingly, Christie has served as an inspiration to others, such as Yukito Ayatsuji, author of the Japanese classic *The Decagon House*

---

1   J. Symons, *Crime Omnibus* (London, 1984), p. 80. See also Camilla Long review of Sarah Phelps, *The Pale Horse* in *Sunday Times*, 16 Feb 2020.
2   James, *Talking About Detective Fiction* (Oxford, 2009), p. 66.
3   M. Edwards, *The Story of Classic Crime in 100 Books* (2018), pp. 48, 52.

Murders. And Then There Were None was the chief influence, one victim is named after Christie, and the cast is of students, all fans of detective fiction, who get murdered while staying on an island house.

Christie is also used as a way to present, and therefore sell, other titles. Thus, Lucy Foley's *The Guest List* (2020) is very much not a Christie in content or tone, but it comes with a back-cover recommendation 'A very modern Agatha Christie', and with acclaim accordingly: 'Confirms her status as this generation's Agatha Christie' (*Sunday Express*) and 'Evoking the great Agatha Christie classics *And Then There Were None* and *Murder on the Orient Express....*' (*New York Times*). These comments are clearly regarded as praise.[4]

Separately, the very restraint of Christie could lead to continued approval. Thus, in 2021, she was among those praised in a depiction of 'Golden Age' fiction as less prurient than its modern counterpart:

> 'Golden-age' detective fiction ... for all the gore, and a sharp perception of human nature, the 1930s to 1950s did not share our 21st-century fascination with sexually motivated woman-butchering. Many of their victims are male, and females are as likely to be rich elderly aunts as pretty girls.[5]

In this context, the great popularity of *Midsomer Murders*, a British television series from 1987 of which 124 episodes had been aired as of 4 February 2020, is an instructive guide to popular tastes, internationally as well as in Britain. The murder rate in *Midsomer* was improbably high and the plots frequently ridiculous, but there were similarities to Christie in the factors explaining success, notably skilful misdirections and attractive settings. Indeed, these parallels were drawn on when season 22 was announced. The executive producer, Michele Buck, remarked on 'an episode with an Agatha Christie-type plot where people are all trapped in one location for 24 hours when a murder takes place', while the journalist Debra

---

4   See also M. Sanderson, 'The best crime fiction for April', *Times*, 29 Mar. 2021, reference to 'a modern-day Agatha Christie'.

5   Libby Purves, 'TV is obsessed with violence against women', *Times*, 15 Mar. 2021.

Craine referred to the series as 'blithely harkening back to a 20th-century tradition of cosy Agatha Christie crime'.[6] That was a critique of Christie that is highly misleading, but it also captured her continual role as a reference point, as well as the popularity that helped lead to a resurgence in the viewing of the David Suchet Poirot versions during the 2020–1 Covid-19 lockdowns.

Christie herself provided plentiful accounts of her writing, as well as an autobiography that, in the manner of the genre, explained as well as concealed. Thus, in her foreword to *The Body in the Library*, she captured the writing process with a degree of reticence:

> There are certain clichés belonging to certain types of fiction. The 'bold bad baronet' for melodrama, the 'body in the library' for the detective story. For several years I treasured up the possibility of a suitable 'Variation on a well-known Theme'.

That, indeed, was a characteristic of her writing. Although criticised for being a conventional writer and for providing a focus on an ingenuity in plotting that led to characters lacking in depth, Christie repeatedly sought to offer variations. To a degree, that was certainly a matter of ingenuity, but that can scarcely be underrated in a genre that deals with battles of wits, wills and circumstances. As with other writers, she was providing novels and not simply technique. For *The Body in the Library*, she noted:

> I laid down for myself certain conditions. The library in question must be a highly orthodox and conventional library. The body, on the other hand, must be a wildly improbable and highly sensational body. Such were the terms of the problem, but for some years they remained as such, represented only by a few lines of writing in an exercise book.

Chance observation of a family in a hotel dining room provides the pivot of a character for which she can endow 'imaginings', for as Christie

---

6   D. Craine, 'Midsomer Murders returns, as whimsical and wicked as ever' *Times*, 13 Mar. 2021.

noted, she did not like to write about people she knew. The relationships in that story are interesting, not least that of Conway Jefferson toward Ruby Keene. In *Hallowe'en Party* (1969), Christie, in the person of Ariadne Oliver, provides some good hints on how she wrote, with reference to her imaginings about people she met, rather than those she knew. The latter, as she pointed out, constrained such imaginings.[7]

She was far more willing to use places she knew. For example, Agatha's eccentric brother Monty was put out on Dartmoor for everyone's safety. Christie visited him often and described the village in *The Sittaford Mystery*. She closes the Foreword to *The Body in the Library* in a light tone: 'In the manner of a cookery recipe add the following ingredients: a tennis pro, a young dancer, an artist, a girl guide, a dance hostess, etc, and serve up *à la* Miss Marple!' This is detective fiction as entertainment, and not simply a way to approach themes in cultural change and continuity.

So also with Christie's openness about the hard work that writing entails, an element she does not disguise. She added a foreword to *Crooked House* (1949) including:

> This book is one of my own special favourites. I saved it up for years, thinking about it, working it out, saying to myself: 'One day, when I've plenty of time, and want to really enjoy myself – I'll begin it!'.... Again and again someone says to me: '*How you must have enjoyed writing so and so!*' This about a book that obstinately refused to come out the way you wished, whose characters are sticky, the plot needlessly involved, and the dialogue stilted – or so you think yourself.... I don't know what put the Leonides family into my head – they just came. Then, like Topsy 'they growed'. I feel that I myself was only their scribe'.

Technique, notably an economy of writing that permits the introduction of several red-herrings, as well as a dry humour that offers an ironic take on characterisation, will take you a long way in presenting Christie's skill. To adopt the language of the military historian, it gives you both the tactical

7   *Hallow'en Party*, chapter 18.

and the operational dimensions, but there is no comparable grasp of the strategic perspective. That perspective can be variously presented, with commercial success appearing the major goal. Yet, throughout, there is a moral purpose. This is not one of some sectional politics, of a backing, for example, by Christie for Baldwinian Conservatism or a *Pax Britannica*. Instead, there is a continual struggle between Good and Evil, one that is present in every soul and in society as a whole. This helps to explain characterisation, dialogue, and plots: there are deceptions and travails, but rightness is a shield and solace, as well as a goal. And, to that end, Christie provides the relevant tactical, operational, and strategic devices and perspectives. The firm Christian theme she enunciated in the short story 'The Call of Wings', published in *The Hound of Death*, is possibly the clearest instance, one of poetic intensity without the complications of a misdirection. In this short-story, Silas Hamer, a wealthy materialist, is made aware of meanings and purposes, and gains an epiphany and redemption accordingly. Whereas Christie's Harley Quin stories to this end are somewhat everywhere, this call is very much set in London, and provides a powerful story.

Yet, alongside the continued sales of the published works, at least two million annually, it is now the visual version that is to the fore. Indeed, that version dominates the account generally presented as in the ITV programme *Agatha and Poirot: Partners in Crime* (2021). Focus on the visual Poirot reflects the extent to which we more generally employ period drama, rather than detective fiction, to learn about and depict a period; and certainly so in popular culture. This tells us something about ourselves and the relative cultural status of period drama. Christie was keen on the visual version, but with a preference for the stage rather than film; she enjoyed the theatre but not the cinema, and some of her plays were impressive, notably *Witness for the Prosecution*. Television and cinema adaptations of her plays and, even more, her novels and short stories, faced the usual problems of such work.[8] The more nuanced aspect of her writing suffered a diminution when adapted, especially for television, but that did not hurt its incredible popularity.

There has more recently been a quite conscious and deliberate reworking of many of her stories, a reworking that is increasingly that of tone

8   M. Aldridge, *Agatha Christie on Screen* (Basingstoke, 2016).

rather than simply plot, notably the BBC serial adaptations by Sarah Phelps from 2015, especially *The ABC Murders* (2018) and *The Pale Horse* (2020). Contrasting with the continuation novels by Sophie Hannah to which Agatha Christie Limited has the copyright, beginning with *The Monogram Murders* (2015), the reworking by Phelps seeks to add Freudian overtones and, linked to this, also to refresh material with which the audience was assumed to be overly familiar.

Ironically, the reworking also pays tribute to Christie's significance. The contrasting approach would simply have been to bypass the plots far more completely as in the recent television versions of the Sherlock Holmes stories. The need for an ingenious murder plot keeps Christie more central to the later versions of her stories than with Fleming and Bond. Both, however, continue for many to play a major role not only in national identity, but also in their genre.

Index

The ABC Murders (Christie)
  The Alphabet Murders film, 96, 161
  cinema, 95
  class distinctions, 98–103
  crime, 7, 14
  economic crisis, 84
  emigration, 79
  food, 100
  industrial development in, 93
  murderers, 19–20
  psychology of suspects, 16
  television show, 190
  World War I, 27
  xenophobia, 76–77
abdication confrontation of 1936, 39
Abney Hall, 29, 100
Absolute Beginners (MacInnes), 149
"Accident" (Christie), 103
Acquittal (Simpson), 45
activist politics, 37–39
"The Adventure of the Bruce-Partington Plans" (Doyle), 36
The Adventure of the Christmas Pudding (Christie), 78, 100, 121, 154–55
"The Adventure of the Egyptian Tomb" (Christie), 41
"The Adventure of the Italian Nobleman" (Christie), 100
"The Adventure of the Sinister Stranger" (Christie), 59
"The Adventure of the Six Napoleons" (Doyle), 73

The Adventures of Arsene Lupin (Leblanc), 21
After the Funeral (Christie), 77, 101, 119, 127, 139–41, 145
Agatha and Poirot: Partners in Crime (television show), 189
Agatha Christie Ltd, 146–47
agricultural depression, 29
air pollution, 156
Airport of London, 47
air travel, 107
Aitken, Maxwell, 7
Alfred, 1st Viscount Northcliffe, 7
Alibi (film), 95
Alibi (Morton), 69, 79
Aliens Act of 1905, 74
All-Russian Co-Operative Society, 69
Alma-Tadema, Lawrence, 63
The Alphabet Murders (film), 96, 161
American crime fiction, 21
American 'rock and roll', 147, 163
anarchist conspiracies, 22
And Then There Were None (Christie), 108, 111–12, 184, 186
And Then There Were None (film), 112
The Angel of Terror (Wallace), 45
Anglicanism, 88
Anglo-American alliance, 131
Anglo-Iraqi treaty of 1922, 81
Anglo-Irish Treaty of 1921, 33
Anglo-Soviet trade agreement, 35
Antic Hay (Huxley), 46
Antidote to Venom (Croft), 15

anti-modernism, 165–66
anti-semitism, 71–72, 74, 89, 103
anti-Socialism, 87–88
Appointment With Death (Christie), 13, 41, 82, 92
archaeology, 80–81, 97, 110, 130–31
architecture, 63, 78, 156–57, 165
The Arsenal Stadium Mystery (Gribble), 96
Ashfield (birthplace), 155
Ask a Policeman (Christie), 7–8
At Bertram's Hotel (Christie), 12, 161
Attlee, Clement, 88
Auden, W. H., 125
"The Augean Stables" (Christie), 8
Austen, Jane, 4
Ayatsuji, Yukito, 185–86

Baghdad, Iraq, 130–34
Baghdad Pact, 132
Bailey, George, 44–45
Bailey, H. C., 78, 94
Baldwin, Stanley, 7, 39, 49–50, 53–54, 85–87, 90–91, 103
The Baronet's Progress (Christie), 139
Barrie, J. M., 62
Batchelor, Denzil, 96
Bath Journal (newspaper), 5
Beatles (band), 162–63, 165
Beeching, Richard, 159–60
Beeching Report of 1963, 159–60
Bell, Josephine, 91
Bellairs, George, 111, 140, 152
The Belting Inheritance (Symons), 118
Bennett, Charles, 65
Bennett, Margot, 145–46
Beowulf, 2
betrayal, 36, 150
Bevin, Ernest, 131
The Big Four (Christie), 52, 68, 116, 174–75
Big Four railway companies, 106

Birmingham Chronicle (newspaper), 4–5
Birthday Party (Kitchin), 62, 97
Black Coffee (Christie), 69
Black Coffee (film), 95
The Black Gang (McNeile), 36
Blackmail (Bennett), 65
"Blackman's Wood" (Oppenheim), 59
black market, 126
Blake, Nicholas, 139, 149–50
Bloody Friday, 34
boastfulness, 76–77
The Body in the Library (Christie), 8–10, 29, 71, 74–75, 93, 95, 102, 111–13, 151, 187–88
Boer War, 80
Bolshevism, 68, 70–71, 91
Bolton Chronicle (newspaper), 5
Bonar Law, Andrew, 37–38
Boyd-Carpenter, Archibald, 181n2
Brandon, John, 118
Brett, Simon, 2
Britain
    British emigrants, 82–83
    Cold War, 68–69
    conservatism, 53
    conspiracy, 49
    cultural changes, 161–71
    diaspora, 154
    economic crisis, 84–85
    and Egypt, 81–82
    extremists, 88–89
    Gold Standard, 51
    immigration, 74
    imperial rule, 131–33, 147
    and Ireland, 33, 179–80
    political extremism, 98
    post-war politics, 31–32
    social change, 104, 150–51, 175–76
    and Soviet Union, 35–36, 48
British Civil Administration, 132

British Empire Exhibition, 40, 78
British Military Administration of
Libya, 132
British Motor Corporation, 158
British Sex Survey, 123
British Transport Commission, 159
British Union of Fascists (BUF), 88–91
"The Broken Toad" (Bailey), 94
Browne, Douglas, 118
Bruce, Leo, 12
Buchan, John, 3, 35–36, 43, 59, 68,
78, 109, 121, 143
Buck, Michele, 186
Bude, John, 64, 72, 106, 118
BUF (British Union of Fascists), 88–91
built environment, 165
Bulldog Drummond (McNeile), 36
Bunyan, John, 3
Burgess, Guy, 134
Buried for Pleasure (Christie), 126
Burton, Miles, 18, 25, 29, 76, 105
bus services, 106–7
Butler, Rab, 141
Butskellism, 141
By the Pricking of My Thumbs
(Christie), 167

Callaghan, James, 163n3
"The Call of Wings" (Christie), 189
Campbell, John, 48
capital punishment, 138
care home murder, 167
A Caribbean Mystery (Christie), 13,
15, 83, 100, 148, 150, 158–59,
176, 185
caricature, 20, 61, 63
Carr, John Dickson, 62, 110
Carry on films, 138, 152, 166
Carter, Howard, 41
"The Case of the Caretaker"
(Christie), 79

The Case of the Constant Suicides
(Carr), 110
"The Case of the Perfect Maid"
(Christie), 28, 111
Case of Three Detectives (Croft-Cooke),
12
Casino Royale (Fleming), 142
"The Cask of Amontillado" (Poe), 1
Cat Among the Pigeons (Christie),
152–54
censorship, 138
Chamberlain, Austen, 6–7, 37–39
Chamberlain, Neville, 50–51, 54, 87,
98
Chang, "Brilliant," 9–10
Checkmate to Murder (Lorac), 111
Chesterton, G. K., 3, 6
Childers, Erskine, 68
children, 8–9
"The Chimeras" (Auden), 125
"The Chocolate Box" (Christie), 14
Christianity, 12–19, 143, 170–71,
175–78
Christie, Agatha
as anachronistic, 143–44, 148
anti-semitism in, 71–72
appearances in, 163–64
archaeology, 80–81, 97, 110, 130–31
architecture, 63, 165
betrayal in, 36, 150
biography, 1–2
book sales, 135–36, 151, 184
Britain as England, 32
Britain's economic issues, 91–92
British diaspora in, 154
caricature, 20, 61, 63
children in, 8–9
Christianity, 12–19, 171, 176–78
cinema, 95–96, 139–40
Condition of England literature,
148

crime, 2–11
criticism, 184–85
divorce, 181–82
Empire in, 40–41
Englishness, 107–8, 110, 116, 170
estate ownership, 28–29
evil in, 142–43
expertise, 67
false identities, 110
food in, 99–101
foreignness in, 73–76
homophobia, 71
human nature, 75–76
imaginings, 187–88
immigration in, 148–49
and Iraq, 131–32
Jewishness in, 70–71
language and settings of, 152–54
masculinity, 119
Middle East, 40–41, 80–83, 110,
130–32, 154
modernism in, 63
modernity, 125–26
morality in, 12, 14–16, 122, 142–
43, 176–77, 189
nationalism, 34
national politics, 39–40
occult, 18, 41
ordered past, 29–30
plays, 189
poison in, 5
politics, 140–42, 154–55
popular interest, 152
psychology of suspects, 16–17
readership, 22–23, 109–10
as reference point, 185–87
reworkings of, 160, 189–90
role of Empire, 82–83
sense of place, 64–66
Shakespeare references in, 182–83
social change, 175–82
sport, 96

technique, 187–89
thrillers, 9, 58–59, 130–34
trains, 104–6
visual versions of, 52–53, 95–96,
189–90
World War I, 24–27
See also individual titles by
The Christmas Egg (Kelly), 153
churches, 170–71
Churchill, Winston, 34, 35, 51–52,
87, 126
Church of England, 170–71
cinema, 95–96, 139–40
The Citadel (Cronin), 46–47
City of Spades (MacInnes), 149
class distinctions, 38, 65, 94–95, 101–
3, 158, 164, 184–85
Clean Air Act of 1956, 156
"The Cleverest Clue" (Christie), 109
The Clocks (Christie), 20–21, 83, 121
The Clock Strikes Twelve (Wentworth),
72
Clore, Charles, 156
"The Clothes Pit" (Dunn), 164
Clouds of Witness (Sayers), 25, 56
coal exports, 51
Coalition, 32–33, 37–39
The Code of the Woosters (Wodehouse),
67
Cold War, 119, 131
Cold War themes, 144
Collier, Doris Bell, 91
Collins, Wilkie, 1, 80
Combes, Robert, 6
"The Coming of Mr Quin" (Christie),
47–48
Committee on Higher Education, 157
Committee on National Expenditure,
85
Common Market, 179
Communism, 33–35, 38, 48, 89–90,
97–98

Compton-Burnett, Ivy, 45
Condition of England literature, 148
conscription, 32, 81, 138
conservatism, 53, 88, 103
Conservatives
    appeal of Christie, 136
    and Baldwin, 103
    Butskellism, 141
    continuity, 137
    cultural changes, 157
    housebuilding, 129
    and Labour, 37–38
    and Liberals, 49, 55–56
    and Lloyd George, 32–34, 37
    modernity, 126
    National Government, 87–88
    social change, 150–51
    social revolution, 175–76
    in *Sparkling Cyanide,* 115
    unemployment benefits, 85–86
    and Watts, 146
    women, 43
conspiracy, 11, 22, 36, 52, 66, 69,
    116, 167, 175
consumerism, 92–94, 151, 158
continuity, 123, 137–40, 147–48,
    166–70
Coolcan, Mary Theresa, 153, 156–57
Cornish Riviera, 105
Cortesi Brothers, 10
cosmopolitanism, 36, 39–40
Courier (newspaper), 5
Courier to Marrakesh (Christie), 59
Craine, Debra, 186–87
crime, 2–11, 15, 134–35
Crime Omnibus (Symons), 185
crime scene investigation (CSI), 67
Crispin, Edmund, 118
Croft-Cooke, Rupert, 12
Crofts, Freeman Wills, 15, 21, 91
Cronin, Archibald Joseph, 46–47
Crooked House (Christie), 17, 60, 75,

102, 107, 120, 125–28, 135, 152,
    188
CSI (crime scene investigation), 67
cult, 174
cultural changes, 137–38, 147, 154–
    60, 161–71
Curtain (Christie), 109, 122, 180–83

Daily Mail (newspaper), 12, 48, 58–
    59, 103
Daily Mirror (newspaper), 12
Daily News (newspaper), 6
Daily Sketch (newspaper), 150
Daily Worker (newspaper), 97–98
Dane, Clemence, 45
Day-Lewis, Cecil, 139, 149–50
D.C. Thomson, 103
Dead Man's Folly (Christie), 11, 110,
    154
"Dead Man's Mirror" (Christie), 27
The Dead Shall Be Raised (Bellairs),
    111, 140
"Death by Drowning" (Christie), 63
Death Comes as the End (Christie), 41,
    148, 151
Death Has Deep Roots (Gilbert), 121
Death in a Little Town (Woodthorpe),
    91
Death in Captivity (Gilbert), 121
Death in the Clouds (Christie), 8, 17,
    27, 71, 76, 79, 91, 99–100, 135
Death in the Tunnel (Burton), 105
Death Makes a Prophet (Bude), 72
Death on the Nile (Christie), 14, 20,
    24–25, 28, 40–41, 61, 82–83, 84,
    96–97, 135, 151
Death on the Nile (film), 184
Death on the Riviera (Bude), 118
The Decagon House Murders (Ayatsuji),
    185–86
"Decline of the English Murder" (Or-
    well), 107

The Decline of the English Murder (Orwell), 130
Defence of the Realm Act, 32
de Gaulle, Charles, 147
Deighton, Len, 150
Departmental Committee on Detective Work and Procedure, 67
design, 158
Destination Unknown (Christie), 15, 119, 144, 174, 182
detection, 66–67
detective fiction
    agency, 136
    American-style, 60
    anarchist conspiracies, 22
    class distinctions, 184–85
    Communism, 90
    conspiracy, 11
    cosmopolitanism, 36
    criticism of, 148
    as entertainment, 188
    as escapism, 98
    evil in, 142–43
    history of, 1–4
    and human nature, 76
    imperial background of characters, 82
    Jews in, 68
    language and settings of, 152–54
    military service, 80
    morality, 15–16
    public knowledge about crime, 134–35
    true-life murders, 9, 93
    women, 145
Detective (magazine), 36
development, 92–94
Devon and Exeter Gazette (newspaper), 6, 47, 50
Dick Barton – Special Agent (radio show), 134
Dickens, Charles, 4, 30

Dictator's Way (Robertson), 89
distribution systems, 135
The Division Bell Mystery (Wilkinson), 98
divorce, 138, 181–82
Divorce Reform Act, 181
domestic conspiracy, 22
domestic help, 65, 94–95, 127, 145, 154
domesticity, 43
Donat, Robert, 109
The Door (Rinehart), 65
Doyle, Arthur Conan, 36. *See also* Sherlock Holmes
Dracula (Stoker), 4
"The Dream" (Christie), 96
Drewry's Staffordshire Gazette (newspaper), 5
drugs, 9–12
The Duchess of Malfi (Webster), 183
du Maurier, Daphne, 45
du Maurier, Gerald, 69
Dumb Witness (Christie), 30, 75, 130
Dunn, Douglas, 164
Durbridge, Francis, 62

economic growth, 47
economy programme, 86
education, 124, 141–42, 157, 171
Education Act, 142
Edwards, Henry, 96
Edwards, Martin, 185
Egypt, 81–83
electoral system, 38
electricity, 92, 94
Elephants Can Remember (Christie), 178
Eliot, T. S., 36
Elizabeth I of England, 143
Elizabeth II, 143
Elks, Florence, 21
emigration, 78–79

Empire, 40–41, 78, 80–83, 131, 136, 178–79
Empire Day, 78
Endless Night (Christie), 10, 154, 170–71, 182–83
Engineering Building, 157
England and the Octopus (Williams-Ellis), 104
English Christianity, 19
Englishness, 83, 107–8, 110, 116, 170
Enter Sir John (Simpson), 45
entertainment, 138
escapism, 98
espionage, 9, 179
estate ownership, 28–29
European Economic Community, 147
evangelism, 175–76
Evening Standard (newspaper), 172
evil, 3, 17–18, 142–43, 171
Evil Under the Sun (Christie), 9, 15, 62, 77, 79–80, 101, 111–12
expertise, 67
extremism, 88–90, 103

Faisal II, 132
false identities, 110
Family Matters (Rolls), 84, 89
Farjeon, J. Jefferson, 20
fashionable architecture, 63
The Fell Murder (Lorac), 111
feminism, 44
Fertility of Marriage Census, 42
Festival of Britain, 125
Fielding, Henry, 3
financial-political crisis of 1931, 39
Firearms Act of 1920, 35
Five Little Pigs (Christie), 111, 113–14
Five Red Herrings (Sayers), 105
Flecker, James Elroy, 154
Fleming, Ian, 72, 142–43, 144, 175
The Floating Admiral (Christie), 80
Foley, Lucy, 186

Folk Songs for the Four Seasons (Williams), 124
food, 99–101, 129
foreignness, 73–76
"Four-and-Twenty Blackbirds" (Christie), 47, 101, 182
4.50 from Paddington (Christie), 121, 127, 139, 145, 154–55, 158
The Four Just Men (Wallace), 22
"The Four Suspects" (Christie), 70
Fourth Reform Act of 1918, 37
free trade, 39
Fu-Manchu stories, 22
functionalism, 165

Gabel, Martin, 160
Gaitskell, Hugh, 141
Galsworthy, John, 62
gangs, 10–11
"The Gate of Baghdad" (Christie), 154
"The Gates of Damascus" (Flecker), 154
Geddes, Eric, 34
General Strike of 1926, 37, 39, 51–54, 69, 90, 106
genteel poverty, 30–31
George, Marquess Curzon, 39
George V, 86
ghost stories, 13, 18
The Ghost Train (Ridley), 105
Gilbert, Michael, 121
"The Girl in the Train" (Christie), 71
G. K.'s Weekly (newspaper), 6
Gloucester Journal (newspaper), 5
Glyn, Elinor, 61
GNP (Gross National Product), 91
Godson, Alfred, 50
Golden Age fiction, 1–5, 67, 185–86
The Golden Journey to Samarkand (Flecker), 154
Goldfinger, Erno, 166
Gold Standard, 51

Gothic novels, 3–4
Gowan, James, 157
Great Depression, 84–85, 106
Great Exhibition in London, 125
The Great Impersonation (Oppen-
    heim), 59
Great Western Railway (GWR), 105
Great West Road, 92
Green, Anna Katharine, 21
Gregson, Garry, 21
Gribble, Leonard, 96
Gross National Product (GNP), 91
The Guest List (Foley), 186
gun ownership, 35
GWR (Great Western Railway), 105

Hallowe'en Party (Christie), 17–18, 72,
    78, 83, 130, 152, 161, 167–69,
    188
Hamilton, Bruce, 84, 90, 96
Hamilton, Guy, 162
The Hanging Captain (Wade), 85
Hannah, Sophie, 52, 190
"The Harlequin Tea Set" (Christie),
    18, 179
Harmsworth, Harold, 7
Have His Carcass (Sayers), 72
Heath, Edward, 175
Henderson, Arthur, 31–32, 38, 87
Henry, 5th Marquess of Lansdowne,
    31
Herbert A. P., 46
*Hercule Poirot: The Disappearance of
    Mr Davenheim* (television show),
    160
Hercule Poirot's Christmas (Christie),
    57, 79, 87, 92, 105, 108, 182
heredity, 16, 17
Heyer, Georgette, 36
Hickory Dickory Dock (Christie), 82,
    128, 149
Highsmith, Patricia, 170

Hitchcock, Alfred, 65, 109
The Hollow (Christie), 8, 66, 123–24,
    128–29, 134–35
Home Magazine, 24
homophobia, 71
homosexuality, 138
Honest to God (Robinson), 170
Hoode, John, 48
Horne, Geoffrey, 153
Horniman, Roy, 68
horror, 1
The Hound of Death (Christie), 18, 26,
    41, 128, 189
housebuilding, 93–94, 129
The House on Tollard Ridge (Rhode),
    64
Housing Act of 1923, 51
housing shortage, 129
Hue and Cry (Hamilton), 84, 96
human nature, 75–76
Hunter, Alan, 150
Huxley, Aldous, 46
Huxley, Elspeth, 82
Hyde Park, 156

ILP (Independent Labour Party), 38,
    89
immigration, 74, 148–49
Imperial Airways, 107
Imperial Preference, 90
Imperial rule, 131–33, 147
impersonation, 83
"In a Glass Darkly" (Christie), 27
"The Incredible Theft" (Christie), 109
Independent Labour Party (ILP), 38,
    89
individualism, 137
industrial estates, 93
inheritance, 31, 131
Innes, Michael, 58
In Search of England (Morton), 13, 30
An Inspector Calls (Priestly), 16

international conspiracy, 52, 69, 116
international intrigue, 59, 66
inter-war Christianity, 19
inter-war style, 140, 153
The Invasion of 1910 (Le Queux), 58–59
Invisible Weapons (Rhode), 94
The IPCRESS File (Deighton), 150
IQ testing, 142
Iraq, 80–81, 131–32
Ireland, 33, 36–37
Irish Free State, 33
Israel Rank (Horniman), 68
Issigonis, Alec, 158
The Italian (Radcliffe), 4

Jakes, John, 1
James, Montague Rhodes, 13
James, P. D., 185
"Jane in Search of a Job" (Christie), 36, 66
Jellett, Henry, 90
Jenkins, Herbert, 65
jewel thieves, 66
Jewish immigration, 82
Jewishness, 70–71
Jews in detective fiction, 68
jingoism, 150
John Bull (magazine), 144
juries, 44–45
justice, 169

Kelly, Mary, 153, 156–57
"The Kidnapped Prime Minister" (Christie), 11, 20, 25, 31
"The King of Clubs" (Christie), 16, 103
Kipling, Rudyard, 62
kitchen-sink drama, 147–50
Kitchin, C. H. B., 62, 97
Krassion, Leonid, 35
Kreditanstalt bank, 85

Labour Party
  appeal of Christie, 135–36
  class politics, 37–38
  Communism, 89
  continuity, 137
  cultural changes, 157–58
  economic crisis, 84–85
  free trade, 39
  housebuilding, 129
  and Liberals, 48–49
  Lloyd George government, 31–35
  MacDonald government, 54–55
  modernity, 125–26
  National Government, 86–88
  New Britain, 163
  social legislation, 164
  social reform, 123–24
  and Soviet Union, 68–69
  in *Sparkling Cyanide*, 115
  strikes, 123
  thrillers, 47–48
  trade unions, 50, 54
  unemployment benefits, 86
The Labours of Hercules (Christie), 151
Ladies' Bane (Wentworth), 156
The Lake District Murder (Bude), 64, 106
Landed Gently (Hunter), 150
landed societies, 28, 30–31
Lansbury, George, 88
Laughton, Charles, 69, 128
Lawrence, D. H., 93
The Leavenworth Case (Green), 21
Leblanc, Maurice, 21
Le Carré, John, 174
Leicester University, 157
Leighton, Frederic, 63
Le Queux, William, 58–59
Leroux, Gaston, 21
Lewis, Matthew, 4
Liberals, 31–33, 37–39, 48–50, 55–56, 86–88, 142

"Linckes' Great Case" (Heyer), 36
The Listening Eye (Wentworth), 137
"The Literary Antecedents of Agatha
    Christie's Hercule Poirot" (Brett),
    2
The Liver Birds (television show), 162
Liverpool, England, 162
Lloyd George, David, 6, 31–35, 37–
    38, 55, 87
Lloyd's Weekly Newspaper (newspaper), 5
LNER (London and North Eastern
    Railway), 105
Local Government Act of 1929, 51
localism, 76
London, England, 65, 156, 170
London and North Eastern Railway
    (LNER), 105
Londonderry House, 156
London dock strike of 1949, 123
London Green Belt Act, 94
Long, Camilla, 16
Look Back in Anger (Osborne), 147
Lorac, E. C., 64, 111, 118
Lord Edgware Dies (Christie), 12, 56–
    57, 68, 70–72, 87, 95
"The Lost Mine" (Christie), 10
Love from a Stranger (MacDonald), 48,
    118
Loy, Myrna, 95
Lucifer theme, 117–18
Lusitania (liner), 26

MacDonald, Philip, 25, 48, 54–55
MacDonald, Ramsay, 85–87
MacInnes, Colin, 149
Maclean, Donald, 134
Macmillan, Harold, 129, 157–59
"Magnolia Blossom" (Christie), 15–16
Mallowan, Max, 40, 120, 131–32
Maltese Messina brothers, 10–11
"The Manhood of Edward Robinson"
    (Christie), 62, 95

The Man in the Brown Suit (Christie), 7,
    24, 26, 35, 41, 66, 75, 95, 156, 182
The Man Who Didn't Fly (Bennett),
    145–46
"The Market Basing Mystery"
    (Christie), 20
Marsh, Ngaio, 90, 136
martyrdom, 134
masculinity, 119
The Mask of Fu Manchu (film), 95
Mass Observation Project, 123
Matrimonial Causes Act of 1937, 46
May, George, 85
Mayfair residences, 156
McCardie, Henry, 44–45
McNeile, Herman Cyril, 36
Meadowbank (girls' school), 152
Mesopotamia (Iraq), 80–81
Meynell, Laurence, 109
Middle East, 40–41, 80–83, 110,
    130–32, 154
Midsomer Murders (television show),
    186–87
military service, 80
Miller, Agatha Mary Clarissa. *See*
    Christie, Agatha
Miller, Clara, 1
Miller, Fred, 1
Miller, Louis "Monty," 119, 188
Miller, Margaret Frary, 29
Mills & Boon, 103
Mini (car), 158
The Mirror Crack'd from Side to Side
    (Christie), 155
misdirection, 58
"The Missing Husband" (Bailey), 78
"The Missing Prime Minister"
    (Christie), 116
Miss Marple and the Thirteen Problems
    (Christie), 40, 151
"Miss Marple Tells a Story" (Christie),
    61, 63

Mitchell, Gladys, 17
modernism, 61–63, 125, 165–66
modernity, 125–26
modern police, 168–69
The Monk (Lewis), 4
Monkswell Manor, 128–29
The Monogram Murders (Hannah),
    190
Moonraker (Fleming), 144
Moonstone (Collins), 1, 80
morality, 3, 11–12, 14–16, 122, 123,
    137–38, 142–43, 176–77, 189
moral panics, 5–6
more than one outcome, 58
Morrell, Ottoline, 61
Morton, H. V., 13, 30
Morton, Michael, 69, 79
Mosley, Oswald, 88–89, 98, 103, 179
Mousetrap (Christie), 139
The Mousetrap (Christie), 128
The Moving Finger (Christie), 30, 114,
    151
The Moving Toyshop (Crispin), 118
"Mr Bennett and Mrs Brown"
    (Woolf), 61
"Mr Eastwood's Adventure" (Christie),
    57, 71
Mrs Dalloway (Woolf), 61
Mrs McGinty's Dead (Christie), 20,
    107, 119, 124, 126–30, 135–36,
    142, 152, 159
Mr Standfast (Buchan), 3
multiple identities, 76
Murder, She Said (film), 139
Murder Ahoy! (film), 160
Murder at the Gallop (film), 139
Murder by Matchlight (Lorac), 111
Murder in Mesopotamia (Christie), 27,
    40, 81, 97
Murder in Retrospect (Christie), 183.
    See also *Sleeping Murder*
Murder in the Mews (Christie), 77, 94

The Murder in the Vicarage (Christie),
    12, 103–4
A Murder is Announced (Christie), 8,
    60, 118–20, 125–28, 136, 159
Murder Is Easy (Christie)
    American-style detective novels,
        60
    class distinctions, 102–3
    cultural continuity, 140
    emigration, 79
    Englishness, 108
    estate ownership, 28
    evil in, 18
    housebuilding, 94
    modernism, 63
    national identity, 96
    and the press, 4
    religion in, 14–15
    social change, 104
    women's issues, 46
The Murder of a Quack (Bellairs), 111
The Murder of Roger Ackroyd
    (Christie), 26–27, 41, 42, 52, 56,
    66
Murder on Safari (Huxley), 82
The Murder on the Links (Christie),
    25–26, 39–40, 64–65
Murder on the Orient Express
    (Christie), 73, 96
Murder on the Orient Express (film),
    184
murder stories, 167–69
Mussolini, Benito, 88
The Mysteries of London (Reynolds), 4
The Mysteries of the Court of London
    (Reynolds), 4
The Mysteries of Udolpho (Radcliffe), 4
The Mysterious Affair at Styles
    (Christie), 19, 23, 24–25, 27–28,
    30, 42
The Mysterious Mr Quin (Christie),
    47–48, 73, 151

The Mystery of a Butcher's Shop (Mitchell), 17
"The Mystery of Hunter's Lodge" (Christie), 14
The Mystery of the Baghdad Chef (Christie), 100
"The Mystery of the Blue Jar" (Christie), 41
The Mystery of the Blue Train (Christie), 40, 68
"The Mystery of the Spanish Chest" (Christie), 8, 100, 151, 182
"The Mystery of the Second Cucumber" (Christie), 57, 71. See also "Mr Eastwood's Adventure"
The Mystery of the Yellow Room (Leroux), 21

National Government, 84–88, 90, 98, 104
National Health Service, 123, 171
national identity, 49–50, 53, 66, 90–91, 96
nationalisations, 123–24, 159
nationalism, 34
National Party, 33
national politics, 39
National Unemployed Workers Movement, 90
National Union of Conservative and Constitutional Associations, 37
National Union of Societies for Equal Citizenship, 44
Nemesis (Christie), 176–78
New Britain, 163
New Brutalism, 157
new houses, 93–94
New Party, 88
News of the World (newspaper), 5, 143
A Night of Errors (Innes), 58
No Friendly Drop (Wade), 85
Norman, Montagu, 85

N or M? (Christie), 15, 79, 116–18
North, Gil, 153
Northanger Abbey (Austen), 4
"Nottingham and the Mining Countryside" (Lawrence), 93
novel, development of, 3–4
The Nursing Home Murder (Marsh and Jellett), 90

occult, 18, 41
occupational classifications, 42–43
The Old Curiosity Shop (Dickens), 30
Oldfield, William, 126
O'Malley, Louisa, 21
One, Two, Buckle My Shoe (Christie), 19, 58, 60, 79, 89, 98, 101, 103, 110
"The Opener of the Crypt" (Jakes), 1
Oppenheim, Phillips, 59, 179
Ordeal by Innocence (Christie), 120–21, 140, 143–44
ordered past, 29–30
Orwell, George, 107, 130
Osborne, John, 147

The Pale Horse (Christie), 171
The Pale Horse (television show), 190
Palestine, 82
Parker Pyne Investigates (Christie), 73, 152
Park Lane, 156
Partners in Crime (Christie), 35, 59, 66, 116
Passenger to Frankfurt (Christie), 117, 133–34, 172, 174–76
peacetime interventionism, 90
Penguin, 62, 135–36, 151
penny dreadful serials, 4–6
people who are not what they seem, 27–28
The Perils of Pamela (film), 66
period drama, 189

permissiveness, 170
Phelps, Sarah, 190
Philby, Kim, 134, 150
Phillpotts, Eden, 105
"Philomel Cottage" (Christie), 48,
  118
The Pilgrim's Progress (Bunyan), 3
Pinter, Harold, 147
"The Plymouth Express" (Christie),
  19, 40
A Pocket Full of Rye (Christie), 8, 19,
  75, 82–83, 101, 119, 123, 127,
  129–30, 140, 148–49
Poe, Edgar Allan, 1
Poirot stories
  in *The ABC Murders,* 99
  in *Alibi,* 79
  attire, 25
  in *The Big Four,* 52
  bus travel, 107
  class distinctions, 103
  consumerism, 151
  cosmopolitanism, 39–40
  and crime in the press, 7–9
  criminal fiction, 20–21
  critical view, 2
  cultural changes, 161
  in *Death of the Nile,* 97
  economic difficulties, 91–92
  education, 141–42
  in *Elephants Can Remember,* 178
  in *Five Little Pigs,* 113–14
  food, 100–101
  in *Hallowe'en Party,* 167–69
  immigration, 74
  international conspiracy, 52, 69,
  116
  justice, 169
  last appearance of, 181
  in *Lord Edgware Dies,* 70–72, 87
  marriage, 72–73
  Middle East, 41

modernism, 165–66
Monkswell Manor, 129
morality, 122
murders/murderers, 19–20, 130
political extremism, 98
popular interest, 152
psychology, 17
and racism, 72
rail travel, 104–5, 159–60
religion in, 14–15
rural England, 66
as 'safe' alien, 83
self-satirical device, 57–58
sense of place, 64–65
Suchet versions, 52–53, 78–79,
  166, 187
television series, 160
in *Third Girl,* 163
visual versions of, 52–53, 95–96,
  189–90
xenophobia, 75, 77–78
poison, 5, 11
Police College, 67
popular interest, 152
popular music, 162–63
The Port of London Murders (Bell), 91
Postern of Fate (Christie), 36, 117–18,
  120, 151, 154, 173, 175, 179, 183
Postgate, Raymond, 74, 111
post-war social policy, 33–34
press, 4–9, 12
pre-war Liberalism, 32
priesthoods, 3
Priestley, J. B., 16
Primrose League, 103
Pritchard, Hubert, 120
The Progress of a Crime (Symons),
  153–54
The Property of a Lady (Fleming), 72
prostitution, 10–11
protectionism, 90
psychology, 16–17

public morality, 11–12
Public Order Act, 89
Pushon, Ernest Robertson, 89

race relations, 149–50
racism, 71–72, 74, 77–78
Radcliffe, Ann, 4
radical Liberalism, 48
Railway Modernisation Plan of 1955, 159
railways, 104–6, 159–60
"The Rajah's Emerald" (Christie), 57, 71, 95, 100
Rand Rebellion, 24
The Rasp (MacDonald), 25, 48
Rathbone, Eleanor, 44
rationing, 123
Rattenbury, Alma, 45–46
Rattenbury, Francis, 45–46
The Reader's Library (series), 59
rebuilding, 156–57, 165
"The Red Signal" (Christie), 17, 26
reform policies, 157
regionalism, 76
Relative to Poison (Lorac), 118
religion, 12–19
Remembered Death (Christie), 114. See also *Sparkling Cyanide*
Restriction of Ribbon Development Act of 1935, 94
Rex v Rhodes (Hamilton), 90
Reynolds, George, 4
Rhode, John, 64, 94
Ridley, Arnold, 105–6
right-wing extremism, 88–89
Rinehart, Mary Roberts, 65
Road and Rail Traffic Act, 106
road transport, 165
Robinson, John, 170
Rohmer, Sax, 22
Rolls, Anthony, 28, 72, 82, 84, 89
Rothermere, Lord, 103

rural England, 49–50, 66, 91, 124–25, 136
Russian Civil War, 35
Rutherford, Margaret, 160

Sabini, Charles "Darby," 10
Sad Cypress (Christie), 7, 27, 28, 87, 94–95, 107, 130, 182
Samuel, Herbert, 51
"Sanctuary" (Christie), 100
Sarsfield, Arthur, 22
satire boom, 157–58
The Saturday Review (newspaper), 1, 98
Sayers, Dorothy L., 25, 45, 72, 105
Scarweather (Rolls), 28, 72, 82
science and scientists, 66–67, 174
Scoop (Waugh), 8
A Scream in Soho (Brandon), 118
Second Anglo-Afghan War, 26
"The Second Gong" (Christie), 27
Second Labour government, 84
secrecy, 3
The Secret Adversary (Christie), 26, 35–37
The Secret of Chimneys (Christie), 17, 29, 146
The Secret of High Eldersham (Burton), 18, 25, 29, 76
secularisation, 170
self-referencing, 166–67
Send for Paul Temple (Durbridge), 62
sense of place, 64–66
Sergeant Cluff novels (North), 153
Seven Days to Noon (film), 126
Seven Dead (Farjeon), 20
The Seven Dials Mystery (Christie), 29, 54–55
sexual conduct, 11–12
sexual policing, 138
Shakespeare references, 182–83
"A Sharp Look at the Mood of Britain" (supplement), 158

Shell Guides (series), 66
Sherlock Holmes, 1, 15, 19, 21–22, 26, 46, 67, 71–73, 83, 118, 136
Sherlock Holmes and the Voice of Terror (film), 118
Sidqī, Bakr, 81
Silence of a Purple Shirt (Woodthorpe), 89
Sillitoe, Alan, 147
Simpson, Helen, 45, 86
The Sittaford Mystery (Christie), 80, 188
the Sixties, 161–70
The Sketch (magazine), 31, 52, 59
Skylon, 125–26
Sleeping Murder (Christie), 109, 183
Slump of 1929, 84
A Small Town in Germany (Le Carré), 174
Smuts, Jan, 24
Snobbery with Violence (Watson), 184
Snowden, Philip, 48, 86
Snow on the Desert's Face (Christie), 61
social change, 42–43, 104, 128, 136, 147, 150–51, 156–58, 169–70, 175–82
Socialism, 33, 35, 38, 47–49, 54
social legislation, 164
social norms, 107, 138–39
Social Realist fiction, 125–26
social reform, 123–24
social welfare, 171
Solomon, Alfie, 10
Somebody at the Door (Postgate), 111
Some Must Watch (White), 43, 84
South Africa, 24, 40, 79–80
Southern Region (SR), 106
South Wales coal miners, 35
Soviet Trade Delegation, 69
Soviet Union, 48, 68–69
Sparkling Cyanide (Christie), 77, 80, 96, 107, 114–15, 182

Spence, Basil, 125
The Spoilt Kill (Kelly), 156–57
sport, 96
Sprigg, Christopher St John, 90
spy stories, 59, 144
SR (Southern Region), 106
Stevenson, Robert Louis, 47
Stirling, James, 157
Stoker, Bram, 4
Stoner, George, 45–46
The Story of Classic Crime in 100 Books (Edwards), 185
Strachey, John, 1, 98
The Strange Case of Dr Jekyll and Mr Hyde (Stevenson), 47
"The Strange Case of Mr Challoner" (Jenkins), 65
"The Strange Case of Sir Arthur Carmichael" (Christie), 41
"Street Haunting" (Woolf), 43
strikes, 34–35, 37, 39, 51–54, 123
Strong Poison (Sayers), 45
A Study in Scarlet, 1
Sturrock, Donald, 180
"The Submarine Plans" (Christie), 36
submarines, 36
suburbs, 93
Suchet, David, 25, 52–53, 78–79, 166, 187
Suez Crisis, 131
suicide, 76
Sunday Dispatch (newspaper), 103
Sunday Times (newspaper), 16, 158
Surfeit of Suspects (Bellairs), 152
"Swan Song" (Christie), 63
Swinging London films, 164–65
Swinging Sixties, 170
Symons, C. T., 67
Symons, Julian, 118, 153–54, 168, 185

Taken at the Flood (Christie), 75, 82, 100, 110, 118, 182

Talking about Detective Fiction (James), 185

Taunton Courier (newspaper), 4–5

taxation, 33, 85, 145, 154

Ten Little Niggers (Christie), 111–12. See also *And Then There Were None*

Terry Street (Dunn), 164

The Test Match Murder (Batchelor), 96

Thatcher, Margaret, 103

The Illustrated London News (newspaper), 6

They Came to Baghdad (Christie), 59, 130–34, 182

They Do It with Mirrors (Christie), 29, 59–60, 124, 140, 159

Third Girl (Christie), 83, 121, 163–67, 170

The Third Round (McNeile), 36

Thirteen Women (film), 95

The Thirty-Nine Steps (Buchan), 109

Three Act Tragedy (Christie), 8, 12–14, 16–17, 29–30, 46, 56–57, 72–74, 79, 100, 102

"Three Blind Mice" (Christie), 128

The Three Hostages (Buchan), 35–36, 43

thrillers, 4, 9, 11, 21–22, 33, 36, 39–40, 47–48, 58–59, 105–6, 130–34, 143–44

Thunderball (Fleming), 175

Times (newspaper), 44

Tom Jones (Fielding), 3

To the Lighthouse (Woolf), 61

Towards Zero (Christie), 17–18, 60, 79, 111, 116

Trades Disputes Act of 1927, 54

Trades Union Congress (TUC), 51–52, 55, 86

trade unions, 33, 38, 50, 53–54, 86, 89–90, 123

trains, 104–6, 159–60

"Traitor's Hands" (Christie), 128. See also "Witness for the Prosecution"

traitor within theme, 134

transport systems, 47, 104–7, 159–60

Treaty of Rapallo of 1922, 36

Trenchard, Lord, 67

"Triangle at Rhodes" (Christie), 14, 77, 80, 92

Tribune (newspaper), 107

true-life murders, 9, 93

TUC (Trades Union Congress), 51–52, 55, 86

The 12.30 From Croydon (Crofts), 91, 107

Twickenham Film Studios, 95

Two New Crime Stories (Christie and Oppenheim), 59

"The Uncrossed Path" (Christie), 103

"The Under Dog" (Christie), 59, 78

Under the Fig Tree (Christie), 61

unemployment, 84–86

Unfinished Portrait (Christie), 76

Van Dine, S. S., 65

Vantage Striker (Simpson), 86

Verdict on Twelve (Postgate), 74

villainess, 45–46, 68, 144

Wade, Henry, 85

Wallace, Edgar, 22, 45, 56–57

wartime coalition, 86–87

wartime novels, 109–22

The Waste Land (Eliot), 36

Watson, Colin, 184

Watts, James "Jack," 29, 146

Waugh, Alex, 11

Waugh, Evelyn, 8, 143

Webster, John, 183

Wentworth, Patricia, 72, 137, 156

Wesker, Arnold, 147

Western Times (newspaper), 138–39

What Beckoning Ghost? (Browne), 118

Wheatley, Dennis, 142

Where is Britain Going? (MacDonald), 54

White, Ethel Lina, 43, 84

"The White Murder" (Chesterton), 6

"Who Cares Who Killed Roger Ackroyd" (Wilson), 148

Why Didn't They Ask Evans? (Christie), 10, 18, 74, 80

Widows', Orphans' and Old Age Contributory Pensions Act of 1925, 51

"The Wife of the Kenite" (Christie), 24

Wilkinson, Ellen, 98, 124

Williams, Ralph Vaughan, 124

Williams, Valentine, 59

Williams-Ellis, Clough, 104

Wilson, Edmund, 148, 163, 163n3, 184

Wilson, Harold, 157

Wilson, Henry, 34

"Wireless" (Christie), 92

Witness for the Prosecution (Christie), 128

"Witness for the Prosecution" (Christie), 128

Witness for the Prosecution (film), 139

Wodehouse, P. G., 67, 140

Wolfenden Commission, 138

Woman's Pictorial (magazine), 116

women, 12, 43–46, 62, 72–73, 102, 145

Woodthorpe, Ralph Carter, 89, 91

Woolf, Virginia, 43, 61

working class, 65, 130, 164

World War I, 6–7, 22, 24–27, 31–34

World War II, 2, 90–91, 109–22

The Worm of Death (Blake), 139, 149–50

Wren, Christopher, 104

Wright, Willard Huntington, 65

xenophobia, 9–10, 75–78, 124

Yellow Iris (Christie), 58

"Yellow Iris" (Christie), 92, 114

The Young Ones (Richard), 152

The Young Vanish (Christie), 88

Zinoviev, Grigory, 48